KAHURANGI STORIES

MORE TALES FROM
KAHURANGI STORIES
NORTHWEST NELSON

GERARD HINDMARSH

pb potton & burton

Published in 2017 by Potton & Burton
98 Vickerman Street, PO Box 5128, Nelson, New Zealand
www.pottonandburton.co.nz

© Gerard Hindmarsh
© Photographs: individual photographers

Edited by Susi Bailey

ISBN 978-0-947503-42-0

Printed in China by Midas Printing International Ltd

This book is copyright. Apart from any fair dealing for the purposes of private study, research, criticism or review, as permitted under the Copyright Act, no part may be reproduced by any process without the permission of the publisher.

CONTENTS

	Acknowledgements	7
Chapter 1	Anaweka Waka	11
Chapter 2	Hopelessly Lost	36
Chapter 3	Taplin's Hut	55
Chapter 4	Little Biddy's Story	66
Chapter 5	The Storekeeper's Lament	80
Chapter 6	The Flying Cray Fishers	97
Chapter 7	River Ports	110
Chapter 8	Mining Magnesite	135
Chapter 9	Ranger's Diary	154
Chapter 10	Heritage Huts	170
Chapter 11	Tracts of Iron	186
Chapter 12	Carbon Footprints	202
Chapter 13	Chasing the Kākahi	220
Chapter 14	Roaring Lion Gold	227
Chapter 15	Modern Controversy	236
	Bibliography	250

ACKNOWLEDGEMENTS

WHEN I LAUNCHED *Kahurangi Calling: Stories from the Backcountry of Northwest Nelson* in late 2010, I could not have anticipated the incredible response I received from locals, who rained down on me a whole bunch of new stories about the place. I felt privileged to record all these, even if each one tweaked my conscience for not including it, or even knowing about it, when I wrote my original book.

For much of the technical information about the Anaweka waka in Chapter 1, I am indebted to canoe conservator Dilys Johns from the University of Auckland, who carried out all the original assessments, and to Geoffry Irwin and Yun Sung, who collaborated with her on producing a most informative paper about the waka: 'An Early Sophisticated East Polynesian Voyaging Canoe Discovered on New Zealand's Coast'. On Huahine in French Polynesia, thanks go to Peter Owen for welcoming me on the day I turned up and showing me around the Maitai Lapita Village Hotel museum, which he set up with New Zealand archaeologist Mark Eddowes. How wonderful to stand on the very spot where the Huahine canoe was discovered in 1978. Huahine thanks also go to Manava, who showed me around sacred marae sites associated with the early canoe builders. Travelling the 4,221 kilometres that separate the Anaweka and Huahine canoes proved a fascinating journey for me. Special appreciation must also go to Tony Nicholls, whose 12-year-old grandson Flynn found the waka. Cheers for sharing your story and for opening up your photo album to me.

For Chapter 2, thanks go to Tony Cunningham for his recollections as the sole-charge Takaka constable who couldn't give up the search for Peter Le Fleming back in 1980. In addition, my gratitude goes to Cliff Turley for digging out his daily search notes from that time, to Pat Timmings for also sharing his diary of events, and to David Young, the *New Zealand Listener* journalist who wrote the 24 May 1980 feature 'Peter Le Fleming: Back from

Beyond'. Such meticulous record-keeping made my job a lot easier. Finally, thanks also go to helicopter pilot Keith Miles, for sharing his memories of flying in on that search and effecting Le Fleming's rescue.

For Chapter 3, thanks go to Robert Atkins of Motueka for contacting me about keen hunter Eric Taplin, creator of Taplin South Hut. And for Chapter 4, old Reefton author William Hindmarsh, who only went by the nom de plume 'Waratah', must get mention for preserving his detailed memories of 'Little Biddy of the Buller' in his 1906 book *Tales of the Golden West*.

For the story of Harry Louis Moffatt, storekeeper of the Anatori diggings and the focus of Chapter 5, the Nelson Historical Society must be thanked for printing this remarkable man's autobiography back in 1966. I am also appreciative of the help of Ken Wright, who let me in on his research into digger James Durdon.

To the families of Godfrey Thomas and John Ryan, who went missing while cray fishing off the Kahurangi coast in 1972 and whose sad tale is told in Chapter 6, I appreciated hearing your family stories. Special thanks here go to Trish Elderton and Jan Studholme.

I could never go past the Karamea stories collected by Barry Chalmers and such comprehensive research should be acknowledged here, in particular the chapter 'Shipping' in his book 'Karamea's Forgotten Footprints'. Thanks for help on Chapter 7 also goes to Dolce McNabb of the Karamea Historical Society, who opened up the Karamea Centennial Museum photo archives to me and gave me much additional information.

For Chapter 8, cheers to Chris Petyt for making available his unpublished notes on the Cobb magnesite mine, and to Garner Teale for his memories and photos of his quarryman father Alfred Teale.

To ex-Forest Service ranger Max Polglaze, you will always have the 'Max factor' when it comes to the backcountry. Thanks for sharing your work diaries for Chapter 9. And on the subject of Forest Service rangers, much appreciation goes to Shirley McBurney for answering my questions about her late husband Jack, who features in Chapter 10, and for loaning me his precious carbon copy field reports. They were a treasure trove of gritty and near-daily diary information that was well worth poring over with a magnifying glass.

Thanks go to Dick Nicholls for showing me his tracks and enthusing me about William Washbourn, featured in Chapter 11. And for Chapter 12, I am particularly appreciative of the information I got about Donald the Puponga

ACKNOWLEDGEMENTS

locomotive steam train from Cary Coburn and John Orchard at the Blenheim Riverside Railway Society.

Thanks must go to Sue Clearwater for getting me passionate about kākahi, the stars of Chapter 13. And to Dave Heraud, cheers for sharing your Roaring Lion stories and photo album with me, featured in Chapter 14.

Thanks also to all the wonderful DOC staff around Golden Bay, Motueka and Westport who helped me as I went around getting these stories.

Last but not least, thanks go to my good mate Paul Kilgour for his astute observations gained from a life spent walking these hills. You added so much colour to these stories.

Writing this book, my life seemed only to get richer by the day.

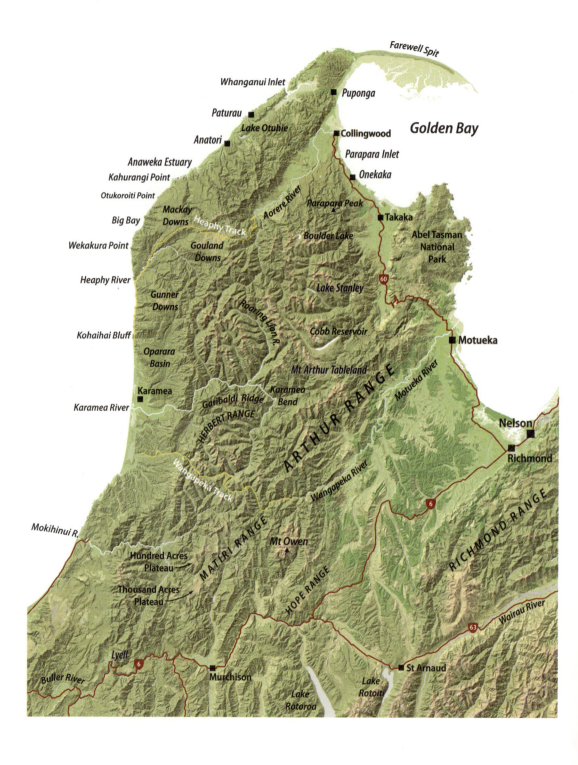

CHAPTER 1

ANAWEKA WAKA

THE DISCOVERY IN EARLY JANUARY 2012 of a 6.08-metre-long adzed-timber hull section from an obviously ancient and complex composite waka (canoe) on the Kahurangi coast was a significant find that was reported nationally. Eventually, news of the discovery spread globally, such were the age and unique features of the piece. It was identified as being no less than part of one of only two known voyaging canoes in existence, dating back to the early occupation of Polynesia, a time when ongoing maritime exploration and inter-island travel were the norm. In comparison, European mariners at that time were still only guessing when it came to navigating the open ocean.

Partially exposed after a major storm event, the complete hull section was dug out of an eroded sand dune behind a natural log jam of driftwood at the mouth of a small freshwater seep some 200 metres north of the Anaweka Estuary. The story of the discovery of the Anaweka waka by a naturally curious boy should not be forgotten. Waitapu Engineering co-boss Tony Nicholls of Takaka had used the Christmas break to take his family, including 12-year-old grandson Flynn, down to camp at the mouth of the Paturau River.

With the tide going out, the family party headed by 4WD vehicle down the gravelled road that leads from Paturau to Anatori and on to the bouldery

Turimawiwi River. They crossed this at the rough ford, before heading out around a driftwood-studded dune to access the hard surface of the outer beach and a clear 3-kilometre run south to the big, broad, open-mouthed estuary of the Anaweka River. Here, they planned to have a picnic and then head back to Paturau in the late afternoon, before the incoming tide would reclaim the beach and make the return impossible.

Ever since the mid-1930s, this long stretch of hard sand running down to Kahurangi Point has been used for vehicular access by the likes of tractors, trucks and all manner of off-road vehicles. This tradition of driving along the beach began when deliveries of the big acetylene bottles needed to power the Kahurangi Lighthouse beacon by surfboat ceased. These surfboats were rowed in from one of the two government supply boats, the SS *Tutanekai* and SS *Hinemoa*, both of which had long-serving and dedicated commanders: Captain Collin Post and Captain John Bollons, respectively. Offloading at Kahurangi was a treacherous business, and was reviewed after one surfboat overturned and its crew nearly drowned. When the surfboat deliveries were halted, surplus Second World War United States Army vehicles from the Pacific theatre were deployed to transport the acetylene bottles and supplies. These were Dodge command cars, purchased by Rex Thompson and Claude Wilkens of Collingwood Motors, who had the monthly delivery contract.

Just before the Anaweka is reached, the driftwood that edges the seaside dunes gives way to a more indented coastline of sea-worn sandstone. Here, the Nicholls family stopped their vehicle, getting out to explore the little coves for any flotsam and jetsam that may have washed up. Running ahead of the others as youngsters do, Flynn disappeared behind a big jam of driftwood. Within a minute he was back, excitedly calling the others to come and look.

Tony knew that the unusual item protruding from the washed-out watercourse was something important as soon as he saw it. A shaped slab of dark timber stuck nearly half a metre out of the sand. It was around 100 millimetres thick, and along its edges at regular intervals were fairly identical holes, each big enough to stick a couple of fingers through. 'It had to be some sort of old canoe,' was Tony's first thought, as reported in the local paper. At first the family dug with their hands, but the slab wouldn't budge, so Tony got out the shovel he keeps in his vehicle in case he ever gets stuck in the sand. The family used this to dig and dig around the slab, but it still refused to budge. At that point Tony returned to Anatori and borrowed a tractor and trailer,

A forest of giant rātā existed around the Anaweka Estuary right up until the 1950s, and was some of the last bush to be cleared for farming along this section of coast. Early Māori made the inlet home, planting sizeable taro and kūmara plots around its more sheltered and sunny recesses. The Anaweka waka was found 300 metres up the coast from the estuary's northern headland (upper centre). Photo: Alex Fishwick

on which he hastily threw an old mattress before heading back off down the beach to fetch his prize. Finally, three hours after coming across the timber, the family pulled it out of the eroded bank of sand, placed it on the mattress and securely tied it on.

I saw the remarkable hull piece the very day Nicholls towed it back to Takaka, parking up around the back of his big engineering workshop off Motupipi Street. I had been tipped off by someone who had spotted it just an hour before, and thought I might be interested – just the small-town grapevine! When I rolled up, the hull section was still securely tied with ropes to the mattress atop the trailer and had not been unloaded. I still recall how it wowed me from the moment I saw it, its smooth-adzed and shapely length protruding over both ends of the trailer. There was no mistaking its uniqueness. Skilfully shaped from a single timber, the fully intact hull

component featured what could only be lashing holes around its edges. Closer inspection revealed something unique: towards one end, the life-sized (around 60 centimetres across) carved relief of a swimming turtle, simple, elegant and beautifully executed. Extending from its tail was a flowing ridge, suggesting its wake through the water. I walked all around the trailer taking photos, before inspecting the far rougher underside and what was obviously the interior of the craft. I counted four transverse raised ribs, along with a straight longitudinal stringer along its entire inside length.

That day, I didn't appreciate that I had witnessed a remarkable piece of boat-building technology far beyond the realm of my experience. At the time, I was doing the odd bit of reporting for the *Golden Bay Weekly*, and my article on the waka section and the photographs that accompanied it in the following issue, distributed on 6 January 2012, was the very first virtually anyone had heard about the exciting find. Local iwi (tribes) and a couple of resident archaeologists expressed surprise that they hadn't been informed earlier. And I received an email from the Ministry for Culture and Heritage (MCH) suggesting that my article should have mentioned the legal obligations of reporting such a find under the Protected Objects Act 1975. My writing philosophy has always been, if it happened, then report the facts. I have never seen it as my job to preach the morality of a situation in the guise of so-called education.

In defence of Nicholls (who incidentally also rang me to complain that I had taken the published photos on his property without his permission and then used them, again without his permission), he had let the Museum of New Zealand Te Papa Tongarewa (Te Papa) know what he'd brought home fairly soon after the discovery. In some ways, Nicholls could be excused for feeling some sort of ownership of the hull strake. His forebears were among the first European settlers to take up land at Sandhill Creek, just north of the Anatori River, and beachcombing along the Kahurangi Coast had long been a Nicholls family tradition.

With all relevant government staff on holiday, the wheels of bureaucracy

An unbelievable find! The Nicholls family of Takaka were out on a 4WD beach picnic in early January 2012 when 12-year-old Flynn came across an unusual piece of wood protruding from an eroded bank of sand. The whole family excitedly got involved, digging out the 6.08-metre-long waka section and taking it back to Takaka. It would be identified as one of only two known voyaging canoes dating back to the early occupation of Polynesia. Photo: Sharon Nicholls

were relatively slow to activate, but Nicholls' tenure of holding onto his prize was short-lived – less than a week in fact. By the end of the Christmas break, everything had swung into action. Dilys Johns, conservation archaeologist with the University of Auckland, had been sailing on the Waitemata Harbour when she received a call from MCH asking her to make a visit to the South Island to inspect the new find.

Johns, a senior research fellow specialising in the study and conservation of waterlogged and 'at risk' taonga (artefacts), travelled down to team up in Takaka with Chris Hill, a representative of Manawhenua ki Mohua, the umbrella group representing local iwi. Together, they visited Nicholls at his workshop, where they found the strake laid on a pallet at the back of the property.

Commented Johns, 'I thought it was going to be just another project, but when I saw the find… it took my breath away. I had never seen something so large and complex come out of a site.'

For around six days, the hull section had lain on the trailer and then the pallet. It was drying out, and fast. Some urgency to secure it was needed because, as it had been dug out of the ground and hadn't been kept wet, there was a risk it would crack as it dried out. Nicholls had little option. 'I just went with the flow and they seemed to want to take it away,' he told the *Motueka–Golden Bay News*.

The section wasn't taken far – just a few kilometres down the road in fact. Nicholls delivered it himself into iwi hands at Tarakohe, where it was locked up in one of the former buildings used by the now defunct Golden Bay Cement Company. It would stay there for the next three years, where it could be examined and kept immersed in a chemical solution of polyethylene glycol, which would remove all the chlorides from the timber. Eventually, at the end of the preservation process, a controlled dry-out over months would produce a curatable taonga ready for exhibiting.

Ironically, Nicholls – the person who found the strake and then gave it up – was commissioned to make the specially designed tank needed for its immersion and preservation. He was the co-owner of Takaka's only engineering shop after all.

Tests subsequently conducted on what was soon dubbed the 'Anaweka waka' were comprehensive and thorough. It took around 2½ years for three internationally recognised canoe and conservation experts – Dilys Johns, Geoffrey Irwin and Yun Sung – to publish a paper on the important find in

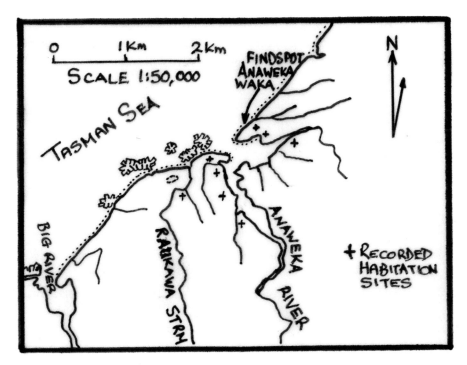

Anaweka Estuary, showing the spot where the Anaweka waka was found, along with recorded pre-European habitation and artefact sites around the inlet.

the *Proceedings of the National Academy of Sciences of the United States of America* (PNAS). It is titled 'An Early Sophisticated East Polynesian Voyaging Canoe Discovered on New Zealand's Coast'. The paper was edited by Patrick Kirch, director of the Oceanic Archaeology Laboratory at the University of California in Berkeley, whose specialist interest is in the origins and diversification of people and cultures throughout the Pacific.

One of the very first tests conducted on the Anaweka waka established that it had been adzed from a single slab of New Zealand matai (*Prumnopitys taxifolia*), while the caulking remains found in four of the lashing holes turned out to be pounded bark of tōtara (*Podocarpus totara*). Radiocarbon dating carried out by three separate laboratories – two in New Zealand and one in the United States – all came in with results of AD 1226–80 for the hull timber, and 40 or so years later for the oldest caulking material. It was normal procedure for composite canoes to be completely relashed every 20 years or so, often before a major ocean voyage or in a staggered fashion as required. Older caulking would be added to, providing a kind of snapshot of the boat's maintenance programme. The PNAS authors concluded from the latest caulking and repair dates that the last likely voyage of this waka would have been in around AD 1400.

Putting this into a global perspective, the Anaweka waka was made in Aotearoa around the same time that, on the opposite side of the world, the ornate Chartres Cathedral was being constructed in France. Who was more sophisticated one may ask, the Polynesian Māori, who had already mastered complex oceanic travel, or the Europeans, who could build elaborate towering churches yet were unable to sail beyond the horizon for fear of getting lost, or worse, dropping off the edge of the world?

Almost certainly, the Anaweka waka was actively used around the exposed open sea coast off the South Island, where it could hardly have operated without a sail. As the hull section was made of mataī, it could only have been built in New Zealand, or at a possible stretch it could have been a replacement piece created for a voyaging canoe made in the islands and sailed out much earlier. After all, mataī is a highly durable timber that would deteriorate at a far slower rate than tropical timbers like breadfruit (*Artocarpus altilis*), which was often used to build boats in east Polynesia. The location, size and sophistication of the find strongly suggest the hull piece was definitely part of a large ocean-going sailing canoe. But the obvious question is: exactly what type of canoe was it part of?

Earlier forms of composite ocean-voyaging canoes, like the one the Anaweka component was obviously from, were the only ones known to have reached New Zealand from east Polynesia. Māori oral traditions state that both double and single outrigger canoes originally came to Aotearoa. Sailing was the primary power mode for these ancient voyaging canoes, the distances obviously far too great to travel by paddling alone.

Having poured over all the possibilities, experts think that the Anaweka waka piece fitted in as one of the upright hull sides near the rear of a big double canoe lashed across with a deck and a shelter from the sun and rain. The vessel had a low bow and raised stern, and an inverted triangular sail set forward just like the historical canoes of the Society and Southern Cook islands. In Tahiti, these canoes were called tipairua and were often an impressive 20 metres in length. The PNAS paper likens the Anaweka find to a single piece of a jigsaw puzzle, or an attempt to reconstruct a new animal from a single bone.

The Anaweka waka section tied tight atop a mattress on Tony Nicholls' trailer, just after he arrived back in Takaka. The family's find was soon requisitioned by the Ministry for Culture and Heritage under the Protected Objects Act 1975. Photo: Gerard Hindmarsh

According to Herb Kawainui Kane in his book *Voyagers* (1991), tipairua typically bore romantic names, two remembered ones translating to *Rainbow* and *Wait for the West Wind*. On some islands their sails evolved locally to be rimmed with pliable wood strips, which were a great improvement on the triangular oceanic sail the Anaweka waka probably sported. In 1769, during the first Pacific voyage of English explorer James Cook, naturalist Joseph Banks explained the improvement: 'With these sails their canoes go at a very good rate, and lie very near the wind, probably on account of their sail being bordered with wood.'

Luckily, a comprehensive historical and well-distributed literature exists on the development of Pacific oceanic canoe designs. More general 'archaic' forms developed into 'classical' designs particular to each island group, adapted to local winds and seas, and local timber resources. So it is possible to speculate fairly accurately which group of islands a particular canoe came from, or where its design originated.

A remarkable feature of the Anaweka waka is the carved relief of a sea turtle, significant to Polynesians as an animal associated with long migrations across open ocean. Relatively rare in Māoridom, turtle motifs are common in the Society Islands, where they were often carved onto the exterior of canoes to help guide mariners on their journeys.
Photo: Sharon Nicholls

Importantly, the design technology and era of the Anaweka hull piece correlates with those of the only other large voyaging canoe ever found. This was excavated in 1978 from a coastal swamp on Huahine, one of the Leeward Islands group (Îles Sous-le-Vent) in the Society Islands, by Yosihiko Sinoto from the Bishop Museum of Hawai'i. His find caused an archaeological sensation, as it was regarded as the last remaining east Polynesian voyaging canoe left in existence, dating back at least 800 years to the early occupation of the region. The finding of the Anaweka waka on the Kahurangi coast in early 2012 now makes that world tally two. The open-ocean distance between the two finds is 4,221 kilometres.

In February 2017, my ongoing interest in the Anaweka waka took me to Huahine (pronounced 'wahine' and like the Māori word wahine, also meaning 'woman'). Clustered together with Raiatea and Taha'a, Huahine rises out of the sea as one of the lushest islands in all Polynesia. It's about 16 kilometres

The remains of a voyaging canoe, dubbed the Huahine canoe, being excavated in 1978 from a coastal swamp on the island of Huahine in the Society Islands. The Anaweka waka and the Huahine canoe are near identical in their construction and are of a similar age.
Photo: Maitai Lapita Village Hotel museum, Huahine

long by 13 kilometres wide, and is actually two islands – Huahine Nui in the north and Huahine Iti in the south. These are joined by a sand spit that is exposed at low tide, and by the modern addition of a narrow, 200-metre-long road bridge for the convenience of motorists today.

Tahitians call Huahine 'the wild island', a reference to its verdant tropical jungle, which on its lower reaches is peppered with coconut and vanilla plantations. Planes from Tahiti (192 kilometres away) arrive three times a day, en route to Raiatea and Bora Bora, dropping off locals, a few tourists and surfies, who come to experience some of the best breaks French Polynesia can offer. The flight in over the turquoise lagoon takes your breath away.

Huahine (current population 6,300) has always stood out on its own. The last island in French Polynesia to resist annexation by France, it's still full of islanders who exhibit a fierce pride and independence. Tahitians have a saying about the people of Huahine: 'Obstinacy is their diversion'.

The vestiges of Huahine's prestigious past and rich culture were first investigated by archaeologist Kenneth Emory of Honolulu's Bishop Museum in the 1920s. He uncovered habitation sites, feasting and council platforms, temples and funerary sites, stone-tool workshops, agricultural terraces, stone fish traps, fortified sites and petroglyph (rock art) sites. It can take weeks just to visit the hundreds of ceremonial marae sites. Emory's work was superseded by that of Sinoto in the 1970s, and was then followed up by New Zealand archaeologist Mark Eddowes, who in 2003 conducted an island-wide survey to document more than 200 of the most important sites.

The Huahine canoe was found during the excavation of an ornamental pond as part of the construction of the original Hotel Bali Hai at Vaito'otia–Fa'ahia in Huahine Nui. Part-owner of the current hotel on the site (the Maitai Lapita Village Hotel) is ex-Californian native Peter Owen, now a long-time island resident and renowned potter. He bought the 3-hectare site after the Bali Hai was demolished following severe damage in a cyclone. Peter took me around his hotel museum, which he set up in consultation with Eddowes, and explained how the canoe was found:

> *During construction work for the buildings of the original Hotel Bali Hai on this site, they were dredging out an area of swampy ground to make some ornamental ponds. Suddenly, the workers began digging up exceptional finds, all totally preserved in the waterlogged anaerobic conditions. Dr Sinoto was working on the island at the time. He was immediately called in and meticulously conducted the subsequent excavation over two years, which came up with hundreds and hundreds of artefacts.*

In addition to a stone war club, near identical to mere (flat weapons) made later in Aotearoa, one of the early finds included a half-finished canoe baler and a 3-metre-long steering paddle, plus a number of other, partially carved, paddles. Then the archaeological team uncovered a mast and, later, sections of a big canoe, which was soon dubbed the 'Huahine canoe'. A feature of the dig was the exceptional condition of many of the artefacts as they were dug up, all preserved in the thick, airless mud. One necklace was totally intact, its woven coconut fibre as good as the day it was made. Some of the artefacts now reside in the Museum of Tahiti and the Islands, others were taken to the Bishop Museum in Hawai'i and some were reburied in accordance with local wishes.

ANAWEKA WAKA

The sea turtle on the Anaweka waka matches exactly the petroglyph of a sea turtle found on a stone block at Marae Rauhuru on Huahine in the Society Islands, and being removed here by archaeologists from Honolulu's Bernice P. Bishop Museum in 1924.
Photo: Fare Potee museum, Huahine

I compared photos on the hotel museum wall of the Huahine hull pieces with the first pictures I took of the Anaweka waka. It is simply uncanny: they are near identical. Because the Huahine artefacts were found covered in a layer of sand, and the larger pieces were all aligned to the reef opening directly offshore, as if being deposited while they were being dragged out, Sinoto later concluded that this important canoe-building site and village were quite possibly hit by a tsunami, or at least a series of big waves from a super-hurricane. In effect, the excavation eerily provided a snapshot of a destructive event that occurred sometime around AD 1100 – quite feasibly a kind of Polynesian Pompeii.

One remarkable feature in an open area of the hotel grounds is a small square pavement of stones. This is the earliest ceremonial marae site yet identified in east Polynesia, indicating that this area was settled sometime between AD 650 and AD 850 – as early as it gets for humans around here.

Being made from mataī, the Anaweka waka hull section must have been created in Aotearoa, although there is a chance it could have been a replacement component that was fashioned and fitted here to an overseas vessel. One thing is fairly certain, however: if the entire craft was made here – and that's the most likely scenario – then the people who sailed her were only two or three generations removed from the original voyagers who sailed to Aotearoa, and that migration would still have lived on in the memory of the society. Could that recent memory (or those recent descendants) have narrowly escaped a natural catastrophe? It is humbling that we now have an artefact of such importance in this country, found on the isolated Kahurangi coast, which matches another one discovered 4,221 kilometres away in east Polynesia.

This needn't come as any surprise, of course. Plenty of artefacts corroborate the immigration link that connects the Society Islands to New Zealand – far more even than the Cook Islands, whose indigenous people we label Cook Islands Māori. These include near-identical fish hooks, necklace styles, clever fish traps, tackle and nets, adzes, mere and even food pounders – the list is long and indisputably all share common characteristics. But perhaps it's language – in particular place-names – that has always provided some of the most compelling evidence that the Society Islands group was the main hub for immigration to New Zealand.

James Cook was the first to chart the past migrational movement of Pacific peoples by comparing their languages. This has been followed through by many distinguished ethnographers, including the likes of S. Percy Smith, who in 1904 published *Hawaiki: the Original Home of the Maori; with a Sketch of Polynesian History*. Twelve years later, Elsdon Best took advantage of the war years to interview indigenous men from the Society Islands who were passing through Wellington en route to training camps in New Caledonia. Among other information he obtained were details about Tahitian place-names, which matched the names of many well-known places around New Zealand. Best collected these names as a way of determining and pinpointing exactly where they had originated, or as he put it, to 'assist to some extent in settling the question as to the islands from which the ancestors of the Maori migrated when they passed down the long sea roads to settle on the shores of New Zealand'.

Best realised that to make sense of these correlations it was important to understand the changes that have taken place in the dialect of the Society Islands since the ancestors of the New Zealand Māori left 30 or so generations ago. While te reo Māori developed in a stately fashion, with more articulated enunciation, the evolution of Tahitian has been marked chiefly by the gradual dropping of 'k' and 'ng' sounds, their place supplanted by a little catch or break in the voice. This has become so pronounced that today some Tahitian words have morphed into a remarkable successions of vowels. Tangata (meaning 'person') has become ta'ata, while kangakanga (meaning 'curse' or 'profanity') has ended up as the almost unwritable a'aa'a. Whakaakaaka (meaning 'having') has become the far softer-sounding fa'aa'aa'a. Half tongue in cheek, Best noted that if this progress continued, it would be interesting to know how long it would be before the Tahitian alphabet were composed of the lone letter 'a'.

As for place-names, Whangarei has become Fa'arei in the Society Islands, while Whangaroa relates directly to Fa'aroa. Large sections of the New Zealand coast bear these exact translated Tahitian names, often assigned in the same order as if you'd walked or sailed along the beach back in the Society Islands. In particular, Best maintained that the place-names of Takaka and Motueka, at the top of the South Island, derived directly from the islets of Ta'a'a and Motu'e'a off the coast of Raiatea, just a canoe hop across from Huahine.

Best noted, too, that Motu'e'a was the abode of a dreaded monster, a destroyer of mankind, known as Ai-fa'arua'i (Kai-whakaruaki in Māori). This story was brought directly to Aotearoa from east Polynesia and localised almost detail for detail as the taniwha (water monster) of Parapara Inlet, 5 kilometres south of Collingwood. It could consume 300 people passing by in one go, and every group of warriors who had ever pitted themselves against it were all quickly slain. In Aotearoa, the taniwha was finally slain by the most fierce Ngāi Tahu warrior, a man so strong he could slay a seal with his bare hands. He made his spear from the last pōhutukawa tree in the area and used it to overcome the monster, which in its death throes gouged out Parapara Inlet.

Interestingly, Best recorded that the collective name of the Society Islands group (excluding Tahiti) in ancient times was Te Aotea. Is this the real origin of Aotearoa? Roa means 'long', given to the long islands the voyagers discovered; modern translations need not apply. One of the oldest Māori whakataukī (proverbs) relates to the *Aotea* waka, one of the traditional founding canoes, and highlights the importance of genealogy and culture: 'He kākano ahau i ruia mai i Rangiatea ('I am the seed that was sown in the heavens of Rangiatea [Raiatea]'). It is pertinent that Māori can often trace their ancestors to the important voyaging waka that brought them to Aotearoa, essentially marking the start of their history in a new land as immigrant peoples.

This emigration history is still well appreciated in oral histories of the Society Islands, the inhabitants of which sometimes infer that those who left were possibly viewed as exiles, or even banished. In 2009, some Taha'a locals held an informal celebration at one of the marae on their island, lifting the tapu (restriction) and allowing the Kiwi iwi to return. The finding of the Anaweka strake was interpreted by some as a sort of completion of this event.

The section of coast that encompasses the Anaweka Estuary was traditionally known as Te Tai Tapu, translated by various experts to mean 'sacred or prohibited territory or boundary'. This coast definitively stretches from the southern end of the Whanganui Inlet to the Kahurangi River, and is defined by a seascape of long sandy beaches, offshore shoals, rocky reefs teeming with kaimoana, and a corresponding landscape of limestone and low-rise clay and sand hills. South of the Kahurangi River, the geology abruptly changes to give way to a steep granite coastline of formidable headlands with numerous offshore stacks. This has always formed a natural rohe (boundary) with southern West Coast iwi.

Well-recorded oral history indicates that the first settlers along the Kahurangi coast and in Golden Bay were the Ngāti Ara people, said to have arrived from Tahiti in around AD 1350. Obviously, the Anaweka waka pushes back this settlement date. Other iwi associated with the earliest settlement of

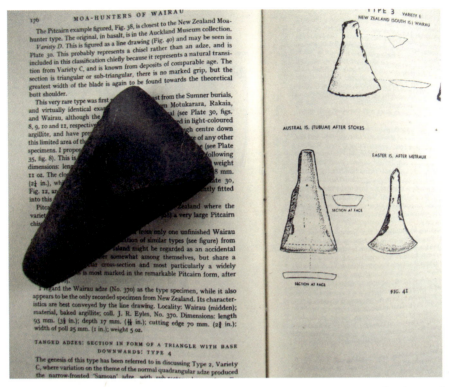

This argillite adze (classified Type 3a), found near the Kahurangi River, is dated around AD 1400, and was most probably used to finish waka. Only one other adze like it has been found in the country, in Wairau. The design technology of the tool matches others from early east Polynesia. Photo: Gerard Hindmarsh

Golden Bay have also been mooted to be Te Rapuwai, Waitaha and Ngāti Wairangi. Their colonisation was successful until they were displaced by the more war-like Ngāti Tumatakoriri in around 1600, the same people who would confront Dutch explorer Abel Tasman off Wainui Bay in 1642. In turn, the Tumatakoriri people were wiped out by northern allied tribes of Ngāti Tama and Ngāti Rārua, the most decisive battle between the iwi being at Paturau in 1830. The invaders sneaked up on the hundred or more inhabitants and cruelly slayed them with patu (clubs), then turfed the bodies up into a long pile, giving the place its name (paturau means either 'lie in a long heap', 'long weapon' or '100 clubs').

New Zealand was the last significant landmass to be colonised. All sorts of theories have postulated that Chinese, Spanish, Portuguese and even Egyptian and Phoenician seafarers came to visit. But in the end, it's only the colonisers who come to stay and inhabit the land that count.

Lia Matisoo-Smith, a biological anthropologist at the University of Otago, has been working on the puzzle of the legendary Polynesian home of Hawaiki for nearly two decades, using variations in mitochondrial DNA (mtDNA) and Y chromosomes to track the migrational histories of the first New Zealanders. The maternal lineage is responsible for inheritance of mtDNA, while Y chromosomes come from the paternal side. Mutations arise in the genes over time, accumulating and being passed down through successive generations. Establishing which mutations individuals have in common is therefore a way of seeing how closely related they are. With permission from the Rangitāne o Wairau iwi, Matisoo-Smith and her colleagues extracted and analysed genetic sequences from the teeth of a man and three women whose remains were uncovered from New Zealand's oldest archaeological site, on the Wairau Bar in Marlborough. This large village, dated AD 1285–1300, has not only revealed human remains but also the remains of extinct species of moa and Haast's eagle (*Harpagornis moorei*), along with those of extant marine mammals. In addition, carved artefacts and necklaces relating to east Polynesian cultures were found, which, says Matisoo-Smith, were produced 'prior to the development of unique Māori motifs and designs'. These remains were dated back 700 years, which Matisoo-Smith postulates 'were within a generation or two of, if not the first colonists, who arrived in New Zealand'.

But one of the most significant findings was the unravelling of the genetic diversity of the four individuals. Explained Matisoo-Smith:

> *One thing we might have expected, given the matrilineal and matrilocal structure of ancient Pacific societies, is that these settlers were sisters and their husbands, or people who are closely related, in which case we would see very little mtDNA variation. So the fact that these individuals were not closely related on a maternal line was quite surprising. It means that there were at least four maternal lineages among the four individuals, which is pretty diverse.*

With all the archaeological and linguistic evidence pointing to Hawaiki being somewhere in central-east Polynesia – an area stretching from the Cook Islands to the Society Islands and out to the Austral Islands – researchers hope eventually to match specific mutations of the Wairau Bar individuals to other populations in east Polynesia. Eventually, Hawaiki – or various Hawaiki – will be found.

As for the relief of the sea turtle on the Anaweka waka strake, these motifs are rare in Māoridom but not completely unknown, and are thought to be associated with the early age of the canoe and in particular tropical east Polynesia. Four prehistoric stone amulets with turtle motifs are documented by archaeologist Nigel Prickett in his 1999 book *Nga Tohu Tawhito: Early Maori Ornaments*, and in B.J. Gill's definitive 1997 paper 'Records of Turtles and Sea Snakes in New Zealand, 1837–1996'. As the PNAS report points out, 'a sea turtle carved into an 800-year-old Polynesian canoe was a powerful symbol'. Presumably the turtle was carved to swim in the same direction as the boat, making that shaped end the back, but was the carving visible underneath the boat or just above the waterline on the side? This is all open to debate.

Excitingly, the Anaweka find not only provides us with evidence about early canoe technology, but also insights into an already well-established seafaring people. As the PNAS report makes clear, those who sailed the waka 'were not that many human generations removed in time from the period of New Zealand settlement by a considerable and diverse East Polynesian population involving many voyages spread over some generations'.

The journey to Aotearoa from Tahiti or any of her islands would have taken anywhere from four to six weeks, necessitating double-hulled craft, which offered far more stability in the running seas. Readying the big canoes for voyaging was an elaborate and ordered process that could take months. Stowed aboard and carefully wrapped were sea rations of dried fish and fruits, breadfruit and taro paste. Enough water for the voyage was stored in large gourds, and copious coconuts were taken. Dogs and chickens, along with specially selected weaned piglets, were often taken as breeding stock for the new land, as were cuttings, seeds and seedlings – it is known, for example, that early voyagers to Hawai'i took at least 24 plant species with them. The finest craftwork and shell ornaments were also often taken to facilitate trade and friendly encounters, just as weapons were stowed aboard should the voyagers face any hostility, along with tools to aid the building of shelters and boats.

As told in tradition, some of these voyages clearly involved returns, quite feasibly in the seafaring Anaweka waka. The Kermadec and Norfolk islands

The ideal length for a multi-hull Polynesian voyaging canoe was 16–18 metres – large enough to handle the relatively tight Pacific swells, yet short enough to recover from the troughs. Vessels that were longer than this tended to twist as they straddled the swells, putting undue stress on the lashings. Photo: Fare Potee museum, Huahine

were visited sporadically, and even the subantarctic Auckland Island (Motu Maha) was reached by Māori.

Hawaiian canoe expert Herb Kawainui Kane makes the point that, from his own experience of Pacific swells, and in consultation with experienced sailors, the ideal length for an oceanic voyaging canoe was 16–18 metres (55–60 feet), large enough to handle the relatively tight Pacific swells, yet short enough to recover in the troughs. This size fits in perfectly with the estimated length of the Anaweka waka. Canoes of greater length tended to twist as they straddled the waves, thus putting too much stress on the lashings.

Maintaining lashings was a top priority. Still practised in Micronesia is the deliberate swamping of canoes when caught out in a bad storm, a concept completely foreign to modern mariners. Wooden craft can be relied on not to sink, and canoes on longer trips always carry coconuts stored under woven nets in hull bilges to provide extra flotation as much as food. In a storm, the deck cabin – along with anything not lashed down – is invariably swept away, but the crew just ride the weather out, crouched in the hulls and keeping their heads and shoulders above the waves. Not only does the canoe hold its position fairly well while in a swamped state, but there is less stress on the lashings – all that is holding the whole boat together after all. Once the storm passes, the crew bale the boat out and get going again, confident their craft is in good shape.

Māori built the longest waka in Polynesia, for war, but by far the biggest multi-hulls were constructed on Tahiti – called pahi if they were used for war, or va'a ti'i if used for ceremonial purposes. In 1774, James Cook witnessed the spectacular sight of 160 of these giant multi-hulled vessels, many more than 60 metres in length, accompanied by 170 smaller double-hulled sailing canoes, all carrying 'not less than 7,760 men to battle' according to Herb Kawainui Kane. The most elaborate vessels could take years to construct, their large keels painstakingly built up with strakes of carved breadfruit planks, all assembled with lashings made of sennit, the plaited fibre from coconuts.

It's amazing to think of the voyages routinely undertaken. Even further away were the Marquesas Islands, which featured bird symbolism on their voyaging canoes rather than the turtles of the Society Islands. Lacking abundant lagoons and plagued by periods of drought, the Marquesas spawned many voyages in search of new lands – Hawai'i and Easter Island (Rapa Nui) may have been among the Marquesans' discoveries. Not all voyages had happy endings, however. One account, titled 'Voyage of Exile', was recorded in the early nineteenth century by Captain David Porter of the United States Navy: 'The grandfather of Gattanewa [a chief in the Marquesas] sailed with four large canoes in search of land, taking with him a large stock of provisions and water, together with a quantity of hogs, poultry, and young plants. He was accompanied by several families, and has never been heard of since he sailed.'

It is said in Tahiti that legendary discoverer Kupe sailed from Raiatea, then called Havai'i, to Aoteoroa and returned to tell of a great mountainous land and forests filled only with birds. Others followed his sailing directions, keeping to the left of the setting sun in November, considered the most settled month for voyaging southwards across the ocean. Oral traditions establish that many voyages to Aotearoa were favourable, being well-planned and well-executed exercises.

It was the Polynesian navigators' intimacy with nature that set them apart. They knew their stars and constellations, such as Pa'e-tea, Ko'oe, Meremere, Matariki. Seabirds were also useful indicators of the probable position of islands, as different species travel varying distances from their island roosts to feed. Sighting a white tern (*Gygis alba*), known as itatae in Tahitian and kota'e in Marquesan, is the sign an island lies within a 10–40-kilometre radius. And when seen flying over the ocean, the white-tailed tropicbird (*Phaethon lepturus*), known as petea in Tahitian and tovake in Marquesan, indicates that land cannot be further than 150 kilometres distant.

But it was their deep and intuitive understanding of the way waves and undercurrents reflected and crisscrossed off islands – the pulse of the ocean – that gave Pacific navigators their major clues. Herb Kawainui Kane tells a story of how, in around 1820, a Tongan fleet lost their way on a long sea voyage. A blind navigator named Tuita Kahomovailahi was brought forward. After asking his son to describe what the clouds looked like and what seabirds he had seen, the old man put his arm in the ocean to feel its temperature and pulse.

'Tell the king we are in Fijian waters,' he called out to the navigators.

'But where is land?' they asked back.

The old man asked where the sun lay, was told, and then announced, 'Tell the king that at noon we will sight land.'

At noon exactly, they sighted the Fijian island of Lakeba.

As Māori established themselves in Aotearoa, it's probably not surprising that migrational return voyages appear to have tapered out from around the fifteenth century or so. Once here, Māori concentrated on developing their own canoe-building technologies, going on to create the 'super-waka' of war, waka taua, often more than 30 metres long and paddled by 120 warriors. These substantial and ornately carved vessels were considered sacred, entities in their own right, with names that commanded great respect. This development was thanks to Aoteoroa's abundance of wide-girthed podocarp trees, such as tōtara and mataī, which meant that not only could Māori build bigger waka but also a more diverse range for everyday use.

Under the Protected Objects Act 1975, all newly found taonga tūturu (original artefacts) such as the Anaweka waka are initially claimed as the property of the Crown, namely the Ministry for Culture and Heritage. Within 28 days, the MCH has an obligation to publish a notice calling for claims of ownership in relevant newspapers, along with letters to iwi with areas of interest related to where the taonga was found. In the case of the Anaweka waka, this protocol was followed.

So who were the historical owners of this canoe? Until now, oral traditions have put the arrival of the original Ngāti Ara people in this area at around AD 1350–1400 at the latest. These original migrants were followed by the Ngāti Tumatakokiri, who took up permanent occupation from around 1600, until they were decimated by Ngāti Tama and Ngāti Rārua allies at Paturau in 1830.

Local archaeologist Jack Walls says there is more evidence of continuous and significant occupation around Whanganui Inlet than in any other place around Golden Bay. In 1846, explorer Charles Heaphy wrote of passing 'old potato and taro cultivation grounds' around both the Anaweka River and the nearby Raukawa Stream, indicating Māori kainga (settlements) had existed on that coast not long before.

Claims of ownership for the Anaweka waka have been lodged by Manawhenua ki Mohua, the local umbrella organisation representing the interests of Ngāti Rārua, Ngāti Tama and Te Ātiawa, and Te Rūnanga o Ngāti Kuia Trust, representing Ngāti Kuia. The Māori Land Court will hear the case, but at the time of writing the hearing date has yet to be set.

In the meantime, the MCH acts as interim custodian, a role that involves appropriate conservation treatment. In this case, the waka is still submersed in a chemical tank in a secure shed at the Fonterra factory in Takaka, having been shifted there in 2014 after its previous lock-up at Tarakohe was demolished. The treatment process is expected to take up to two more years to complete before the hull section can go on display.

Exactly where this remarkable artefact ends up is anyone's guess of course. Any facility to house it outside of Te Papa would have to be purpose built. Personally, I agree with many locals who think it should be displayed locally, exactly where it belongs.

A similar strategy is being applied to the Papanui waka, a 6.17-metre-long by 0.59-metre-wide waka hī ika (fishing canoe) that was recovered in October 2014 from under 1.6 metres of sediment at the edge of the Papanui Inlet on the Otago Peninsula, along with a quantity of plaited fibre in its hull. After the Anaweka waka, it is now the second-oldest existing canoe relic in the country, aged at between 500 and 600 years. Like the Anaweka waka, it was adzed into shape with stone tools. This method differs from that used on many historical waka held in New Zealand museums, which are more recent (constructed within the last 250 years) and were created with the use of European tools. The Papanui waka likely relates back to the Ngāti Māmoe

Members of Manawhenua ki Mohua, the Golden Bay group representing local iwi, help place the Anaweka waka in a specially built tank at the defunct Golden Bay Cement Company plant. It stayed soaking here for some years in a solution of polyethylene glycol to remove all the chlorides from the timber, before being moved to a Takaka location. The final part of the process will be a controlled dry-out over several months. Photo: Sharon Nicholls

occupation of that part of the Otago Peninsula, or the Waitaha before them. That the waka appears to be smashed up along its gunnels indicates it may well have been regarded as a spoil of conquest and worthy of destruction. This sort of scenario is the intrigue that follows the recovery of such a relic. A special glass-topped tank on the Ōtākau Marae (Ngāi Tahu) now houses the waka while it undergoes chemical restoration and its eventual controlled drying out, so it can be exhibited for all to see. Along with the Anaweka waka, recovered taonga such as the Papanui find will continue to inspire us and even push back the record so that we can truly appreciate our past.

The last traditionally trained master canoe navigator in the Pacific died in 2010, aged 78. As an infant, Pius 'Mau' Piailug, of the tiny island of Satawal in the Caroline group in Micronesia, was often placed by his father in open rockpools so that he could 'feel the pull of the ocean currents'. At four, he started his full-time training in learning about the 'stars, swells and birds', and at 18 he earned the title of palu (master navigator), with status equal to a chief.

Luckily, this great man shared his knowledge with the Polynesian Voyaging

Society, which was set up in Hawai'i in the mid-1970s to revive the ancient art of non-instrument, wayfinding navigation. The outcome has been the construction of seven modern replicas of ancient ocean-going canoes, each now owned by a Pacific nation associated with voyaging. New Zealand's replica, the 22-metre-long *Hinemoana*, has recently returned home after five years of ocean voyaging. The waka is currently used in youth development training around the East Coast of the North Island. It is heartening to know those voyaging skills will not now be lost.

CHAPTER 2

HOPELESSLY LOST

KAHURANGI IS A RUGGED WILDERNESS that has claimed its fair share of victims and produced some incredibly close calls. John Reid Hut, a 1,200-metre-high grunt up from the Wangapeka River, is named after the Wakefield-based helicopter pilot who performed the first ever aerial cave rescue in the country, retrieving keen speleologist Lee Merchant from 20 metres down a deep shaft on Mt Owen in 1963. Luckily, the young caver had landed on a small shelf sticking out of the marble rock, otherwise he would have plummeted all the way down to the bottom. With severe spinal injuries, Merchant had to wait two days before Reid, ready and poised, could sneak his helicopter down through the first break in the heavy clouds and winch him out. Conditions were atrocious, but Reid flew the severely injured caver out to safety through conditions of near-zero visibility.

Top New Zealand caver Kieran Mackay describes the marble landscape of the 1,875-metre-high Mt Owen massif as like a glacier wrought in rock, struck through with crevasses. These twisted drainpipe contortions lead down from the sieve-like surface to the underworld, making it some of the most treacherous country that Kahurangi has to offer. In 2004, a 25-year-old Christchurch tramper named Anthony Goile broke all his front teeth and suffered a back injury on the southern side of the mountain when he sat down to edge over a lip covered in slippery snowgrass. Instead of controlling his slide, he took off down the steep hill, cartwheeling over a cliff and landing on a ledge. Only his pack and helmet saved him. His tramping mates used their cellphone to call for help, but Goile had to stay on that ledge for 24 hours before a helicopter could make it in to rescue him.

Sadly, some become lost and are never found. Californian tramper Roselyn Rae Tilbury, 23, disappeared without trace somewhere on the Gouland Downs in 1972. Her male tramping mate searched more and more frantically for her for three days before raising the alarm, but an extensive two-week search revealed no sign of the young woman. The Heaphy Track may be safe, but anywhere off it – even a few metres – can be disorientating and downright treacherous in places.

Alistair Levy, 54, a relatively experienced tramper from Christchurch, was another who was not found. He was last seen alive on Sunday, 23 December 2012 as he set off on a ragtag circuit of the broken stonefields of Castle Basin. The treacherous minefield of crevasse-studded and jagged bouldery terrain was a route he'd tried to take with a mate 20 years earlier, but they'd run out of light and were forced to return to Granity Pass Hut. Levy was definite how he wanted to retry it, his last 'intention' in the Granity Pass Hut book being: 'Going out through Bulmer, not Mt Owen/Sunrise'. It was an ambitious route, and when he didn't turn up at home for Christmas, his wife called New Zealand Land Search and Rescue (LandSAR). They looked for a week, but no sign of the tramper has ever been found.

As the popularity of the Kahurangi wilderness increases, so must more people be rescued, now relying ever more heavily on the modern availability of rescue helicopters and personal locator beacons. Call-outs are reported in the *Nelson Mail* with monotonous regularity, like the small inside-page story 'Tramper Winched from Kahurangi Park' on 29 February 2016. This report tells of the rescue of a 51-year-old male tramper from Wellington, who was on the steep and rugged Boulder Lake Track when he simply 'ran out of steam'. Running out of water on the dry, forested karst landscape hadn't helped him either, and after spending the night camped out in the open, he activated his rescue beacon the following morning. A rescue helicopter soon found him, set up in a clearing ready to be winched up and airlifted to Nelson Hospital, where he was qualified as having 'moderate injuries' from his ordeal.

The record for the longest time spent lost in the New Zealand wilderness – a dubious sort of title to hold – goes to Peter Le Fleming. He went missing, not on Mt Owen, but off the Heaphy Track for just short of 30 days in January and February 1980. From the very start, the circumstances of this 21-year-old's ordeal were highly unusual. Because he had suffered a head injury, he did not follow what could be considered normal patterns of expected behaviour for a typical lost person. What's more, the clues he purposefully left were positively baffling, leading searchers initially to look in the opposite direction. It was only a miracle that Le Fleming was finally found in a totally unexpected catchment just as the search was about to be called off. He was close to death and probably wouldn't have lasted another day. Nowadays, profiling techniques and more sophisticated terrain analysis used by LandSAR crews arguably mean a lost tramper like Le Fleming would be found sooner. But then tramping alone has always carried its risks. Throughout New Zealand, around 8,000 people are reported missing annually, but nearly all turn up within two weeks. Currently, the list includes 333 people who have been missing for more than a year, although only a handful of these relate to wilderness disappearances without trace. Luckily, Peter Le Fleming did not end up one of them.

The parks and reserves gardener from Palmerston North had recently finished his apprenticeship, and his idea of doing the Heaphy Track in his next summer holidays was a celebratory one. His parents, Bill and Avis Le Fleming, had raised seven children on their modest 25-hectare dairy farm at Kopane near Rongotea, 16 kilometres out of Feilding. Peter was their fifth child and still living at home. Slight of build but wiry, and sporting a full beard that had earned him the nickname 'Yeti' among his mates, he had been brought up to be extremely comfortable living the outdoor life. He was even an avid rugby player, a front rower for the local senior B team – an unusual position, it could be said, for someone so lightly framed.

So when Le Fleming flew from Palmerston North to Nelson to walk the Heaphy Track in early January 1980, he never bothered to write down his exact 'intentions' like everyone is urged to do today, nor did his parents think anything amiss with that. They were OK with just knowing his return date – after all, their son was a natural in the big outdoors and could survive anywhere. That strong sentiment of confidence from Avis Le Fleming in particular was reiterated several times to the media after her son was miraculously found

Based in Takaka, Constable Tony Cunningham was the sole-charge policeman in Golden Bay when 21-year-old Peter Le Fleming went missing off the Heaphy Track for just short of 30 days in January and February 1980. Cunningham, whose job included coordinating Search and Rescue, never gave up hope of finding him alive, and eventually he did.
Photo: Gill Cunningham

alive. 'A stubborn, honest, loyal and true streak,' she told David Young in his piece for the *New Zealand Listener*. Young also tracked down Peter's old school teacher, who commented, 'He always was a brave little boy.'

But Peter's omission to let anyone know his exact intentions cost the search team ten days – the time between when he did go missing on what was supposed to be the last day of his tramp, and when his family became worried enough to phone the police and report him missing.

From its start at Brown Hut to its finish at Kohaihai, the Heaphy Track is a robust 84 kilometres. Le Fleming was more ambitious than most who tackle the walk. He flew from Palmerston North to Nelson, and then caught the bus and several rides to Brown Hut. When he finished the track (which took him four days), the already tuckered-out tramper then turned around at Kohaihai and walked back again, effectively doubling the distance. It was suggested in one newspaper afterwards that perhaps Le Fleming had underestimated the

South Island terrain, which was far more extreme than he was used to in the Manawatu foothills. One thing is certain though, which is that January 1980 turned out to be the wettest on record. The track was being used heavily and in many long stretches became extremely muddy, boggy and slippery. Rivers and streams rose dramatically, breaking their banks and forcing trampers to hole up in the huts.

The subject of conversation in the all the huts would have been what the weather was going to do, and Le Fleming stayed an extra day at James Mackay Hut to let the rain clear and maybe even find someone to walk with. He whiled away his time playing 500 with his hut mates, but was disappointed no one seemed to be going his way. He wasn't a loner, and well appreciated that it made sense not to walk alone with so many torrents around. That stop at Mackay cost him a precious day's food, and he had calculated his provisions exactly to the very last day. So now he was one day's food short.

Le Fleming's return trip from James Mackay Hut across the largely treeless and marshy Gouland Downs the following day was miserable. He fell into a deep hole of water up to his elbows and managed to eat virtually all the food he had left. A party coming from the opposite direction found him at Gouland Downs Hut 'soaked through to his matches'. Condensation had permeated through the plastic liner protecting the matches, something he would later pay for dearly.

Feeling sorry for the young man, the trampers lit a fire and cooked up some soup and a little stew for him, which he had with some of their bread. The sunset that night was gorgeous, sneaking in under heavy cloud cover, indicating to Le Fleming that the weather was clearing, so he took off around 6AM the following morning on what was supposed to be his last tramping day. But the weather was doing anything but clearing. On that day, 19 January, 151 millimetres of rain was recorded at Bainham down in the valley, causing a flash flood in the Aorere River that would claim the lives of two experienced kayakers in a vicious whirlpool just upstream from the Quartz Range Road bridge. As LandSAR recovered the bodies later in the day, they were unaware that another situation was developing off the Heaphy Track just upstream.

The day had started relatively well for Le Fleming. He made good time along the easy 6.5-kilometre section to Perry Saddle Hut, where he met a trio of Canadian trampers. They would be the last people to see the young man for almost a month.

HOPELESSLY LOST

Before leaving Perry Saddle, Le Fleming recorded in the hut book that he intended to finish the track that day by walking out to Brown Hut, a relatively undemanding 15-kilometre graded track down the hill into the head of the Aorere Valley. The first part from Perry Saddle Hut is actually slightly uphill until you get to Flanagans Corner, which at 915 metres is the highest point along the whole Heaphy Track. On the day Le Fleming passed through, the open tops along this section had attracted some overnight snow, and the fractured schist and shale rocks of the track were wet and slippery.

Somewhere beyond here, and with more heavy rain imminent, Le Fleming stumbled and took a serious fall, banging his head in the process. The exact details of when and where this accident occurred will remain a mystery because the young tramper could never recall them, apart from saying to one of his rescuers later that he thought he fell about 10 metres down a bank. This was never verified and to some searchers did not quite add up, because the track along here is wide and has a consistent grade. But one thing is certain: whatever happened that day gave Le Fleming a huge concussion, because the next four days were fairly unaccountable in his memory. 'I just remember walking in a fog,' was all he could recall later, along with a brief few moments when he 'discovered' his wounds and roughly bandaged them up. Later in hospital, terrible scarring wounds were recorded on his lower back, along with cuts on his head and thigh, all consistent with a fall.

It rained for much of that week, apart from on 25 January, when there was a temporary reprieve in the weather. In that eerie, still aftermath of wet weather, a group of trampers reported hearing strange sounds coming from the direction of Shakespeare Flat, a forested area beside the upper Aorere River that can be reached down a 2-kilometre side track 7 kilometres up from Brown Hut. The trampers stopped and listened, but decided it was not a cry for help but more repetitive 'gong-like' sounds. After conferring, they decided it was not worth investigating further and so tramped on.

After his fall, there are two distinct possibilities for what happened to Le Fleming, desperately hungry and now seriously concussed. Either he regained the Heaphy Track and stumbled down it before turning off to Shakespeare Flat, or he continued down the slope he fell over, carrying on through the bush to end up at the flat. He didn't have any recollection of either.

Back in 1980, the turn-off to Shakespeare Flat was marked by a fairly large New Zealand Forest Service sign saying 'Shakespeare Flat 1 hour', but there was no mention of, or arrow indicating, the continuation of the Heaphy Track, as would be standard practice today. Despite having come up this way a week before and no doubt noticing the sign then, Le Fleming may have naturally taken the turn-off and stumbled down the roughish track to the forested flat on the true left bank of the Aorere River. The other possible scenario, in which Le Fleming continued down the slope after falling off the track, which may have been as far down as Aorere Shelter, also puts him in the direction of Shakespeare Flat. Either way, he would eventually find himself by towering stands of lush podocarp forest. Shakespeare Flat is a far different terrain from the ascending beech forests, tussocky downs and coastal forests of the Heaphy Track. The difference was perhaps beginning to dawn on Le Fleming as he stumbled along the river and pitched his tent in fading light near two dunes of flood-deposited sand beside a stand of rimu trees. Things were starting to register in his memory, but still only on a very basic level. As he would later recall, 'There were sandflies and bees which annoyed me to dark, and very quick-flying flies.'

Le Fleming spent five full days camped at Shakespeare Flat, eking out the last of his meagre rations, which included a bag of salt. For the first three days he put his energy into gathering stones to build a 'HELP' sign in metre-high letters that could be spotted from above. Searchers would later describe it as an elaborate construction – Le Fleming had even used his orange plastic plate to carefully curve the circle for the 'P' before filling it in with white stones. He also built a double arrow nearby out of fallen ponga logs, but confusingly one arrow pointed upriver and the other down. Apparently, he couldn't make up his mind which way he should head to get out, upstream or downstream, so he put in both. He explored his territory, even fording the swiftly flowing Aorere River on at least one early occasion, when he started banging for help at Flanagans Flat on a rusty old track marker that had been made from a disused 44-gallon drum. These were the 'gong' sounds heard high up on the Heaphy Track by the Canadian trampers who had stopped to listen, but in the end decided were nothing untoward. Down on the flat, Le Fleming later recalled banging everything in sight – anything that would make a noise or that could be recognised as a cry for help.

Somewhere between the fourth and eighth days, by Le Fleming's later reckoning, he felt fortunate to spy a sizeable trout, perhaps sickly, floundering and flapping about in the shallows along the river. He raced in and scooped

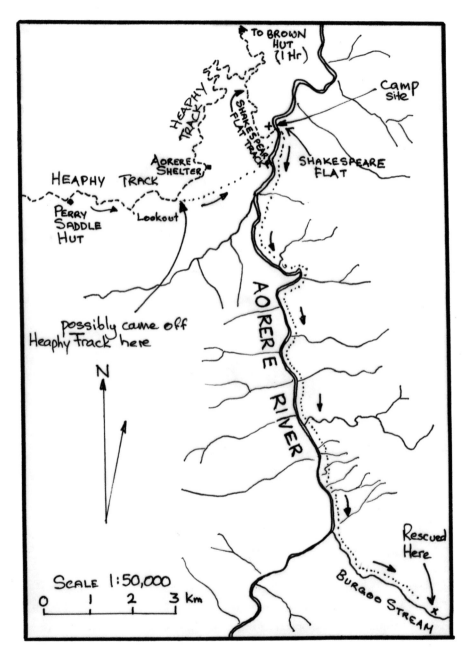

Map showing the probable route Peter Le Fleming took after coming off the Heaphy Track somewhere between Perry Saddle and Brown huts. Confused after a fall, he set up camp at Shakespeare Flat on the Aorere River for around four nights, before heading upstream and into the catchment of one of the Aorere's tributaries, the Burgoo Stream, where he was eventually found.

it out, rubbing it in and out with salt from his pack to preserve it before hanging it in a tree. Sodden from condensation, his matches were useless, so he knew he would be eating that fish raw. Amazingly, the trout was his only food for the next 3½ weeks, apart from native 'asparagus' or fiddlehead ferns, which he knew from home were edible, and a few worms he would pop down with salt.

The young tramper claimed that once he got used to the feeling, he never felt hungry during his ordeal. He did admit to dreaming of milkshakes and fried chicken, but he wasn't the type to pine for food. He'd been brought up on a dairy farm, and was tough. 'Breakfast was what was important. Tea – [dinner] you slept overnight, so it was wasted.' His mother also said later that he always ate well, but never indulged in hot drinks. Perhaps it was lucky for Le Fleming that he wasn't a hot tea or coffee addict, because it may well have added to his torment. He was Spartan in his approach to food – 'All you need is water and a bit of salt' was his approach to surviving in the great outdoors. And that philosophy worked for him, even if it did bring him within a hair's breadth of survival.

Holed up at Shakespeare Flat, in weather that never seemed to let up, Le Fleming tried to conserve his energy as best he could, often playing clock patience with a pack of cards he'd brought along, or even just sorting and resorting the cards into groups. His mind whiled away the time with word association games. He would look at his boots, and then his mind would race with 'shoes, sandals, sandshoes, rugby boots'. If you let your mind go, then you're nowhere, he thought to himself emphatically.

The extensive Shakespeare Flat area has long been favoured by hunters because of its deer and wild pig populations, but Le Fleming never saw any game, even though every morning when he struggled out of his tent there would be hoof prints neatly incised all over the sandbanks around him. 'Pig or deer, it was one of these two. I was too weak to wake up… a sort of half-pie sleep.' He recalled the birdlife as being minimal, except for the screeches of the kiwi at night, which he initially found a bit scary. Later, he would comment to his rescuer, Constable Tony Cunningham, on how his tired mind and hungry body had played tricks on him during his ordeal: 'Man you get some way-out visions here.' He never elaborated, except to say that the worst, most scary ones came at night.

But if Le Fleming's nights were hard to bear, by contrast his days turned into a reverie, a state defined as thinking about pleasant things, and occupied by dreamy meditations and fanciful musings. He spent hours one day carving his nickname 'Yeti' into a tree. Searchers looking around where he had camped found strange things, like his return air ticket folded and carefully stashed under a log, as if ready for collection later. The mornings were always misty, heavy cloud and rainy weather blotted out the rest of the days, and even during the long, dark nights the moon and stars barely showed themselves. Although the days seemed to merge into each other, the young tramper did make the effort to take a dip in the river to keep himself clean.

When Le Fleming did break camp, sometime around 1 February, he never thought about heading back up the track that had possibly led him down to the river flat. Instead, he gathered up his stuff and decided, for some unknown reason, to head upstream into the interior of the great North-West Nelson Forest Park wilderness. From things he said later, it is quite possible that he thought he was heading downstream, a type of disorientation not unknown among lost individuals suffering confusion or injury.

The tramper's memories from this time moving on were highly fragmented, little more than snippets or flashes of information strung together, as he would later recall: 'Crossed river near rapids, so I would come up against rocks to avoid whirlpools. Crossed with pack and did breaststroke. Had to cross a lot of waterfalls in steep country.'

The first day of February 1980 was also the day Le Fleming was expected home in Palmerston North. The first anyone knew something was up was when his parents drove out to the airport to meet him off the plane he had booked for his return home. 'When we went to meet the plane and no one was there, I suddenly went cold,' recalled his mother. The authorities were immediately alerted.

Le Fleming's mind-boggling traverse – of which little is really known – would see him end up 15 kilometres away from Shakespeare Flat in the Burgoo Stream, a rough, gorge-riddled tributary of the Aorere River, where he would stay for around a week before finally being found on the point of death. How he got there is not an impossibility. Only a handful of the hardiest trampers to this area know that an old, overgrown benched track put in by goldminers in the 1870s exists along the true right side of the Aorere River. Starting across the river from Shakespeare Flat and quite possibly still indicated by that old drum, it tracks through the bush all the way to the

Burgoo Stream. Skirting an impassable river bluff where the contours of the map almost touch, the old track cuts inland to meet the river again further up. It is quite possible that Le Fleming followed this overgrown benched track for at least part of the way, leading him further and further into the Kahurangi interior.

Once the police had been alerted that the young tramper was missing, a LandSAR operation was soon organised by sole-charge Takaka Constable Tony Cunningham. Unlike today, when there are dedicated LandSAR teams, local police back in 1980 coordinated any searches in their area of jurisdiction. Forest Service rangers were promptly radioed through and asked to check all the hut books. They soon ascertained that Le Fleming had passed through Perry Saddle Hut on his way out – a lucky break considering he did not sign all the hut books along his route. And there were no reports of him arriving at Brown Hut.

Checking the sides and banks along the Heaphy Track and the steep shortcut route – which diverts off at the old Skiltons Hut site and cuts out a wide loop of the track, saving an hour's walking – revealed nothing untoward, so attention then turned to Shakespeare Flat, at the end of the only turn-off between Perry Saddle and Brown Hut. Le Fleming's abandoned camp was soon found just downstream from the bushy flat. Collingwood farmer Mark Strange was in the team that found it:

> *It was teeming with rain when we came across it, this big HELP written with stones on the sand. We thought we were really onto something, but then it became confusing when we found the double arrow made out of ponga logs, which pointed both upstream and down. I spent seven days on that search, frustrating too in that we didn't quite know where to really look.*

LandSAR's technique today is big on profiling. A typical person picks their way through rough or uncharted terrain by 'purposeful wandering'. Nearly everyone will naturally choose open trails, be they animal tracks or natural partings and clearings. The mind intensely concentrates on finding the best, most convenient and fastest way forward, often at the cost of ignoring all non-essential information. Modern searchers are encouraged to stop every few metres, imagine themselves in the middle of a cube and look all around it,

Searchers thought they were onto something when they spotted Le Fleming's big 'HELP' sign – seen here from a helicopter – carved in a gravel bank just below Shakespeare Flat on the upper Aorere River. Confusingly, however, the nearby driftwood arrows (partially obscured by scrub, lower centre) pointed both upstream and downstream. Searchers decided to concentrate their search downstream, but Le Fleming had gone upstream, which was the reason it took so long to find him. Photo: Tony Cunningham

checking for any clues they would otherwise have missed. Only 'despondents' don't want to be found, but everyone else leaves clues, and usually plenty of them. The searchers on Le Fleming's case may not have known all the modern lingo, but they knew instinctively how to track someone who was hopelessly lost in the bush.

After five days with few clues, the search was stepped up and all available civilian searchers were called in to help. Pat Timmings was a high school teacher on LandSAR's list, which drew heavily from the Golden Bay Alpine and Tramping Club, of which Timmings was a keen member. Takaka District

High School was used to finding relief teachers when Timmings was called out on searches. The now retired teacher has kept an informative daily diary for much of his adult life, and his record for the Le Fleming call-out starts on 10 February 1980:

> *I got a call from Tony Cunningham to initiate another search and tomorrow two Club teams will head for Shakespeare Flat on the Aorere River. A bloke named Fleming... alias The Yeti... HELP in stones, arrows of logs pointing upstream and downstream... sounds like we might have a nutter.*

A typewritten 'Description of Missing Person' was distributed by the police to all searchers:

> *PETER LE FLEMING: 5′ 8″ in height, blue eyes, slight build, scar on inside of right leg, dark hair with full beard. WEARING: brown rubber soled shoes, blue Swandry* [sic] *jacket, brown corduroy hat, shorts, sandshoes. PACK: khaki canvas pack, top flap, one pocket. SLEEPING BAG: green with white lining inside. TENT: orange pup tent, orange ground sheet. CAMERA: Olympus 'Trip' camera, black transistor camera, orange plate/bowl, dessert plate found at camp site below Shakespeare Flat.*

Le Fleming was obviously in distress, indicative from the big 'HELP' sign he'd left behind, but the biggest red herring was the double arrow clue he had left pointing both downstream and upstream. Assisted now also by Nelson Police, Cunningham and all the initial searchers at Shakespeare Flat presumed Le Fleming would naturally have headed off downstream, which is the obvious way out for most people. So they concentrated much of their search downstream from the young man's camp. Since the day of his disappearance, the Aorere River had come up on several occasions and there was a possibility now he could have been swept away in the strong current and even drowned. Several seasoned Collingwood men were recruited to don wetsuits and float down the river rapids on a tractor tube, checking all the pools and snags along the way.

Timmings kept a meticulous record of the following day, which started with a 4AM wake-up. He headed to Brown Hut, where he was joined by Peter

Riordon, Peter Coote, Ralph Douglas, and brothers John and Allan Rose – all keen local men who knew the terrain well. Rather than head off up the track, they split into four two-man teams to scour both sides of the Aorere River, in particular an area directly below the Heaphy Track from where some trampers had reported what sounded like distant cries of 'Help! Help!'

Timmings recorded the arduous dawn-to-dusk search: 'Usual grim business of heading through swamp and supplejack, trying to dodge boulders and bush lawyer, enduring vagrant sunshine and falling over logs. We found no trace of Le Fleming, but then, no one else did either. Big highlight of the day was heading off a big kiwi which showed it was not appreciative of our attentions.'

The reason no one found anything, of course, was because Le Fleming had trudged, waded and swum some 15 kilometres upstream, in exactly the opposite direction to where all the searchers were looking. And then, deep in the wilds of the upper Aorere Valley, the young tramper suddenly turned up one of the river's tributaries, the Burgoo Stream – named by goldminers after their stodgy porridge – and started trudging up it. Now in no condition to build any more direction arrows or even pitch his tent, Le Fleming would subsequently remember little of events from this point on. Utterly exhausted, he abandoned his pack and tent, along with his groundsheet, under a big rock.

With nothing to protect him from the elements, Le Fleming lived for a whole week up in the incredibly isolated Burgoo. When it got cold around dawn and in the late evening, he would use the little energy he had to walk around, and during the day he slept as much as he could. Vague, misty recollections came to him later about two blue ducks that showed up every day to feed in the river. But his rural unsentimentality came out, with no such thing as companionship read into any of the sightings of fauna that some lost folk can experience. In particular, two hawks that flew over every morning and evening felt downright sinister to Le Fleming.

How the lost tramper was discovered by sheer chance and rescued is remarkable in itself. After extensive efforts, the ground search was scaled down and Cunningham was reported in the *Nelson Evening Mail* on 13 February as saying that the prospects of finding Le Fleming alive were not bright: 'We would have expected some signs by now.' The constable reiterated that the close-contact searches had covered extensive areas of the Aorere River and the surrounding flats – virtually everywhere Le Fleming could be expected to have wandered.

When all the ground crew pulled out, a helicopter was used to carry on the search up the upper Aorere Valley. Each day it scanned different sections of the riverbank for clues, no one even remotely suspecting that Le Fleming had diverted well up an isolated upstream tributary. Cunningham was ready to call it off and conferred with his boss, a district commander from Christchurch who was relieving in Nelson. The order was to carry out one last helicopter search to exhaust all possibilities and 'keep the family happy'. No searcher likes giving up on a 'no trace', especially when it comes to informing the family.

That very last search for Le Fleming lifted off from a paddock in East Takaka around 10.30AM on 18 February. The Hughes 500 chopper was piloted by experienced deer-recovery bush pilot Keith Miles, and also on board were Cunningham, search stalwart Trevor Solly of Collingwood and Cunningham's wife Gillian, on what was her first ever helicopter ride. Gillian had been recruited at the last minute for her great eyesight, a useful asset over the exceedingly difficult terrain they were expecting to cover in the next few hours.

Miles took his chopper up the Anatoki Valley, climbing steadily so that he could pitch over the sharp line of ridges and come down the catchment of the Burgoo. This was a direct shortcut to the planned search area, and Cunningham thought the course might also 'save the taxpayer some money on what had proved to be a costly search'. Everything had to balance out in the end.

As they came down the narrow Burgoo Valley, Cunningham was the first to spot a reddish-orange tent 'looking like it was hooked up in a tree or something'. Unable to manoeuvre down into the tight catchment with a full load of passengers, Miles dropped Trevor and Gillian off by a small lake formed by a slip upstream. The pilot was then able to bring his chopper almost down to the river so Cunningham could jump out and collect it. He recalled, 'I knew we were onto Le Fleming as soon as I saw his pack with the tent, everything matched the description of his stuff. His boots were there too, just discarded.'

With Cunningham back in the chopper, they descended right into the steep-sided creek so that the helicopter could do a slow search of the vicinity. In some places the overhanging trees forced them to climb above the canopy. Around 400 metres downstream from the spot where they'd found the ditched gear, they finally saw the missing man himself, lying on his side on a large rock. They waved madly to him but he was too weak to respond, barely managing to turn his head as he feebly twirled a twig at them. Finally, he must have summoned all his energy, lifting his head barely to give his rescuers a feeble wave back. Recalled Cunningham, 'He was very lucky we spotted him. He was wearing a black parka on black wet-looking rocks. We had already been over that spot three times without seeing him.'

As the terrain was too steep and narrow to allow a landing anywhere nearby, Miles circled high to pick out a small, flat area upstream where they could land. Cunningham jumped out here and headed downstream. Le Fleming, almost certainly only hours away from death, wondered if he had been hallucinating. The big thumping helicopter had been there, hovering, and then it was gone, nowhere to be seen. Four times he had heard helicopters fly overhead while he was up the Burgoo, and four times he'd thought he'd imagined them.

Around ten minutes after it all went quiet, Le Fleming saw his rescuer picking his way across the boulders towards him. 'Gidday, how the hell are you?' Cunningham greeted him with genuine amazement before smoothing out some of the gravel bank so that the young man could lie down properly. Carefully, Cunningham gave him water, which Le Fleming did not have the strength to get himself from the river just metres away. Le Fleming later recalled that his rescuer was 'quite a good joker. Six foot, broad with a mo and Swanndri and blue jeans', but could remember nothing about what words went down between them. In fact, it was an hour before Le Fleming could say anything, and that only came out in a whisper, which Cunningham had to bend his head close to hear.

Rescuer and rescuee stayed together until the early afternoon, when a Lama helicopter from Helicopters New Zealand in Nelson could be flown in to winch the man out, something Miles's Hughes 500 was not capable of. Lama pilot Ray Wilson came with two passengers, Dr Mark Patrick and Constable Brian Nicholls from Nelson, the latter having been involved in the ground search around Shakespeare Flat. The passengers were dropped off on a convenient flat nearby, lowering the weight and increasing the manoeuvrability of the chopper, then Wilson hovered above the tight gorge and lowered a lightweight stretcher to Cunningham, who loaded Le Fleming onto it. As Wilson said later, 'Then came the tricky bit!' The winch rope – actually just a climbing rope – was lowered 36 metres and tied to the stretcher before Le Fleming was lifted out, dangling on the end of the rope, and ferried into the

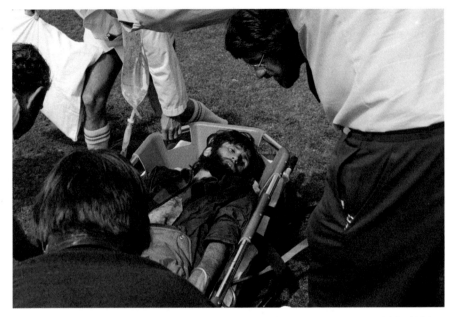

A rescued Peter Le Fleming being unloaded from the helicopter on the lower field of Nelson College, from where he was whisked across to Nelson Hospital. Normally weighing 70 kilograms, he was down to just 45 kilograms after his month-long ordeal – an average weight loss of around 860 grams per day. According to doctors, Le Fleming's superb physical condition when he set off aided his speedy recovery, and he was discharged from hospital after just five days.
Photo: Nelson Provincial Museum, Nelson Mail Collection, 3863_fr16

arms of the waiting doctor and constable. From here he was loaded into the security of the Lama cabin and ferried straight to Nelson College playing field, where he underwent the final brisk transfer by waiting ambulance to Nelson Hospital.

Cunningham recalled afterwards to a reporter the fragmented conversation he had had with Le Fleming as they were waiting on the side of the river for the Lama helicopter:

> *He recalled having his fall but then nothing at all two days after that, how he'd taken the 'path' down to Shakespeare Flat. He talked about how he'd found a fish, and all he'd had left was the jawbone and a tiny bit of skin. He ate everything else, even the bones – he ate the flesh, then dried the bones and ate them. That fish lasted him five days. He thought he was walking out, but instead he was walking upstream.*

That confusion between downstream and upstream did not surprise Cunningham, a seasoned searcher who, when stationed in Christchurch, had been called out to find a young hunter who had picked up his rifle by the barrel and accidentally discharged it into his stomach. Attempting to stagger out, the hunter had gone upstream thinking he was heading down. Said Cunningham, 'Confusion resulting from an injury can do strange things to your perception. Peter must have had an immensely strong will to have survived the way he did.'

Talking from Kopane, Peter's mother Avis agreed with that, with a newspaper reporting her saying, 'Prayers and scout training had saved her son. All the denominations around here were praying for him.' It had been a lonely vigil for Peter's parents, who were advised by the police to stay at home and wait for news. Every night, Avis would check the weather report for Nelson. 'They were atrocious for the Nelson area, there was even snow there, at that time of year, it always seemed so bad.' Every time the phone went, she jumped, then on the afternoon Peter was lifted out, she got the call from the police that she had been waiting for.

'Don't raise your hopes too much,' the policeman started by saying, 'but your son has been found. He's in a very weak condition, but he's alive.'

After hanging up the phone, Avis ran all the way to the bottom paddock, where her husband was working, to blurt out the news. She then ran back to the house to phone the school, where Vicky, her 15-year-old daughter, was in class, so that she would know too. Along with Peter, Vicky was the last of the Le Fleming kids still living at home. The daily Palmerston North–Nelson plane had already left, so Avis and Bill would have to wait until the following day to see their son.

Late that night, while packing and organising for someone to milk their cows, they got a call from Nelson Hospital, where Peter was now recovering in the Intensive Care Unit. The doctor reported to Avis that he wasn't too bad, and that they could talk to him. Peter came on, weak and faltering, but as Avis would say, 'It was him alright.'

The Le Flemings knew no one in Nelson, but a stranger who met them at the hospital offered them a place to stay, which they happily accepted. But their son was only a vestige of his former healthy self. Normally 70 kilograms, he was down to just 45 kilograms. Peter had lost 25 kilograms over the course of his 29-day ordeal. Barely holding on to survival, his body had lost around 860 grams a day.

Avis and Bill stayed with Peter for the week, visiting every morning and not leaving until late at night. His feet, which had suffered from exposure and were cut and bruised, responded well to treatment. His rapid recovery surprised even the doctors – indeed, the hospital medical superintendent, Dr W.B. Jackson, commented to a reporter that Le Fleming's extraordinarily fit physical condition continued to surprise him. His patient was discharged on Friday, 22 February, just five days after he was rescued.

During his spell in hospital, Le Fleming did not want to talk to reporters or be photographed, although hospital staff did say that he'd taken a keen interest in all the newspaper and television coverage of his dramatic rescue. Later, he did give an extended interview to David Young from the *New Zealand Listener*, which provided the material for the fullest feature about his ordeal.

In the year following the event, Constable Cunningham and his wife Gillian received many letters from a most grateful Avis. She outlined how the papers and radio had been a real trial to the family in their incessant search for news, 'and I will feel deeply for others in situations of grief in the future'. She always gave the Cunninghams news of Peter, like how his physiotherapy had helped rebuild the muscles in his legs, and how he'd been promoted to caretaker at Memorial Park in Palmerston North.

All in all it was a happy ending, and one that in some way initiated changes to procedures when looking for lost trampers. When Le Fleming was in hospital, officials from LandSAR interviewed him to find out more about his mindset during his ordeal, in particular errors made at decision points of the trip, so that finding others would be easier. Today, profiling is used with precision to predict where a missing person may have gone. In Le Fleming's case, if Constable Cunningham hadn't gone down the Burgoo Stream and spotted his orange groundsheet, the chances are that the lost tramper would almost certainly have died. Nowadays, people don't generally stay lost this long – they are usually found a lot sooner through profiling and extensive contact searches. A postscript to this story is that Le Fleming did get lost again, in the North Island, but he was found much more quickly second time round.

And Constable Tony Cunningham, now retired, looks back on the Le Fleming search as 'one of the best buzzes I ever got in my whole career as a cop. I was as high as a kite the day we found him. To save a man's life is a great feeling.'

CHAPTER 3

TAPLIN'S HUT

AFTER MAKING COMMENT in *Kahurangi Calling* that makeshift miners' huts used to be a common sight in the wilderness of northwest Nelson, I received one wonderful letter from Avelon (Ave) Thorn, the Cobb Valley's last grazier, who kindly corrected my caption for a black-and-white photo of a 'birch' sapling log cabin that used to stand 'on the corner' at Upper Junction, where the Salisbury Track branches off to Flora Hut. Remains of the cabin were well remembered by passing trampers into the early 1960s, and I described it as a typical miner's hut. But Ave's letter told me that the cabin was built and occupied by Matt Robinson and his wife for the duration of the Second World War, the purpose being to provide support for their two sons, who were actively evading conscription into the military forces. The Motueka area generated many a conscientious objector, mainly associated with Riverside, a community with pacifist ideals that still thrives at Lower Moutere.

Rather than face unfair treatment or even confinement in a punitive labour camp – to which the boys would be subject for refusing to enlist – they all headed for the hills. Not only did they construct the log cabin that everyone came to know, but also another smaller and much more secret hut 500 metres up the hill through the beech forest. Here, the two sons would hang out, evading anyone who passed through the area and coming down for meals only when the coast was clear. They had a prearranged system of alarms, whereby both vocal calls and hammering on tin cans strung up in the trees were used to alert them when someone was heard or seen coming. Whenever the alarm was given, the boys would head up the hillside and keep their heads down. Increasing their options, the family also kept a third hut further up the Flora. While the Robinsons lived there, Ave regularly took sheep past on his way between the Cobb and Ngatimoti, but never once did he meet the two sons. He recalled that on one particularly wet, cold day he arrived with a mob of sheep at the Robinson clearing and was invited into their hut for hot soup. 'Good folks' is how Ave describes the parents. The couple had a vegetable garden by the hut, which Ave had no doubt they must have shared with the prolific 'wood hens' (weka). After the war, the two sons handed themselves in and were given community service. For them, Kahurangi was a place of refuge where no one would find them – a place to keep their peace.

Another letter I received after *Kahurangi Calling* was published was from Robert J. Atkins of Motueka, who filled me in on Taplin South Hut, a photo of which (on page 166 of the book) depicted the slab hut on a lean not long before it finally collapsed under snow in around 2006. This hut became a feature of the route to Granity Pass and Mt Owen. Again, my caption called it a miner's hut, but Atkins sent me an extract from his unpublished 'Memories of the Past. Vol. 2', which featured some of the adventures of Eric Taplin, including an account of how he'd built the hut in around 1954 for the purpose of having somewhere private to stay while shooting deer in the area. Taplin's application to the Forest Service to build the hut was on the basis of it being a prospector's hut, his miner's right (under the name Eric John Taplin) entitling him to construct it. Taplin certainly fossicked for gold, but mostly he liked to go hunting for deer. Like many deerstalkers, he had his favourite patch, and he built his hut dead smack in the middle of it.

Leaning against the hut in an earlier photo is the 6-foot two-man saw Taplin carried in atop his pack and used to cut mountain cedar into lengths for splitting into slabs and shingles to build the hut, as well as a rusty old gold pan perched in the antlers above the door. This gold pan was set at 45 degrees to catch rain, which could then be poured into a billy below, Taplin's theory being that when you turned up there'd at least be enough water for a cuppa to get you going again.

TAPLIN'S HUT

Taplin's hut was situated in the headwaters of Blue Creek, around three hours' walk up from Courthouse Flat near Rolling River, and was built over 14 days in 1954 by Eric Taplin and four mates. This photo, taken some 40 years later, shows the effects the extreme weather and later lack of maintenance had on the hut, which became a fine feature on the track to Granity Pass and Mt Owen until heavy snow caused its collapse in around 2006. Photo: Bleyden Taplin

The building of the hut took 14 days, Taplin being assisted by his mates Doug and Trevor Goodall, Taffy Gwylliam and John Jones, the latter an old hand of the Howard Goldfield whose skills proved indispensable. Between them, the men shot 53 deer over the course of the two-week construction. The crosscut saw was used to cut the trunks of selected mountain cedars into 3-foot lengths, before they were split with a shingle knife. All the best lengths were used on the roof, while anything inferior was used for cladding the walls. The 16-foot-long bunks, each big enough for two men to lie end to end with their gear in the middle, ran the full length of the hut and were made from heavy jute sacks sewn onto frames of 'birch' saplings, ready to take the occupants' sleeping bags. To save carrying everything in, smaller tools and essential equipment like splitting knives and a camp oven were stuffed into a bale of hay attached to a rudimentary parachute, which was then tossed out from a fixed-wing aircraft. Hut-builders often cultivated relationships with local bush pilots, and Taplin was no exception.

The shallow basin Taplin chose for the hut had its own microclimate, keeping it sheltered and relatively warm, even in a storm. Not only that, but water was available just out the back from nearby Blue Creek, which flows underground along this stretch – all you needed to know was the spot where you could use a shovel or stick to scratch among the loose rocks and dirt to get the water flowing out. Taplin sited the hut intentionally just out of view from the track, but over time it became plainly visible and passers-by would detour to see it. Many trampers who came by before the hut collapsed in 2006 will remember it.

To get there from Nelson, Taplin would drive his Chevrolet truck to the Dart River, where he would often stay the night with whomever he'd taken up. His hut slept five comfortably, so he often took a whole crew with him. The next day, they would ford the Dart and walk to Courthouse Flat (altitude 360 metres), the site of the former goldmining settlement of Gladstone. During its heyday in the 1870s, several hundred hard-working (and hard-drinking) souls lived up here, but now only an old brick chimney of the former courthouse stands resolute as the last real vestige of that hopeful community. Completely gone are the several hotels, jailhouse and skittle alley. If you follow the tracks through the blackberry scrub into the hills, you will find endless tailings, abandoned mines, and even a huge overshot waterwheel and five-stamper battery, which Doran's Company kept fed by an aerial tramway.

From Courthouse Flat, Taplin, with his crew of mates in tow, headed up the long ridge that runs between Granity and Blue creeks. This route, called Billies Knob Track, is named after William Flanagan, a storekeeper and gold-digger at Courthouse Flat who later turned to farming, running his sheep on the grassy tops. One of his sons, Frank, took over the sheep grazing, moving north to the upper Baton Valley, where he built the original Flanagans Hut. On a hot summer's day, Billies Knob Track can be a hard slog, especially as you have to carry water all the way to quench your thirst. After the steep ascent through beech forest, Taplin and his crew would stop to catch their breath on the grassy tops, burnt off for years by Flanagan, and take in the great views north and west, including to Mt Patriarch at the southern end of the Wharepapa/Arthur Range. It was always a relief when they could pick their descent along the Staircase around the forested marble bluffs, before turning left at the bottom to find the hut a kilometre or so on. Atkins recalls as a young man the first time he visited the hut with Taplin, saying that he was absolutely 'beggared' by the time he got there.

TAPLIN'S HUT

Keen to fight overseas for his country, Eric Taplin declared himself to be 18 when he enlisted in the army. But his worried mother marched onto the troopship as it was about to set sail from Wellington, pulling her 17-year-old son off and substituting his older brother instead. Photo: Loise Taplin

The hut was comfortable and always kept well equipped with gear and food, ongoing supplies often dropped by fixed-wing plane whenever the opportunity arose, and all carefully stashed. Still up there, wrapped in greased canvas and buried in rocks not far from the hut, is the crosscut saw, which was never taken out, along with over a thousand live .303 rounds stashed in a cream tin. You could never have enough ammo when there were plenty of deer around. A guaranteed evening meal at Taplin's hut comprised a camp oven full of venison stew, which all agreed improved as each day progressed. It was too far to carry any meat out, but the deer skins were a different matter – they were rolled up and tied, carried out and then sold. Demand for them had been high since the Second World War, when many British Spitfire pilots were seriously burnt when their forward fuel tanks were hit by enemy fire and erupted into flames around them – particularly dangerous when they were trying to parachute out. It was discovered that lining fuel tanks with deer skin reduced flaming incidents to near zero, the skins self-sealing as the bullet went through and also acting as a fire retardant.

Taplin relied on a perfected hunting technique, and he arranged everyone in his crew accordingly. The 'daily programme' was that they would hunt in pairs in different areas. The cook – invariably an older man – would stay behind, not only to attend to hut duties but also to fill in his spare time fossicking for gold or hunting close by. There was never any shortage of deer, this being before the days of hunting from helicopters – their numbers were simply out of control and they were eating out the bush. The method of shooting was quite straightforward, as Atkins recalled: 'When you came across a mob of deer, you gut shot as many as possible. Once shot in the stomach, the deer tend to stay standing, barely staggering with the shock of being hit. Only then would you move in to shoot them in the head and put them out of their misery.'

One day, on approaching a basin, the hunters spotted an alert and fidgety deer that was the obvious lookout for the rest of its herd. Keeping deadly quiet, they crested the basin just in time to count 23 deer walking into cover and out of range. That was one mob that escaped without a shot being fired. Taplin never missed the roars in there, when the stags would bellow around them all night. Birds, too, called out – mostly morepork and kiwi. A typical stay for Taplin's hunting crew was a week. Carrying the heavy bundles of skins added two hours to the trip out, meaning they could get caught out in the dark if they didn't leave early enough. According to his son, Taplin ended up installing some 'fibreglass windows' at the entrance of a small cave just beyond Billies Knob so they wouldn't be caught out without shelter. Before that, they just slept anywhere they could. Atkins recalls one trip back out when they ran out of daylight:

> *I remember I had to sleep against a tree so that I didn't roll down the steep hill. Not only that, but we also had no food and after tramping all day it wasn't funny. Next day we reached the Wangapeka Track that led to civilisation and picked up some of the valuable deer skins that had been carried out previously. For a lad not long out of school, the whole experience had been both challenging and exciting.*

When Taplin built his hut, both he and his wife Loise were leasees (and licencees) of the Bush Tavern in The Wood, Nelson. But before that (from 1947 to 1953) they had the licence to the Owen River Hotel (now the Owen

Eric and Loise Taplin leased and ran the Owen River Hotel from 1947 to 1953, here pictured around halfway through their tenure. It was during this time that the ever-keen hunter Eric came up with the annual Owen River Pig Shoot, which became the forerunner of similar competitions run in conjunction with rural pubs all around the country and still going today.
Photo: Loise Taplin

River Tavern and Motel), situated along State Highway 6 at the confluence of the Owen and the mighty Buller. This is great pig-hunting country and Loise became a keen shooter just like her husband, something she says was a bit of an oddity at the time. But who could blame them – after all, chasing wild pigs is a sport like no other. Every human skill and every dog is tested. Bailing up a pig is a close-combat competition, and if you don't get it right, you can be seriously injured. No other animal in this country can be relied on to fight back with such veracity when cornered or wounded. As the saying goes, 'Dogs look up at you and cats look down at you, but pigs look you straight in the eye'. In many ways, wild pigs are an equal foe, which is why pig hunters get off on hunting them so much.

James Cook is largely credited for releasing the first pigs into New Zealand (hence the name Captain Cooker), although that claim may go to French explorer Jean-François-Marie de Surville, who gifted a sow and a boar to Māori in Doubtless Bay in 1769. A succession of successful liberations saw the

With Eric and Loise both keen hunters, pig hunts became a family affair. A day out chasing pigs was never complete until all the gutted animals had been brought home for processing and then hung in the cool shed. Photo: Loise Taplin

North and South islands, along with the Chatham Islands, soon all overrun. Shooting pigs for sport is recorded as far back as 1840, and many early colonial Australians routinely referred to New Zealand as 'the pig isles'. During the 1930s, 'two bob a snout' was the government bounty paid to hunters, while in the 1940s it morphed into the choice of a shilling or three live .303 bullets for every tail. Poisoning was carried out on a large scale in the 1950s, but it made little overall dent in the pig population. One reliable estimate for 1988 put the number of pigs shot that year at around 100,000. Wild pigs have long been present throughout Kahurangi, especially around its ferny fringes.

One thing Taplin did that would have a nationwide effect was to set up what was almost certainly the first ever weekend pig-hunting competition in the country. He offered his pub as a venue for local hunters to bring their pigs for weighing and auctioning, not to mention hosting the community party afterwards. Entry fees essentially paid for the event, which offered sponsored prizes for each of the different categories: average weight, heaviest boar, best jaw, heaviest sow and longest tail. The idea took off, the success of the Owen River Pig Shoot being copied by scores of backcountry pubs around New Zealand. It is a uniquely New Zealand institution that started in Kahurangi, where some of the heaviest single boars in the country can still be found. One 1960s story from the Owen River district describes one mean giant boar that ranged over the adjoining catchments of the Tutaki, Nuggety and Granity. It would take on any pack of pig-hunting dogs sent after it, often ripping them open and sending them all flying, before grumpily marching off snorting into the scrub. No one in the pig-hunting fraternity ever claimed to have shot that pig, so it may well have to go down in the annals as undefeated.

Back when Taplin started the Owen River Pig Shoot, pigs averaged 65 kilograms gutted. Today, the average for a three-day competition comes in at 57 kilograms, while at the Collingwood Tavern on the other side of Kahurangi, they average 52 kilograms. It is probably true that the good old days of routinely bagging big pigs are gone, or at least going, thanks simply to the pressure imposed by a whole new generation of keen young hunters.

When Taplin took over the Owen River Hotel, there were still a few working goldminers in the area. Back in 1886 there had been huge excitement when gold-bearing reefs were discovered by Matt Byrne and C. Bulmer about 12 kilometres up the Owen Valley. Some of the claims that were pegged out carried names like Better Times, Wakatu, Comstock, Golden Crown and Enterprise. Two stamping batteries of 15 and 20 heads were installed and a thriving settlement sprung up, along with a 15-room hotel. Brewery Creek, further up, was named for the brewery that operated there. Because the lower valley is so narrow, a dray road was carved over the hill from Owen Junction, where another accommodation house stood around 6 kilometres up the Buller Gorge from the current Owen River Tavern and Motel. But despite all the hopes, the field proved a let-down for those early miners. Chemical weathering had concentrated all the easily won gold at the surface of the reefs, but underneath the colours petered out. In addition, faults had broken up the lodes into little more than big blocks of barren quartz. The place became more suited to the small-scale prospectors who would ferret here and there.

Although he was not a licensed gold buyer, Taplin occasionally 'did these goldminers a favour' by buying their booty after weighing it on his gold scales, even trading their small loose amounts of gold for a bar and bottle

Eric John Taplin, 22 January 1924– 9 July 2011. Photo: Loise Taplin

tab. But for years Taplin didn't sell on any of the gold, instead building up a considerable stash that eventually became an embarrassment. Finally, he decided to take his hefty bag of gold to Wellington to sell it, his rationale being that an established Chinese community there would be interested. They loved gold, after all, and many were descended from the country's earliest Chinese goldmining immigrants.

But not long after he arrived in the capital, Taplin's wife, Loise, got a telephone call informing her that her husband was being held for questioning at the Wellington Central Police Station. The incident concerned a Gowan Valley miner who had been found dead in suspicious circumstances, rather dramatically blown to bits by his own gelignite. After a lot of questioning and explaining, Taplin was released by the police, who eventually accepted that he had absolutely nothing to do with the man. Heading to the capital to sell his unexplained gold had, however, certainly flagged their interest. The time Taplin spent in Wellington selling his gold would go down as one of his great adventures, perhaps second only to the tramp he did from the head of Lake Rotoiti to Hanmer Springs. Ever since he was a boy, Taplin had pined for adventure. At 17, he'd even falsified his age so he could enlist in the army, so keen was he to go to war. But his mother found out and marched up the gangway of the troopship as it was ready to sail, taking him off and substituting his older brother in the process.

After a life spent on the edge of a great wilderness, Eric Taplin passed away on 9 July 2011. His hut preceded him by a few years. Even though the remnants of history are soon obliterated in the Kahurangi wilderness, may the exploits of Eric Taplin never be forgotten.

CHAPTER 4

LITTLE BIDDY'S STORY

IF EVERY GOLDMINING TOWN has a belle époque, Lyell's started in 1863, when it went off with a bang. 'Good nuggety gold' was found over the summer of 1862, the first European miners drawn to the area by a Māori prospector called Eparara, who knew of patches of coarse gold up Lyell Creek. Eparara eventually teamed up with four other miners, and the party was credited with finding a dumbbell-shaped nugget weighing 19½ ounces as they prospected their way through a solid-rock tunnel 1.6 kilometres upstream from today's highway bridge. Some finds were spectacular – one group of five miners scored 500 ounces in five days. Around a hundred good-sized nuggets were found in 1863, including ones weighing 17 ounces, 30 ounces and 52 ounces. A 109-ounce nugget from Lyell reputedly found in 1880 was not officially recorded, the story being that it was whisked off to Australia and sold. If this is true, it would have been the largest gold nugget ever found in the country, that title still officially going to a 99.68-ounce hunk found in Ross in 1909 by John Scott and Arthur Sharpe. The Ross nugget was named the 'Honourable Roddy' after Minister of Mines Roderick McKenzie, and was purchased for £420 by the New Zealand government and presented as a coronation gift to King George V. It was subsequently melted down to make a tea service for Buckingham Palace.

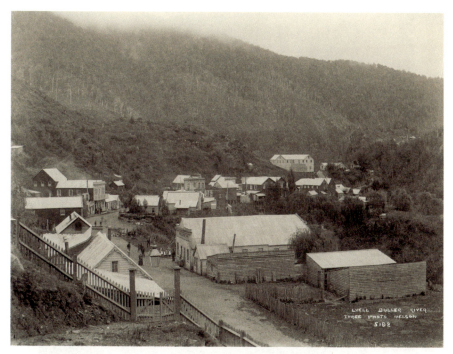

This Tyree Studio photo, taken in 1890, shows Lyell to be a thriving goldmining settlement with many boarding houses. In the centre is the Welcome Inn, above which is the Criterion Hotel. The Commercial and Empire hotels are to the right at rear, and the Alhambra is the pale building on the spur. Photo: Alexander Turnbull Library, 10x8-0736-G

But it wasn't until the quartz reefs were probed in 1863 that Lyell's true wealth became wildly apparent. The biggest and richest reef was at Irishmans Creek, 4 kilometres northeast of the town in the lower Lyell Valley. That mine became the basis for the town's prosperity for the next 40 years, employing no less than 60 miners, who were all housed at nearby Zalatown. The thoroughly astute Swiss and Italian miners who discovered the 60-metre-wide, inclined reef formed the United Alpine Company to work it, procuring an impressively steady return of amalgam equal to 1¼ troy ounces of gold per ton of crushed material. Proclaimed the *Westport Times* on 24 June 1879, 'With plenty of good stone and an efficient battery, with water as the motive power, the Alpine Mine is certain to take its place in the front rank.'

Nearly all the reefs around Lyell were initially probed by horizontal tunnels, called adits. Once crushing got underway, the non-gold-bearing soil was dumped to the side of the mine mouth as 'mullocks', while the gold-bearing

quartz was trucked out and laid onto paddocks for crushing later (while a paddock today refers to a grassy field, to the goldminers it was a holding area for the spoil). From these holding paddocks, a tramway or chute delivered the spoil directly into the crushing battery, which was invariably driven by an overshot waterwheel. After being crushed by the huge metal stampers, the powdered quartz was washed over copper tables coated with mercury. Here, the gold combined with the mercury, which was later boiled off in a retort. Berdans, revolving metal dishes containing heavy steel balls and mercury, were among several common methods used to collect all the gold missed by the first process. Victorian gold technology was efficient and ensured a recovery rate close to 100 per cent, the reason Kahurangi gold fossickers today find only scant dregs when working through tailings of old diggings.

Even back then, the vapour given off by the waste mercury waste during the process was a known hazard, suspected of causing tremors, emotional instability, insomnia, memory loss and headaches. But those side effects were all just regarded as a necessary evil. Apart from the obvious effects of mining and mercury leaching, the local environment was also affected by the catastrophic felling of millable trees, invariably needed to build the mining structures and huts. Radiating out from Lyell today is a vastly altered landscape, although the beech forest and its luxurious understorey are gradually coming back. It wasn't only people, though, that have brought about recent change here. Both the Murchison earthquake of 1929 and the Inangahua earthquake of 1968 wreaked absolute destruction in the area, causing slips along the steep bush hillsides. Luckily, nature's regeneration has been vigorous.

Lyell developed quickly into a tumultuous society and took on the atmosphere of a Wild West town. Within its very first year, its citizens created the first dedicated police unit on the West Coast, a 12-man 'vigilance committee' that deterred claim jumpers and other troublemakers by plainly threatening to lynch them, and on at least one occasion effecting a mock execution to get their point across.

As the local population swelled, the Lyell goldfield warden in 1869 called for a permanently manned police station to be built, reporting, 'Some notoriously

Around 40 residents were buried in the Lyell Cemetery between 1870 and 1900. This grave of Mary Edge, wife of miner James Edge, reveals she died aged 48 after prolonged illness: 'Afflictions sore, long time she bore, Physicians were in vain'. Lyell could be a hard place to live, and those buried in its cemetery rarely made it to 50. Photo: Gerard Hindmarsh

bad and ruffianly characters have found their way to Lyell. Some serious breaches of the peace have occurred and on more than one occasion it had become necessary to dispatch constables specially to this locality to apprehend offenders of this sort.'

Among the disturbances that year was a one-man drunken riot involving a headstrong Irish miner known as 'Dublin Jack', who 'kept the township in a state of alarm for some hours, fighting and throwing stones indiscriminately'. Not one window was safe and considering every pane of glass had to be imported, it was a great loss to have your windows smashed. Storekeepers were all forced to close their businesses for self-protection. The miner's rampage went on all afternoon, and he couldn't be restrained by the succession of men who tried to tackle him. The incident ended only when Dublin Jack began fighting yet another man next to a cliff, tumbled over it and was badly injured.

Any sort of glamourous social event in particular seemed to provide good reason to have a fight. One 1872 report describes an otherwise successful miners' ball 'to which the fair sex mustered strongly and in elegant costume. But the Ball finished up in the usual style with two or three major brawls shortly after daylight – a common occurrence at Lyell – but we are all nonetheless friendly afterwards.'

The incident that gave Lyell its wildest notoriety, however, was the fatal stabbing in 1866 of Denis Quinlan at the local brothel, an establishment referred to in the newspapers as Lyell's 'house of ill repute'. Quinlan's killer, John Davidson, tried to get rid of the body by dumping it in the Buller River, but it became snagged on some branches and ended up being retrieved. While serving a life sentence in Nelson's gaol for the manslaughter of Quinlan, Davidson managed to grab a warder's gun, shot the man dead and then turned the gun on himself. The entry to one end of the Lyell township was called 'Devil's Elbow', while the other would become known as 'Murderer's Point' after the Quinlan killing.

This little town of diggers held on as a goldmining hub and way-stop well into the twentieth century. One 1910 photo looking up the street shows the Victorian Hall and three hotels still open for business. It wasn't long after that though, in 1913, that the last mine closed, while the last surviving wooden building was burnt down in 1963, reportedly by passing drunken hoons. Today, the site of this once lively goldmining settlement is a camping ground maintained by the Department of Conservation (DOC), a layby for campervans and passing traffic along State Highway 6, not to mention the southern end of the Old Ghost Road (see Chapter 15). It's all pretty visible, including the strewn remains of machinery and gear, the last surviving miner's hut up near Irishmans Creek, and a few interpretation panels down at the carpark to make sure it's never forgotten. But there's nothing quite as poignant as the old cemetery, a ten-minute walk around the hillside from where the town once stood. Up to 40 people were buried here between 1870 and 1900, and a few still legible gravestones lie scattered among the trees, showing that life at the time could be short and death dramatic indeed.

Lyell's most famous citizen by far was Bridget Goodwin, who became known as 'Biddy', 'Little Biddy' or 'Biddy of the Buller'. If anything defined this remarkable woman, it was her diminutive stature and her 'questionable' morality. Exactly 4 feet nothing in height, and not an ounce over 7 stone in weight, she shocked the rough but still essentially Victorian standards of the goldfield by living and working with two men at the same time. These men were referred to as either her first or second mate, and she was married to neither. She didn't see the slightest thing wrong with the romantic arrangement, a ménage à trois, and she never cared a damn what anyone else thought or said about them all either. She loved both of her men, although one, many suspected, was her clear favourite. Together they made a queer combination indeed. 'Two's company, three's a crowd' goes the saying, but in their case they came to be a decided exception. And, not hurting anyone, quietly toiling away with their lives and not preaching any form of immorality, they came to be highly respected.

From a distance, Little Biddy could easily be mistaken for a young teenager, but close up there was no way you could miss her age – a pipe was invariably gripped staunchly in her mouth, and her furrowed, wrinkled, sunburnt skin looked like parchment stretched over her small but wiry frame. Like her male mining counterparts, Biddy always wore moleskin trousers and boots, the only concession to her gender being a smock-like apron to keep off the worst of the mud. She sported a wild crop of iron-grey hair, usually tied back with a loose kind of scarf. But close up, it was her face that got you. One writer described her thus: 'the furrows and wrinkles on her sunburnt features, the colour of parchment, the iron grey hair, the washed out expression in her far away pale blue eyes, evidence, so plainly visible, of the daily struggle for existence this little woman had passed through in the open, seeking for gold, precious gold, under circumstances of extraordinary hardship'.

The trio – Biddy and her two mates – did have a way of alleviating their wearisome lives though. Whenever they had earned enough gold, they would go to the store and trade it for some basic supplies, but also for enough whisky to get them rolling drunk for several days at a time. They would live it up to the very last drop, leaving them utterly broke again. Once they sobered up, they would start mining again to fund the next splurge. So on through the years they went, which worked well while they all remained healthy.

Biddy's first and favourite mate took ill with an undiagnosed complaint sometime in the 1880s. She took him to hospital in Quartzopolis (early Reefton), where he eventually died and was buried. It was said that the little woman wept sorely at losing this rough companion, and in later years the memory of him and all his kindness to her would often bring tears to her washed-out blue eyes.

Her second mate, 'Old Bill', didn't last much longer. When he fell sick a few years later, he stopped helping Biddy altogether – as the straight-talking woman described it, 'he just took to loafing around'. So Biddy had to fossick for gold herself, and buy tucker and hump it on her back to their little hut, which was situated near Iron Bridge. Later, talking about her life, she describes how it turned out: 'I got so bad with rheumatics. And Old Bill getting worse we went to the hospital in Quartzopolis, where he died and was buried, and I wasn't sorry a bit… for I felt my days were numbered.'

In her old age, Biddy eventually settled into a two-room cottage in Reefton, and in her time there was admitted to the local hospital on at least two occasions with unrecorded conditions. Old Biddy, as she became known in her later years, died peacefully on 19 October 1899, aged 86, and is buried in the Reefton Cemetery. By then she had become a staunch Anglican, probably encouraged by the practicalities of support offered by the Church, and was often visited by the vicar or his curate and numerous ladies of the parish. Her loyalty, generosity and wry humour earned her many friends over the years, and no one would ever think of visiting her empty-handed. One thing she never gave up was her pipe, filled with the strongest tobacco. From the time she got up in the morning, it would hardly ever leave her mouth, the only exception being when the vicar came to see her, in which case she'd quickly hide it by slipping it under a cushion.

Many of the details of Biddy's life story would have been forgotten had they not been documented by Reefton writer William Henry Scott Hindmarsh,

Clenching her trademark pipe and dressed in moleskin trousers and boots like any self-respecting miner, Bridget Goodwin's only concession to gender was an apron to keep off the worst of the mud. Known as 'Biddy of the Buller' or 'Little Biddy', she stood exactly 4 feet tall and never weighed an ounce over 7 stone. But what she lacked in size, she made up for in spirit, becoming the lynchpin of a successful goldmining venture that utilised the two men she lived with. Photo: Nelson Provincial Museum, Tyree Studio Collection, 39942

who only ever wrote under the pseudonym 'Waratah'. He was born on Norfolk Island in 1835, where his father, Ralph, was commissariat of the store at the penal colony. Hindmarsh Sr. later fell out badly with his superior, prison commander Major Joseph Anderson, and took his family to live in Sydney, where his grievance was well reported in *The Colonist* newspaper. Later, William and his wife, Mary Frances, went to live at Ipswich near Brisbane, but moved to Reefton with their young family in around 1868 after being influenced by the get-rich-quick stories coming from the goldfields of New Zealand. Hindmarsh found he was a better writer than a goldminer though, his 'Little Biddy of the Buller' becoming a chapter in his 1906 book *Tales of the Golden West*, which contained 19 individual stories that had previously appeared in the columns of the *Grey River Argus*. Mary Frances died in 1915, aged 80 years, while William died in 1919, also aged 80.

Hindmarsh's account was obtained from the long conversations Biddy had with an unnamed 'lady confessor and tobacco conspirator' in Quartzopolis, an active church member who had no scruples about procuring and slipping Biddy her tobacco. The scene painted at their sessions is of them both sitting beside the open fireplace of Biddy's residence:

> *her kettle singing merry tunes above the hot fire, which she always kept going to keep her old bones warm. Refilling and lighting her pipe was her ritual, occasionally leaning forward to blow a cloud up the chimney, where it would join the smoke from her fire, ascending heavenward by way of incense. Biddy, under the influence of the fragrant wood, would commence her general confession.*

Hindmarsh's use of the word 'confession' is entirely his and no doubt alludes more to his own morality rather than that of Biddy's. As he writes:

> *but one young visitor, knowing Little Biddy's infirmity, conveyed plugs of tobacco to her surreptitiously and under strict secrecy, so her enjoyment of the fragrant weed was not stinted… Biddy's confessions to her one and only lady confessor (the tobacco conspirator) were somewhat of a startling nature, and much of it given under the seal of secrecy must pass forever into oblivion; although it is sincerely to be hoped that she has long since received absolution for the sins and errors of her life on earth.*

LITTLE BIDDY'S STORY

Biddy originated from Ireland, but amazingly she genuinely seemed to have forgotten exactly where from, the name of her village and even county completely escaping her in later life. As she recounted, 'I was born in Ireland, Miss, but when and where I cannot say. My education as a child was neglected, for I cannot read or write. I'm a believer in the Church of England, and I like the parson you've got in this place. He reads to me and does his best for me.'

She left Ireland in the waves of emigration that characterised the country in the nineteenth century, and ended up in Australia. Her first recollection of looking for gold was in Bendigo. One scene she could never forget took place after a terrific storm that raged all night. In the morning, nuggets of gold were seen clearly clinging to the roots of the trees that had been uprooted. Biddy saw hundreds of people – men, women and even small children – panning the ground all around as quickly as they could. 'It was wonderful, Miss!' she said excitedly as she described the scene, causing her to take an extra draw or two on her pipe. Biddy had gold fever, and she had it bad.

She met her two men, both fellow miners, in Ballarat and came out to New Zealand with them, landing in Nelson sometime in the early 1860s. They'd heard about the riches of the Collingwood goldfields, and they wanted to be part of what the Aorere Valley had to offer. But those riches didn't 'pan out' for the trio, and they tied up their swags and trudged overland to Tadmor, eventually making it into the headwaters of the Buller River. Here, they set about seriously fossicking in all the stream beds and river tributaries, working in degrees all the way down to Inangahua Junction and Murchison. The occasional sight of rich patches would encourage them to go like mad with their picks, shovels and cradle. It was no easy life, but together they worked like a well-oiled human dredging machine. Always in firm charge but working equally was Biddy, organising her two-man team to secure the best result. That was her strength, but it took its toll.

Recalled Biddy of that time, 'It was a hard, rough life for a woman. I seen us working all day long, up to our hips in water… and in all sorts of weather, but me and my mates stuck together, and we managed to make sufficient for tucker, and something over, and we would go to the Lyell, and sell our gold to the banker there.'

When she was timidly asked by her 'confessor' if she had put any of the money away for the future, Biddy replied:

Miss, I won't deceive you. After buying tucker, we knocked down the rest of the money in a long boose [an excessive drinking bout, now booze], *and when it was all spent we would stir ourselves up a bit, swag our tucker on our backs, and return to our hut, and to the claim, and begin fossicking about for more gold. When my first man died in the hospital, I cried very much of losing him and even now, when I think of him, the tears come in my eyes.*

Old Bill, Biddy's second mate, was a different story. She describes him as 'quite another sort, hard to get on with'. In particular, as he got older Bill had a 'funny complaint', for when he raised his head to look up, he would get giddy and fall over, and go out of his mind for a bit. Biddy rightly assumed that prospecting and working on the river beaches, always peering down for gold, had caused his condition, because it was common among older miners and became well reported over the years.

Their hut was situated just where the Iron Bridge crosses the Buller River on the way to Lyell, and one day Biddy glanced out to see Old Bill cutting down a small tree for firewood, not looking where it would fall. Before she could run out and stop him, the top branches of the felled tree came down among the telegraph wires, tangling them up. When the telegraph inspector came and saw the mess, he went to the little shack and frightened the pair, saying they would have to go to jail. Biddy pleaded with him to let them off, saying it hadn't been done intentionally, and told him of Old Bill's infirmity. She was relieved when the inspector forgave them, and the visit ended with Biddy making him a cup of tea.

When Old Bill passed away, Biddy was half relieved. Her body was worn out and she didn't have the strength to look after anyone else, let alone herself. She was happy to tell her 'confessor' all about him, and how she really felt, and after bidding her another cheery goodbye, she would settle back in her chair with her pipe and thoughts of long ago.

When Biddy moved to Reefton she was encouraged to live at the hospital, such was her great age and frail condition. But she declined to live 'sumptuously everyday there' and instead secured a two-room cottage whose rent was guaranteed by a church benevolent society. Later, she joined the army of old age pensioners created by the Old-age Pensions Act 1898, and couldn't

Biddy and her two mining mates lived in a one-room cabin near where Iron Bridge now spans the Buller River along State Highway 6 at Lyell. Crossing this rocky gorge, which is known for its 12-metre flood rise, required the building of massive masonry piers anchored into concrete footings. Andersons' Foundry of Christchurch fabricated all the bridge sections, which were shipped from Lyttelton to Westport and carted up by bullock teams from there. The bridge opened in 1890, its only serious set-back since then being the Murchison earthquake in 1929, which sheared off many bolts that then had to be replaced.
Photo: Nelson Provincial Museum, Tyree Studio Collection, 182001

believe her luck in the sunset years of her life to receive the magnificent sum of one shilling per day. This, Biddy said, caused her to pray monthly to 'Seddon – and the Lord's name be praised'. The Act allowed means-tested pensions to be paid to people who could prove they were over 65 and had few assets and a good moral character. As she had no birth certificate, Biddy would have relied on the parson to vouch for her obvious old age, and for her good character, which was undeniable despite her past living situation. The full annual pension was £18, with the eligibility criteria set at £34 of maximum allowable income and £50 of property assets. Claimants also had to have lived in New Zealand for 25 years, although all Chinese were excluded.

Despite this and the trouble many elderly Māori had in producing a birth certificate, bringing in the old age pension was one of the major achievements of Richard Seddon's Liberal Government. For the first time in the world, it acknowledged that the state had some responsibility for elderly folk who had no other means of support. It made a huge difference to the old retired miners like Biddy who had operated in northwest Nelson.

On the occasion of Queen Victoria's Diamond Jubilee in 1897, Little Biddy was visited by many of her lady friends of the parish, who brought with them all manner of delicacies and creature comforts. Among these, a bottle of finest port wine made its way into Biddy's larder, with the strictest instructions to drink to the Queen's health at a rate of only two or three teaspoonfuls at a time. Another young lady visitor supplemented the morning's gifts with a 'wee drap' of Scotch, of which Biddy was particularly fond. In the afternoon the visitors left the old lady to enjoy her banquet in honour of Queen Victoria.

Later that day, the parson made one of his usual random passing visitations. First, he attended to Biddy's firewood pile, cutting and splitting up a good stock for her. His reverence was well known in Reefton as an expert with the axe, which he was able to wield with as much force and power as he could deliver a sermon. His task finished, and with no Biddy about – which was unusual considering all the wood chopping – the parson knocked on the door and called out, but got no reply. Tentatively, he ventured inside the cottage, and to his dismay found Biddy spread out and looking quite comatose, in what he presumed were the last stages of her passing.

Off on his bike the parson hastily flew, returning speedily with the town's doctor. But a quick examination had the doctor laughing heartily, for it appeared that Biddy was simply 'dead-drunk'. Together, they wrapped her up tenderly and let her sleep it off. The next day she was very penitent, with the result being that – among the parish folk anyway – any future contributions of wine and whisky were stopped.

It was another two years before Biddy really did pass away. The little lady goldminer of the Buller was laid to rest in the quiet new Reefton Cemetery, one of the first to be interred there. Her brief mention in the register of deaths in the parish church of Quartzopolis simply reads:

LITTLE BIDDY'S STORY

No. 126
BRIDGET GOODWIN
Died 19-10-99
Buried 20-10-99
Aged 86

For the day, and despite all her hard labour, this remarkable 'mere morsel of a woman', as she was once described, lived to a ripe old age. And thanks to William Hindmarsh, the personal details of her story were recorded. Most of all, may she be remembered for the true way she lived her life, unfettered by Victorian standards. Hers was not an easy life by any means, but she bucked the system and lived how she thought was right. RIP little Bridget Goodwin, a big part of the Kahurangi story.

CHAPTER 5

THE STOREKEEPER'S LAMENT

IN THE EARLY 1870s, the gold diggings around the Anatori River on Golden Bay's western flank were regarded as some of the most isolated in the country. The best gold was won from the Independent Stream tributary, but the whole valley proved largely auriferous. At the height of the rush, some 500 diggers were recorded as trying their luck in the catchment.

Little remains of their efforts today, bar one lonely grave on a small terrace overlooking the Tasman Sea, a kilometre or so north of the mouth of the Anatori River. It's only a stone's throw from the modern road, the protruding top of the concrete headstone just visible as you pass a small tannin-stained pond on the right – park there on the upward bend and it's a short scramble through the flax to get to the grave. The inscription can still be clearly read:

Erected in the memory of
JAMES DURDON
Native of New South Wales
August 1872

I have heard many differing and confusing stories about this grave, even that the surname inscribed is wrong – some say that the monumental mason in Nelson who carved the headstone was given the incorrect spelling by Durdon's fellow miners and that it should have been 'Durden' or even 'Durdun'. Being the son of parents who were originally convicts sent out to Australia's penal colony may not have helped in recording the family line of this man, who was born and raised in Parramatta, Sydney. It is quite likely Durdon grew up largely illiterate anyway, so the spelling of his name possibly changed with the years, especially after he came out to New Zealand to try his luck in the goldfields.

The most reliable and full account of Durdon's demise comes from the memoir of Harry Louis Moffatt (1839–1913), who before becoming the Motueka harbourmaster was one of two storekeepers at the Anatori goldfields. He describes how Durdon worked by himself in a remote and inaccessible gully, with only one other man nearby, a kilometre further up the hill. A week before he died, Durdon went to his neighbour and jubilantly told him that he had gained a few ounces of gold, so was going to Collingwood for a spell and would be back soon.

'He evidently got into a spree,' wrote Moffatt in his memoir *Adventures by Sea and Land*. 'Then with his money done, he started to come back and ultimately arrived back at his camp one evening. His neighbour noticed the smoke from his fire and thought he would go and see him first thing in the morning to hear the latest news.' Gossip was everything in the goldfields – what you knew gave you the edge.

But the next day, when the neighbour reached the tent and looked in, Durdon was lying on his stretcher, looking much like he was still fast asleep. Getting no answer, even after making much noise and calling out, the neighbour went in, only to find the occupant dead and stiff. At that point, the neighbour hurried back down to the store to spread the news. In another account, the stricken Durdon was discovered alive but died of a slow and painful heart attack, surrounded by his mining mates.

However he died, word was soon sent around and a big muster of men went up the gully to bring the body out. Durdon was not a slight man, and they arrived at the store after a terrible journey over rocks and through bush. Continues Moffatt, 'We laid him out, rolled him in a blanket and placed him in a roughly made coffin. We concluded that an inquest was out of the question and that it was evident the man had died from exhaustion after a drinking bout. A written statement was made to that effect and signed.'

The grave of Australian goldminer James Durdon protrudes from a coastal terrace just off Cowin Road on the way to Anatori. The New South Wales miner had come out to the remote Anatori goldfield to try his luck, staking out a claim in the upper reaches of Independent Stream. After his lonely death there in August 1872, his goldfield mates banded together to bury him and raised a headstone on a terrace along the beach. Locals still refer to the winding section of the road that passes close to the grave as 'Tombstone'. Photo: Gerard Hindmarsh

To the practical, no-nonsense miners, there was no need to complicate the matter with any sort of legal proceedings – it was patently obvious no one else was involved. Durdon had died simply as a result of his excessive drunken bout in Collingwood, exacerbated by the huge effort he would have exerted travelling the 56 kilometres back home in a hungover state. This was long before any road was put in. Trudging back across Whanganui Inlet was an ordeal in itself – roughly 10,000 paces, and much of that through mud. Death by drunkenness, that was all there was to it, plain and simple.

The next morning, a few men went up the beach to choose a place to bury Durdon. The perfect spot was found 'about a mile northward of the Anatori' on a terrace overlooking the sea, where they dug his grave easily in the sandy soil. The following day, 60 miners gave up their work to follow the coffin respectfully to the grave. Not a single prayer book or anything faintly resembling one could be found among the gathered assembly, so the funeral service was improvised by the obvious candidate: a miner descended from one of the oldest Scottish baronetcies. This digger had rightfully inherited the title of 'Sir', which he admitted was somewhat out of place considering that now, in the second half of his life, he roamed rather free with only a swag. But the consensus among the Anatori miners was that this man's gracious manner rendered him fairly deserving of that title, rather than his given name of William.

Despite the lack of religious detail, the funeral service that day proved both moving and impressive. Moffatt says that even though there was 'an entire absence of mourning trapping or dress, there was a rough but genuine feeling shown by all present. After marking the grave, they took up a subscription and £25 was collected so that a suitably inscribed tombstone could be brought from Nelson.' This arrived in the next delivery of cargo and provisions for Moffatt's store – incidentally, the last he received there – and was put up along with a fence around the grave.

The storekeeper long appreciated the necessity of providing essential stores to the various goldfields, many of which he had personally tried himself in his search for the precious metal. Moffatt's worldly adventures had started in 1851, when at the age of 12 he answered an advertisement in a London newspaper for 'Apprentices for the sea wanted for first class ships. For premium and other particulars apply Fenchurch St'. After borrowing some money from his parents to pay a tailor to make him a navy blue sailor suit with gold buttons, he sailed from Blackwall, London, on the *Bolton* bound for Australia and returning to England via Callao, the chief seaport of Peru. But as they were coming back up the coast of Chile, the ship foundered in a terrific storm and the crew only just managed to get off in the longboat. At age 13, Moffatt found himself a shipwrecked sailor in Peru, with only three worldly possessions, all of which he was wearing – a pair of trousers, a cotton shirt and a hat made from dungaree trousers.

From there, Moffatt talked his way into a job on a guano boat, which headed out to the Chincha Islands to load the fertiliser for Mauritius, where they backloaded sugar, hides, rum and jute bound for England. The young man saw exotic ports all over the world, and first visited New Zealand in 1857, when he came out as an able seaman on the *Mariner* bound for Nelson and Port Chalmers, a 112-day voyage with 127 immigrants. That visit impressed

Moffatt, and he actively looked for a one-way ship back to New Zealand. His opportunity came in 1859, on a 2,000-ton wooden American ship that was chartered to ferry 170 emigrants and one prisoner from the London Docks to Auckland. It was the largest and fastest ship he'd ever sailed on, with the voyage taking only 92 days. When he was finally discharged, Moffatt's first job offer was as an oarsman on the surfboats that delivered supplies to the soldiers fighting the 'Native Wars' along the Taranaki coast. Instead, however, he fell 'for the free life of the digger', trying his luck in New Zealand's goldfields, first at Collingwood, then at Buller, Otago, Mangles and Matakitaki, and finally at Wakamarina. But in all these, his luck was sporadic at best, and he came to suspect that the real riches to be made came not from searching out the gold, but rather supplying the diggers in these remote locations.

First, Moffatt set his sights on Hokitika, after hearing that beef was in short supply there and fetching the phenomenal sum of two shillings and sixpence a pound – around five times the going price elsewhere. Several thousand diggers in the area were literally starving for beef, and it was impossible to get any supply of the meat there except by sea. Moffatt purchased 36 live bullocks in Nelson at around sixpence a pound, and started for Hokitika with the first eight quarters of beef aboard a low-powered steamer. But negotiating the Kahurangi coast in a heavy sou'wester proved arduous, and after burning nearly all his coal the boat's skipper was forced to turn around and take refuge in Whanganui Inlet to wait for the vicious wind to change. It didn't, and Moffatt's unrefrigerated beef all went bad and had to be thrown overboard to the fish. Not only did Moffatt incur the financial cost of losing his precious meat, but also the £16 he'd paid for freight on the boat. Eventually, the boat did make Hokitika and Moffatt erected his tent to await the arrival of more of his beef. But it was not an easy game. In the end, out of the 36 bullocks Moffatt slaughtered in Nelson, he managed to sell only four in that rollicking West Coast frontier town.

Many more mishaps followed as Moffatt struggled to make a sea-based living between Blenheim and the West Coast. First, he joined the *Nelson*, which was promptly broadsided by a monster wave as it negotiated the Greymouth bar, piling up on North Beach. Next, he joined the steamer *Lyttelton*, regarded as one of the slowest boats around, having taken a full 15 months to sail out from England. Moffatt made the point that she was a splendid boat though: 'she might starve her crew to death through being

THE STOREKEEPER'S LAMENT

To access the Anatori goldfield in the 1870s, diggers had to cross over Pakawau Saddle from Collingwood and then traverse Whanganui Inlet, which could be problematic. A rudimentary corduroy track evolved along the edge of the estuary, made by laying down mānuka trunks and covering them in gravel. Some sections, like this one, still remain alongside Dry Road, which itself was built during the 1920s by workers from the Public Works settlement at Rakopi.
Photo: Gerard Hindmarsh

too long at sea, but she certainly wouldn't drown them'. He then switched ships to become a steward on the *Charles Edward*. For two years Moffatt kept that job, until early in 1869 he got wind of an opportunity to start up a store on the new diggings around the lower Anatori River, on the western coast of Golden Bay. The prospects looked bright, with almost daily reports of payable gold being discovered in the new field.

Having a new wife, Theresa, provided no real impediment to his plans. They decided that she would stay in Nelson, and when he had everything established she would be able to join him at the Anatori. It was the grand plan of every colonial adventurer, even if it usually didn't work out that way.

Determined now to make his living at the Anatori goldfield, Moffatt quit his job and, after obtaining credit from a well-known Nelson merchant, purchased some 30 tons of goods and supplies to set up his store. He certainly extended himself with the deal, and had some trouble scraping together enough money to pay the freight. The cargo was consigned to a small chartered steamer, with instructions to land it all in the mouth of a river near Kahurangi Point, quite a few miles from the diggings but by far the safest landing spot for supplies. Moffatt, meanwhile, set off overland from Nelson to Collingwood and on past the Anatori, where he immediately began building a shelter to house the goods, which arrived the day he finished.

Moffatt immediately did a roaring trade, attracting gold-digging customers from near and far, simply because their only alternative was humping in supplies themselves. But before he had sold around half his stock, retail competition came in the form of a rival storekeeper, who cleverly used a king tide to negotiate his small vessel laden with goods into the Anatori River itself, giving him a decided commercial advantage by being closer to the diggings.

Moffatt had little choice but to hike to Collingwood, buy several bullocks and drive them back to the Anatori. He then used the animals to shift his entire operation, lock, stock and barrel, along the beach to Anatori, setting up his new shop directly alongside his rival just up from the river mouth.

At first it was hard to know who was going to win in the store stakes, but the tables quickly tipped to Moffatt's advantage. Running out of basic supplies first, his competitor consigned his small vessel to fetch more provisions. But as the boat was crossing the little Anatori bar, it struck the stony bottom and broke up in the waves, washing up on the beach – much to the horror of its owner. One man's disaster is another man's profit, and Moffatt immediately took advantage of the situation. He bought a small boat in Nelson, which he had towed to Anatori behind a passing steamer, which also carried his new load of supplies. Moffatt's rival gave up after losing his precious boat, but the monopoly situation did not last long, as yet another competitor set up in his place. It was common knowledge that storekeepers made good money trading in the goldfields, doing far better than most of the diggers, and there never seemed to be a shortage of up-and-coming rivals.

Through 1870 the population around the Anatori River continued to increase and a fair amount of gold was won. However, the disadvantage of the goldfield was that all the workings were in dry gullies at high elevation, so it was possible to sluice up only when it rained. Darkening clouds would be treated with jubilation, and the men would be ready with their sluice boxes as soon as the first drops of rain fell. Rather than hide away under their

Harry Louis Moffatt (1839–1913) became a storekeeper at the Anatori goldfield during the height of the rushes there in the early 1870s. His experiences proved highly colourful but his fortunes were mixed, and he went on to become a long-serving and well-respected harbourmaster at Port Motueka.
Photo: Nelson Provincial Museum, Tyree Studio Collection, 38694

rudimentary tent shelters like they did in other goldfields, Anatori diggers typically worked their hardest in drenching rain, when they would see some 'colours' for their efforts.

Despite having a new longboat, Moffatt still faced problems with bringing in supplies. One day, a schooner pulled up close to the mouth of the Anatori. The crew indicated that they had supplies to land, but conditions looked too tricky to Moffatt. Eventually, two men volunteered to go out in another boat to see if they could at least bring back some sacks of flour, as stocks of that most essential of essentials were getting mighty low. They managed to load these onto their boat with great difficulty, but as they were coming back over the bar, a big roller struck and bowled the boat clean over, tossing the men and their precious cargo into the water. The miners ashore watched anxiously as the two men struggled, trying to make for shore. Finally, when the men were close, the onlookers joined hands and waded out to rescue them. It was a close call, and the pair were fairly insensible when pulled out. Later that day, the boat was found washed up and smashed to pieces along the beach.

Only screw steamers could be really relied on to drop supplies along this beaten section of coast. Moffatt remarked how unreliable sailing boats were, citing that his neighbouring storekeeper had dispatched his sailing boat with stores from Nelson five weeks earlier, only to hear that it was still in Collingwood waiting for a 'slant', or favourable wind, to get around Cape Farewell. This delay resulted in his latest competitor almost completely running out of stock. But with the gold rush in full progress, it wasn't long before Moffatt's store was also down to just a few lines. So, hoping yet again to get a lead on a competitor, Moffatt purchased a whaleboat in Nelson and once again made arrangements for it to be towed around by the steamer, which would carry his newly ordered goods.

Arriving off Big River on a splendidly fine and calm day, the steamer offloaded Moffatt's supplies into his whaleboat, which made for Flat Rock, just inside the mouth of the river. This perfectly flat rock pavement was a safe bet for unloading, if conditions were right. Moffatt waited until the following morning's high tide to take his laden whaleboat up the coast from Flat Rock and sneaked into the Anatori. Pleased the run had been so successful, the storekeeper now concluded that Big River was by far the best place to offload stores, and so had two more big loads brought in that way. Moffatt's biggest problem proved to be getting a boat crew to help him – everyone was so occupied in the diggings that spare labour came at a premium.

On another occasion, as day was breaking, Moffatt heard the steamer's whistle, indicating it would be offshore in around three minutes. However, the waves coming over the bar were rough, so Moffatt and his crew hesitated. They had another cup of coffee, but everyone was getting impatient – the steamer captain included, who was liable to just sail off. Finally, Moffatt and his crew decided to risk it, managing with some difficulty to get out alongside the steamer. The captain gave them all the mail and newspapers for the miners, but suddenly refused to unload the stores, saying he now considered it too unsafe and advising Moffatt to get back to shore as quickly as possible before the sea rose any more. The men in the whaleboat let go and made off for land. But just at a critical moment when they were going back over the bar, the boat took a bad steer when one of the hired rowers lost his stroke. The heavy strain Moffatt put on his 20-foot-long steering oar as he tried to correct their line wrung the stern post off the boat, and over the whaler went!

Suddenly, five men were struggling for their lives in the heavy surf.

THE STOREKEEPER'S LAMENT

With difficulty, they all managed to keep hold of the upturned boat, which threatened to roll over the top of them with every new breaker. But, knowing the boat was slowly being driven to shore by the relentless waves, they all hung on for grim life. As they neared land, four crew let go and attempted to swim the last stretch. Overcome by the waves, they had to be rescued by men watching from the shore, who all linked arms and pulled them in one by one. Moffatt clung to his boat, eventually feeling the bottom with his feet some 3 kilometres north of the point from which they had set off. He combed the beach, picking up the waterlogged letters and papers scattered along the tideline, later writing that he was 'not feeling any worse for wear for the experience'.

Moffatt was taken aback, though, when he made it back to his store, only to find it had been forcibly opened by rescuers 'keen to get stimulants for the half-drowned men'. He wrote:

> *Fortunately my* [store] *neighbour had acted the part of a man and taken charge of the store or things would have been much worse. After dinner we went along the beach and, as it was low water we hauled the boat above high water mark and ultimately she was repaired and did good service later on a small lake* [Lake Otuhie].

Things at the Anatori didn't turn out for Moffatt quite as he had planned. The largely seaborne, store-driven pioneer had turned up with a strong vision of establishing 'a money making store with a house and garden close to it in which my wife and children would be comfortably settled'. But instead of having time to build his homestead, Moffatt found his middle age becoming more and more strenuous, every month seemingly busier than the last. He lamented, 'My wife had to live a lonely and anxious life. We only saw each other about one in three months, but I still hoped things would improve.' The reality was that the day of her move from Nelson to be with her husband at Anatori constantly had to be put off.

Although the district became increasingly populated, the Anatori goldfield always had the disadvantage that rain was needed to wash up. A long dry spell saw many diggers living on credit, and Moffatt had little choice but to carry them. But as soon as the rain came, business could be relied on to boom. Moffatt could count on a big buying spree as the miners, all washed up with alluvial gold in their pockets, would come in to trade their findings for supplies. Notes and coins may have been legal tender, but as in most goldfields, flakes of the precious metal were the everyday currency. All you needed was a set of simple balance scales and weights to verify the gold's value. Moffatt would weigh each miner's gold as the men came in, then give them a pound and pence value so they knew how much they could spend or how much credit they could pay off. Wrote Moffatt:

When the rain came there would be a big spree at the store, but I would probably miss some well known face and, on asking what had become of Jimmy I would probably learn that he had gotten sixteen ounces out of his washdirt and left yesterday to catch a boat to Sydney. I would then go back through my book and find that Jimmy owed twelve pounds and that his last purchase was a pair of boots and a shirt. I would draw a line through that account and write 'bad' across the page, while I congratulated myself that was only Jimmy – it could have been worse!

After one post-rain buying spree, Moffatt took a sizeable amount of gold – around £60 worth – which during the day he kept in a bag in a locked drawer near his gold scales. At this time his store was only a stone's throw away from some large dormitory huts that had been built to accommodate miners when they came down from their diggings. Moffatt walked back and forth between the store and the huts quite often that day to talk to the men, but finally they were all quiet and went to sleep. As the miners intended to return to their diggings early the next day, Moffatt got up before them and headed back to his store, ready in case they wanted to buy supplies. Immediately on his arrival, however, he noticed that the drawer by the gold scales was partly open and the gold had gone. He made a coffee and contemplated the theft. Once the men made a start along the sea beach, Moffatt took a shortcut through the bush, intercepting them to explain that someone had taken his gold.

'Well,' said one cryptically, 'there was only two of us at the store and one of us has got it.' The man opened his swag, emptied it on the ground and began stripping off his clothes as well. Then all the others started doing the same. As Moffatt expected, there was no gold to be found on any of them. However, they all voluntarily returned to the store and 'two miserable days were spent each watching the other'. Moffatt never did find out who stole his gold, and the men gradually drifted away. The storekeeper had a few customers during the week and took a few ounces of gold, which he secreted away when no one was about.

In addition to the alluvial diggings in the Anatori catchment, the nearby Golden Blocks mines beyond Lake Otuhie were also coming into their own for their quartz-bearing gold. Because heavy stampers were required to crush the quartz, this goldfield – the most isolated in the whole country – became controlled by companies with sizeable capital. Workers congregated in tent-camp towns with names like Dogtown and Pennyweight. Moffatt saw opportunity up there, too. He purchased two packhorses in Nelson and used them during the week to pack in goods up to the lake, and also to drag his whaleboat overland to the lake. By packing in and rowing his goods up Lake Otuhie, he could get his merchandise to within 3 kilometres of the principal diggings. When Moffatt got ahead of himself packing in supplies, he would turn the horses out to forage for a week or two. Occasionally, they would return to the store on their own account to get a handful of sugar and salt, after which they would go off again and not be seen for several days.

During spells of good weather when all the miners were busy at their diggings, Moffatt might not see another person for days, but that did not mean he could drop his guard:

> *On one occasion I had not seen a soul for eight days, only the horses who had been there the day before. I woke in the night, hearing an animal sound and found the horses had come, which was strange after such a short interval. I spoke to them and gave them something and then they went away. I turned in again but felt nervous about the horses. At daylight I went to the chest of tea and felt for the gold – it was gone! I was startled as I knew it had been there the day before. I went down to the beach, saw the horses' tracks coming and going and, just at the low tide mark, the footprints of a man. I spent that day going to every tent in the diggings. Of course I said nothing about the further loss of gold, but found out where every man was the night before, with one exception, and he left during the night on his way to Collingwood.*

Around this time several larger gold-bearing reefs were discovered further back in the hinterland. Huge excitement swept through the Anatori goldfield as claims were pegged off along the supposed lines of the reef. Many of the alluvial miners abandoned their claims to work the gold-bearing quartz. Suddenly, Moffatt found the miners demanding not only supplies but also heavy-duty mining equipment like blasting powder and rock drills. The trouble was, despite the excitement and optimism of the new ventures, little gold was being returned to pay for these items. The storekeeper could only give so much credit, and he put his foot down, irritating many miners. 'I used to get told it was about time another store started and so on, however some went back and got a little gold which kept things moving.'

Later, a big reef was found and outside capital brought in. It was an exciting day when a ten-head stamper battery was landed at the Anatori and then taken along the beach to Sandhill Creek, floated on a huge raft of logs and pulled upstream to the head of Lake Otuhie. To Moffatt, this signified a confident future, and he immediately embarked on building another store 'at the extreme end of the terrace' along the lake, to which he would pack in goods even further from his Anatori store.

But there were just as many ratbags to contend with up at the new lake store. After he was well established there, Moffatt was walking along the side of the building when he noticed two charcoal marks on one of the boards. He recalled:

> *I suppose I had got suspicious or nervous, but I counted the boards and went inside and found the marks were exactly opposite the gold scales. I came to the conclusion that another robbery was contemplated and supposed the idea was to bore holes through the marks on the boards, knock the piece out, pass the hand through and get what was wanted.*

Moffatt seldom, if ever, had visitors at night, so he made preparation for the would-be thief by first making sure his revolver was in order. Then, every night for three weeks, he crouched in the dark behind his counter and just waited. Sometimes he would doze off and wake with a start to the cry of a morepork in a tree outside or to the call of a seagull. At last, in the early hours one morning he heard 'scroop, scroop' sounds coming from the side of his building. It was a cold winter's night, but sweat began rolling off his forehead as he waited. The sound went on and on, until finally, as the day was breaking, a rat ran across his foot. It had been gnawing to get into a wooden box of biscuits. After that, Moffatt came to the conclusion that the marks on the boards had somehow appeared by accident and he gave up his nightly watch. Lamented the storekeeper, 'I should say that a majority of diggers I knew were good honest men, it was the small minority that caused a deal of trouble and loss.'

The alluvial diggings around the Anatori gradually lost more and more diggers as they joined the reef prospectors up beyond the head of Lake Otuhie. From Moffatt's point of view the transition was worrying, because unless some fresh discoveries were made, his main store would have to close.

One of the last significant discoveries in the Anatori goldfield was made at Friday Creek, and it was typical of all that had come before.

Heavy black rain clouds rolling in had marked an otherwise quiet Sunday night, and everyone knew they would be waking up to rain the following morning. Many miners had been turning up at Moffatt's store since Saturday night, but all had left to return to their diggings in anticipation of rain. The storekeeper expected to be left alone for a few days at least, barring maybe the arrival of some newcomer calling in to ask for two weeks' tucker on credit, or at best half-payment. Moffatt read a three-week-old newspaper and turned into his bunk, idly wondering that night if Long John or Scotch Bill would ever square their store accounts with him. He thought about his wife and children in Nelson before drifting off to sleep, but later woke to the sound of the wind blowing and heavy rain falling… and a voice enquiring after candles.

Moffatt turned out to meet his customer and asked what was happening. He was given a hurried and garbled account about a rush somewhere up the Anatori River, and how two miners called Ned and Joe had suspiciously left for Collingwood with a big bag of quartz. It was all hastily explained. Dungarvon Tom had been at West Whanganui Store when the pair went through: two men who had stopped for only one drink before heading on into the night. That had immediately aroused everyone's suspicions. Then some men coming from Collingwood had excitedly proclaimed that Joe's quartz was half gold. 'Tom let us know, and here we are,' said the midnight customer, who, with his newly purchased candles, asked if Moffatt could spare any Old Tom bottles to make lanterns. The storekeeper gave the man three or four he had lying around, the bottoms of which were soon knocked out with a sharp pick, turned upside-down and their necks plugged with the

The largest dune lake along Golden Bay's western flank is Lake Otuhie, today accessed up the Lake Otuhie Walkway, which starts just over the Sandhill Creek bridge along Cowin Road. Miners faced a long haul up beyond the head of the lake to reach the rich quartz reefs of the 'Golden Blocks', touted as the most remote goldfield in the country. Moffatt set up a general store here, in addition to the one he ran at Anatori. Photo: Gerard Hindmarsh

lit candles. The miner then disappeared out into the night, assured that his candles, thus protected, would not go out in the wind.

Moffatt got little sleep that night, for soon another lot of men called in, blurting out about the same discovery, except now the story had become more exaggerated and the find a bit richer. This second lot were positive that the previous caller had got it wrong, and that the discovery was up Independent Stream. After a quick drink, they set off into the dark too. Almost on their heels, a third excited party arrived out of the dark, and even more turned up in the morning as the news spread like wildfire around the diggings. The only trouble now was that the river, which had been steadily rising all night, was in high flood. Still, all day the place was abuzz with the news, one man coming back late afternoon to report excitedly that most of the prospectors had headed up the wrong creek. He said that Long Don, Woodhen, Kangaroo

Jim and some others had found out that Joe and Ned had been working in Friday Creek when they discovered the run of broken quartz rich in gold, and that they had followed it into the hill until they struck a 2-foot reef showing gold all over it. Pegging out a double claim, Joe and Ned had then rushed into Collingwood to formalise it. Within just one day, the entire hill for a mile around that prospecting claim had been pegged out. But everyone had been so overcome by the excitement that no one was quite sure what the truth was. That didn't stop the speculation though.

One of the gold-claim peggers, P.B. Jack, let it be known that he would sell a quarter-share in his 'No. 3 South' claim for the astronomical sum of £400. Confusion reigned more than ever, as bedraggled men came out of the bush after flaying around on wet hillsides trying to find the rush, for many to no avail. The flood lasted all the following day and did temporarily curtail the movement of diggers, but those who passed through the store kept Moffatt up on all the latest news as it was developing. The surrounding country was becoming increasingly pegged off, and the miners had turned to talk of floor-walls, hanging walls, strikes of reef and machinery, which would now surely be needed. Values of quarter-shares were discussed in detail, along with plans for new townships, business sites and water rights. 'The end of it,' wrote Moffatt, 'was more skittles, more rum, little money and strained credit. A diversion was briefly caused by a row between "Grummety Ned" and "Okarito Joe", which ended in more rum [being purchased]... and gradually quiet reigned once more.'

Despite the optimism that the latest rush had brought, business slowly declined at Moffatt's two stores to such an extent that he became worried that there were simply not enough people to sell his goods to anymore. Not only that, but he worked out that it wouldn't even pay to pack all his lake store stock back to Anatori and then freight it out by ship. He travelled back to Nelson to consult his merchant friend and business partner. The venture had proved a bit of a disaster for the Nelson man, and Moffatt also had to admit that he had spent three years in a situation that was not to be envied. His greatest regrets were not only the financial loss he had caused his friend, but the solitary and anxious existence his wife had been put through while he attended to business at the Anatori. He went back once more to tidy up his affairs there, sold everything he could at rock-bottom prices and abandoned the rest. It was the end of the Anatori store. After arriving back in Nelson,

Moffatt got a job working for the contractor charged with putting in the Nelson Railway, then in a store, before being offered the new position of looking after the wharf and harbour at Motueka. He accepted the offer and moved there with his wife, children and all their belongings. For the first time in his life, he knew what it meant to have a proper home.

For 30 years Moffatt remained harbourmaster at the Motueka Wharf, resigning only when 'warnings of old age were beginning to show'. Expressions of appreciation poured out at a public meeting in the town to mark his last day on the job: 'many nice things were said and I was the recipient of a handsome piece of plate, a purse of sovereigns and many written testimonials in appreciation of services rendered, and of expressions of good wishes for the few remaining years of our lives'.

One of the last things Moffatt mused in his autobiographical memoir, which first appeared as a series of articles in the *Nelson Evening Mail* and as a small book called *A Digger's Story* by 'Kiwi', was that the Durdon grave would probably become overgrown and hidden by vegetation, but that some day it might be found by people who would wonder about its history.

But when road-builders extended the public road from the mouth of the Paturau River 15 kilometres south to the Anatori River in the 1940s, the new route swept close to Durdon's grave, which until then had been accessible only via a scramble up from the beach. Locals still refer to the section of Cowin Road that passes the grave as Tombstone. The seascapes from here all the way down to Kahurangi Point are truly wild, notably the crumbling Kaipuke Cliffs, which start just south of the mouth of the Anatori.

Brett and Michelle Hart purchased Anatori Station 32 years ago, moving from their tobacco farm at Riwaka to continue farming here. A decade or so ago they subdivided some of their land, and around the same time Michelle commissioned a website advertising her 'one woman at a time' retreat. She now spends around half her year commuting and living in Takaka, where she works as a wellness advocate.

Even the most remote areas change and develop. Half a dozen places out on Golden Bay's west coast now offer accommodation and lodgings, and you can even get a real coffee on the way out there at the Nugget Café in Mangarakau. It's lucky then that we still have the odd reminder – like James Durdon's grave and Moffatt's account – of what life in this remote spot was once like.

CHAPTER 6

THE FLYING CRAY FISHERS

I AM ALWAYS IMPRESSED by the bravery of those who reject conventional jobs and earn their living in the wild, especially so in such a vast wilderness as Kahurangi. The park's 450,000 hectares of untamed country, with its unforgiving coastline and mountainous interior, have attracted a succession of prospectors, hunters, eelers, trappers, fishermen and others of the backcountry fraternity, who have defied the odds and managed to eke out a living here.

In the early 1970s, one such venture saw two Nelsonians combining their respective talents to fly over to the Kahurangi coast to catch crayfish and then fly them out. It was certainly an ambitious plan, and one that ultimately cost them their lives in mid-October 1972.

John Rodney (Rod) Ryan, 49, was a Nelson-based cray fisherman with many years of experience under his belt. Fishing and seafaring ran in his blood – both he and members of his family before him had had a long association with both Stewart Island/Rakiura out of the port of Bluff, and the Chatham Islands.

Ryan became involved in the cray-fishing boom around the Chathams in the mid-1960s, the boat he captained back then being the *Kalimarus*. He also took the role of navigator and unofficial 'commodore' of small venture fishing convoys going to or returning from the islands. Back in 1964, the main fish caught there was blue cod, but this changed dramatically the year after, following a visit by the fishing vessel *Picton*. The crew caught 2 tons of crayfish around the islands, before returning to Wellington to sell them for a substantial profit.

The subsequent rush, spurred by a fashionable demand for 'lobster' from the well-heeled American market, lasted little more than four years. The best year was 1968, when nearly 5,900 tons was shipped out. Although the official reported catch from those heady years was 14,427 tons, the truer estimate of extracted crays was 20,000–25,000 tons according to a timeline history on the Ministry for Primary Industries website. This was a similar quantity to that taken in Fiordland during the entire 1960s. However, what differentiated the two fisheries was the high degree of risk associated with the Chatham fishery, where far more fishermen drowned as boats foundered across the Chatham Rise and on the risky crossings to and from 'mainland' New Zealand. Although freezing and processing plants were built on the Chathams, the argument against the boom was that little money was retained in the local economy. And as crayfish stocks steadily declined after 1970, the so-called 'looters' – fly-by-night fishermen – left to follow more lucrative opportunities around New Zealand's exclusive economic zone. The reality for some fishermen involved in the boom had been anything but big profit. Working between the Chathams and the mainland incurred huge costs, with much of the profit being spent on operating expenses and high wage bills.

It was following his involvement in this adventurous industry that Ryan headed back to Nelson, a regional port that in the early 1970s was beginning to process an increasing amount of wet fish, scallops and crayfish. This opened up new possibilities for entrepreneurial fishermen like Ryan, who was multi-skilled. In particular, he was a qualified private pilot and had been a navigator in the Royal New Zealand Air Force (RNZAF) in the Second World War, when he was little more than a lad. In effect, Ryan was a man capable of any mission, whether it be on land, sea or in the air, and he was up for it.

It was this love of flying and his connection with the Nelson Aero Club that brought Ryan into contact with another pilot who would become his business partner for the Kahurangi venture. Godfrey Elliott Harrington Thomas was just 23, but nevertheless an experienced flight pilot who, until he teamed up with Ryan, had been an instructor with the Nelson Aero Club.

In 1972, Nelson men John Rodney (Rod) Ryan and Godfrey Thomas combined their respective fishing and flying skills to fly in to Kahurangi Point and fly out with crayfish they caught there. Their early morning routine involved flying over from Nelson and landing their Auster aircraft on the long, hard stretch of beach that runs alongside Lagoon Creek. Photo: Lois Benjamin

Thomas's sister Patricia (Tish), two years older than her brother, recalls his incredible passion for flying, and how they grew up in the area:

> *We lived on a farm at Orinoco just out of Motueka. It was 550 acres and we ran cattle, sheep and tobacco. There were three of us kids, two sisters and Tom* [the family's nickname for Godfrey] *in the middle. We were really lucky growing up, we were a close family. Our father bought the farm by ballot after returning from fighting in northern Africa and Italy in World War II. Because he'd been shot in the heel during active service, they made him undertake a tractor ploughing test to show he could handle the farm before they'd hand it over. Our parents supported us in anything we did. My brother Tom became passionate about flying and took up flying lessons while still enrolled at Nelson*

College. At 16, the youngest possible age he could get his private pilot's flying licence, he'd already clocked up his 40 hours beside an instructor and went solo. Flying was all he wanted to do.

When he left school, Thomas enlisted as a trainee pilot in the Royal Air Force in England, and moved there to continue his career. But when his father (also called Godfrey) was tragically killed in a tractor accident on the family farm at Orinoco in December 1968, the younger Godfrey decided to return to New Zealand to be closer to his now widowed mother, Joan. Still keen to pursue an aviation career, he soon enrolled at the Whanganui Commercial Pilot School, where he spent a year gaining first his commercial licence and then his instructor rating, both of which he passed with flying colours. On his return to Nelson, Thomas took up as an instructor with the local aero club, which was when he met Ryan.

The two men, although 26 years apart in age, hit it off, and together they put their heads together to come up with a unique joint business venture that had the potential to earn them both a lot of money. First, it entailed purchasing an Auster aircraft from a farmer in Methven and flying it up to Nelson. Then they acquired an 18-foot jetboat called *So-Big*, which they custom-equipped with cray-fishing gear, pots, and a swing-around hoist arm with a pulley for bringing up the pots.

Their final acquisition was an old tractor, which they transported on a flatbed truck to the end of the public road near the mouth of the Anatori River. There they unloaded the tractor onto the gravel bank and hooked it up to the jetboat trailer, which they had towed down with them.

After crossing the Anatori and heading down the farm road that winds through old dune country, they crossed the Turimawiwi and made their way to the outer beach. It would have been an easy run along the hard sand all the way to Big River, although no doubt the pair would have tied their jetboat down onto its trailer for the Anaweka and Big River crossings to stop it floating off – or if it did float, to ensure that the trailer would stay firmly with it. Finally, at an old woolshed that used to stand in the lee of some macrocarpas 500 metres or so north of the Kahurangi Lighthouse keeper's house, behind Conical Hill, they parked their tractor and boat up on the grass safely beyond the tidal zone.

Then the men returned to Nelson and began a very carefully scripted procedure, flying over to Kahurangi every day the weather was reasonable enough to permit the trip. Depending on the wind direction, they would approach Kahurangi by sweeping the beach for any sign of driftwood or soft-looking spots, then come around to land on the long stretch of hard sand that runs parallel to tannin-stained Lagoon Creek, its ink-black water trapped behind a line of old dunes smothered in coastal bush bristling with nīkau. This locality is reminiscent of any Pacific paradise, thanks to a warm offshoot current of the Queensland Convergence that flows south from eastern Australia to brush the Kahurangi coast. It is for this reason that nīkau palms thrive in great numbers from here all the way down to Greymouth, where they peter out.

After taxiing back along the beach, the two men would wind up the engine to full throttle to cross the final line of soft, dry sand above the high-tide mark, then continue onto the open grass in front of the dilapidated woolshed, an area kept relatively chewed down by both sheep and browsing deer. Sometimes, if the wind had deposited an excess of loose sand, they had to use the tractor to pull the plane up the last few metres.

Once the plane was secure, the pair would then waste little time launching their jetboat into the surf with the tractor. Along this stretch of Kahurangi coast, launching a boat of any description – not to mention landing it again – is no mean feat. Almost certainly, Ryan and Thomas would have chosen what used to be called Landing Beach, tucked in at the end of their beach runway, to launch their craft. This slightly curving bank of sand at the far end of the beach lies between two rocky reefs, which used to be marked by two white posts in the paddock immediately behind, now long since eroded away.

Landing Beach got its name because it was once regularly used by the surfboats rowed in from the government coastal supply ships *Tutanekai* and the *Hinemoa* to deliver supplies to the Kahurangi Lighthouse (see Chapter 1). These tenders originally landed directly below the lighthouse, but after one rolled over and its crew nearly drowned, the drop-off was moved to Landing Beach, from where a horse and cart would convey the stores to a holding shed. After the 1929 Murchison earthquake devastated all the houses and sheds that stood by the lighthouse, a new keeper's house was built near Landing Beach. This was subsequently towed a kilometre north to its current position after sea erosion threatened to demolish it and what was left of the paddock. Today, it is known as Kahurangi Keepers' House, administered by DOC.

To get their Auster off the beach and onto the hard grass beside the old woolshed, Ryan and Thomas had to taxi or sometimes tow their plane up through the last line of soft sand. Every second counted in this operation. Photo: Lois Benjamin

After a day out on the water pulling in and resetting their cray pots along the rocky offshore reefs, Ryan and Thomas would return to shore. They would drive the jetboat directly onto the trailer as best they could, then use the tractor to pull it out of the water and return it to the woolshed. After loading their crates of wet crays into the plane, the pair would take off for the return to Nelson. This was virgin fishing territory, and they had no trouble getting a full load for their plane every time.

It is likely the men would have been confident in pushing the payload capacity of the plane to its maximum. Their choice of a Taylorcraft Auster was not only an economical one but a sensible one as far as workhorses went. The plane was developed as a British military liaison and observation aircraft during the Second World War, when it was used mainly in battle as an aerial observation post to direct fire from Royal Artillery units. It went on to become one of the most successful post-war British light aircraft ever built, with more than 400 snapped up by individual pilots, aero clubs and small charter firms for everything from passenger flights to freight carting, and from banner towing to photography. Austers still operate today in most African countries, Scandinavia, Europe, the Middle East, South America, Australia and New Zealand. With their large overhead wings they can be flown at incredibly slow speeds, making them ideal for observation flying or landing on roughish ground like riverbeds and beaches, the big, bouncy wheels and sturdy undercarriage adding to that security.

In terms of specifications, the reliably robust Auster became one of the most altered aircraft in aviation history, sporting more variations than virtually any other plane of its type in the world. In New Zealand, Austers sprouted spraying gear and cradles to carry 44-gallon drums, and were even adapted for venison recovery. All these modifications should have been approved by Civil Aviation Authority (CAA) inspectors, but some owners couldn't see the point of this. In his book *Hunting for Trouble*, Auster owner Charlie Janes of Hawke's Bay saw nothing wrong with repowering his Auster with a Rover V8 car engine. The CAA wouldn't approve it beyond flying around the airfield, so Janes just used to take off, later claiming a big wind had suddenly come up and flung him and his plane out over the ranges.

With the rear two seats taken out in Ryan and Thomas's Auster, the luggage compartment became spacious, capable of carrying around 200–250 kilograms of crays for the return flight home. In its early days their plane had been powered by its original 130-horsepower de Havilland Gipsy Major engine, but this had later been legally modified to a more powerful 150-horsepower Lycoming engine, which could increase their payload even further. Not only that, but the pair had added tail flaring to give the plane more stability in the ferocious winds it could sometimes be expected to fly in along the Kahurangi coast. For aircraft buffs, these standard Auster Aiglet modifications had the effect of changing an original Auster J/1B into an Auster J/1Y Alpha. In plain language, Ryan and Thomas had chosen the perfect work vehicle, slightly modified but well within CAA requirements.

Ryan and Thomas launched their boat at Landing Beach, a couple of hundred metres south of the woolshed, directly in front of the lighthouse keeper's house. A 25-metre-wide channel was blasted in the reef offshore here by the Lighthouse Service after a surfboat attempting to land supplies was overturned and its crew nearly drowned. Photo: Lois Benjamin

On the way over to Kahurangi every morning, the plane would be full of miscellaneous gear, fuel and bait for the pair's jetboat, but on the way home it was jammed with crayfish, plus the odd empty drum of boat fuel for refilling. It's quite possible Ryan and Thomas took 44-gallon drums of avgas down the beach with their tractor, keeping the plane payload dedicated to payable crayfish. That would certainly have been worth doing. Even if they fished 200 days a year – ambitious on the Kahurangi coast, but possible – they could have expected to make roughly $500,000 in that time, not bad for a business that probably cost little more than $12,000 to set up. But not everyone could have done what these two men did. They had an edge, including the daring and all the skills to pull it off.

Without a doubt, Ryan and Thomas played the conditions to a very fine line, but not every day was a success. Lois Benjamin, daughter of Alva and Jean Page, the last Kahurangi Lighthouse keepers, recalls a time when she visited the lighthouse on a holiday break and witnessed the pair attempting to land: 'The weather was obviously too rough to launch their boat, so they did a fly over the keeper's house where we were staying and threw their loaves of fresh bread out for us to have, before turning back for Nelson.'

The two men fished successfully for two months, flying in and out of Kahurangi every day the weather allowed. On 17 October 1972, probably their last day alive, they landed on the beach soon after first light, pulled their plane above the high-tide mark and had their jetboat launched into the surf by around 7AM. Where they went that morning and how far out is anyone's guess now, but the best crays around here are out at Kahurangi Shoals. This notorious undersea rocky rise, 7 kilometres out in a north-northwesterly direction from Kahurangi Lighthouse, used to be known as Stewart's Breaker. Even the very lowest spring tides do not actually expose the reef, but at such times it is within around 6 metres of the surface. The stretch of coastline along here was the scene of more than a dozen shipwrecks before mariners' demands were finally met in 1903 and a lighthouse was erected at Kahurangi Point. The flash signature of the lighthouse, serial number K4236, runs white–red–white, the middle sector indicating the position of the Kahurangi Shoals, which on a bathymetric chart can be seen as a cluster of undersea mounts. All manner of fish can be caught from the swaying kelp forests beneath the waves here, including blue cod, snapper, trumpeter and kingfish in summer. Massive groper are pulled from its canyons, and big crays still abound today.

When the duo's aircraft failed to return to Nelson that evening, Thomas's flying mate at the Nelson Aero Club scrambled a plane and went looking for them, getting there as the light was fading. The pilot spotted their Auster pulled up above the high-tide mark, as well as their boat trailer hooked to the tractor nearby. Ominously, however, there was no sign of *So-Big* anywhere. The pilot flew back home along the coast, hoping to spot them coming in somewhere, but there was nothing, just row after row of whitecaps rolling in off the Tasman.

Nelson Police were soon alerted and the two men were declared missing at 10PM. The RNZAF was called in on the search, and an Orion maritime patrol aircraft flew down in the dark from Whenuapai. It swept the area from 2.45AM to look for any flares the men may have fired, in the hope they were drifting out to sea or even clinging onto wreckage. From first light, the Orion began a more intensive search of the area the men were known to fish. In addition, a Nelson-based Lama helicopter from Helicopters (NZ), piloted by Peter Tait, joined in.

The search intensified as the day wore on. Members of Nelson Police and Golden Bay Search and Rescue scoured the 10-kilometre section of coast between Kahurangi Point and the Anatori River, while searchers in 4WDs covered the coast north to Farewell Spit. Two aircraft from the Nelson Aero Club also joined in the search, and a fishing boat skippered by Ron Henderson of Nelson combed Whanganui Inlet. The 2-knot drift current in the area at the time would likely have taken any debris northwards from the point where the two men had been working, but there was still hope the small vessel was intact, broken down or even overturned with the men clinging onto it. Their boat was known to be well equipped with flares, a marine radio, life jackets, food, water and enough fuel for five hours of engine use. Ryan in particular was an experienced sailor, who knew the drill and what to do in the event of an emergency.

The first clue that disaster had struck was when a sizeable section of *So-Big*'s bow, along with the windscreen, was spotted from the helicopter, stuck on a rocky section of reef around a kilometre from Kahurangi Point. This was picked up by Tait, who came across it after being alerted to a floating object in the sea that the Orion's radar had picked up. Tait hadn't managed to locate whatever the radar had detected, but had come across the bow section instead.

The photo in the paper the following day showed Sergeant Dave Allen of Nelson Police examining a depth finder and fire extinguisher that had been attached to the recovered bow section, now confirmed as being that of the *So-Big*. The situation was not looking good. Police said the search would continue for another two days before being reviewed.

No one wanted to give up though. During the early hours of 19 October, two local residents who were assisting the searchers found two life jackets, several seat squabs, a number of small buoys, a torch and an oil container washed up at the mouth of the Anatori River. All were thought to have come from the *So-Big*.

It was a heart-rending end to a hugely ambitious fishing venture. Sadly for the families of the two victims, neither body was recovered. Both men

While Ryan and Thomas were fishing, their parked-up plane became the subject of interest – on this day for the children of the Benjamin family of Pakawau, holidaying at the lighthouse keeper's house in September 1972. Photo: Lois Benjamin

were married, Ryan leaving behind three children and Thomas a newlywed of just 11 months. For Thomas's family, the tragedy came all too soon after the death of his father on the family farm at Orinoco. His mother and two sisters later moved to Wellington. As one family member put it to me, 'The fate of the two Godfreys was a tragedy which reverberated in the family for years.'

A coronor's inquest the following year concluded that the men probably died from drowning on or about 18 October 1972. Sworn depositions were received from several local farmers, one being Phillip (Phil) Win, a farmer at Paturau and Search and Rescue organiser for the local area. He said that he first met Ryan when he assisted him taking his fishing gear down to Kahurangi during their set-up. As the two fishermen started flying in, Ryan would often

Aerial photo of the Kahurangi coast, from Kahurangi Point on the left to Big River at the right. Ryan and Thomas would land on the long stretch of hard beach showing as whitish sand. The small recessed bay at the western end of their beach airstrip is Landing Beach, where they launched their boat – the channel through the reef here is clearly visible. Photo: Airwork (NZ)

phone the Win homestead to enquire about the weather conditions along the coast. On three occasions when Win was near Kahurangi Point attending to his farm block down there, he watched while the two men launched their boat to go fishing: 'I noticed each time they put their boat in the water, they put on their life jackets before they started the engine. I took notice of this because they were the only ones I have seen in the area wearing life jackets while in their boats.'

Another deposition came from Victor (Vic), Phil Win's brother, who farmed land at Anatori and also at Big River. He reported that the weather on the 18th deteriorated to gale force from around 11AM. The wind direction was west to southwest, which would have whipped up the sea all along the coast, making conditions dangerous for boats close in to shore.

Many Kahurangi locals suspected that the coroner had been hesitant to say that Ryan and Thomas's *So-Big* jetboat was actually *too small* for the rough conditions that are experienced along that section of coast. No one will ever really know what happened to the pair, but it is easy to speculate. Commercial fishermen invariably didn't wear life jackets back then (and still don't), claiming it inhibits them in their work, but Phil Win's evidence suggests Ryan and

Godfrey routinely wore them. It was strange then that two lifejackets were found washed up with other gear from their boat. When pulling heavy pots from a relatively small boat, the craft can easily be put into a lean and then become swamped in heavy seas, or even just struck by a rogue wave. When explorers Charles Heaphy and Thomas Brunner walked down this section of the Kahurangi coast in 1848, they spent hours watching wave patterns to work out exactly when they could dash across a memorised series of boulders to reach safety before the precipitous coast would once again be inundated. Heaphy's observation was that every seventh wave or so was larger than the preceding ones, and that around one in every 500 was a monster that had to be avoided at all costs. Perhaps it was one of these monster waves that got Ryan and Godfrey?

To my mind, no blame should ever be afforded, and the pair certainly get top marks from me for the adventurous way they decided to go about earning a living in an environment that has always precluded anyone but the most daring.

CHAPTER 7

RIVER PORTS

WHILE HE WAS ALIVE, Karamea seaman Adolphus McNabb had the dubious distinction of being the only person to have crossed Cook Strait in an upside-down boat. This happened in around 1920, when the schooner he was captaining, *Te Aroha*, capsized as it was coming around the top of the Marlborough Sounds in rough weather, losing most of the crew in the process. McNabb was trapped inside the upturned hull, which then drifted almost right across the strait before he was finally rescued nearly a day later.

That traumatic experience never seemed to put McNabb off the sea though. His maritime career had started when he was a lad straight from school in the 1890s, sailing under his father, Captain John Fyne McNabb, who'd started the same way, sailing under his father, Captain Robert McNabb. After leaving Karamea as a lad, much of Adolphus's early sailing was on coastal vessels around the North Island. There he earned his master mariner tickets in both steam and sail, an unusual double qualification in the day, before heading back home to take command of the 100-foot, 57-ton schooner *Te Aroha* for the Karamea Shipping Company.

Originally built for the Wairoa and Mohaka Steamship Company and launched in May 1909 under the command of Captain Tomkin, *Te Aroha* was converted to a motor vessel in 1948, around the same time it was purchased by the Karamea Shipping Company. It had a maximum speed of 7 knots and regularly plied the route between Karamea and Wellington, taking primary produce, including timber and coal, to the capital. One of the final remaining coasters that once ploughed up and down our seaboard, it made its ultimate Cook Strait crossing – the last of more than 10,000 the little ship made – on 21 July 1976, long after it had turned keel up with McNabb inside and subsequently been refloated. But even that wasn't the end of the ship. From the 1980s, *Te Aroha* found a new purpose, taking up to 6,000 people a year out on historic cruises, first in the Hauraki Gulf and later around Kaipara Harbour. Reputedly built from a single kauri tree, this remarkable ship has since been through many hands and faced mooring conflicts, but at least it still lives on to bear witness to the 'phantom fleet' of small coasters that once plied our coast.

Also largely forgotten today is the relatively small band of merchant seamen like the McNabbs, who were largely responsible for opening up and supplying the coastal settlements along Kahurangi's western sea flank. These sailors made it their business to know every inlet and waterway here, using the tides and even 'fresh' water levels to take their shallow-draft vessels up rivers to load and unload their essential cargoes.

They weren't the first, of course. Early Māori appreciated the navigable tidal waterways of Kahurangi and knew them just as intimately. Their Māori names, from north to south along the Kahurangi coast, are Whanganui (Inlet), Paturau, Anatori, Turimawiwi, Anaweka, Awaruatu (Big River), Whakapoai (Heaphy River), Kohaihai, Oparara, Karamea, Wanganui (Little Wanganui), Mokihinui and the mighty Kawatiri (Buller River). The latter translates as 'deep and swift', a particularly pertinent name since it has by far the greatest flood flow of any river in the country.

The dangers of crossing these West Coast rivers was well appreciated by the region's earliest inhabitants, unlike the later Pākehā (European) travellers who lost their lives while trying to ford them. Mokihinui, meaning 'big raft', was the name given by Māori to the lazy-moving, tannin-stained waters of that river's lower reaches, best forded as every travelling Māori knew by making a raft from dried kōrari, the tall branch-like flower stalks that sprout from harakeke (flax), which have near-identical flotation properties to balsa. Just like the wood of this South American tree, whose name incidentally means 'raft' in Spanish, the coarse, open-grained, air-filled inner cells of dried kōrari are extremely buoyant and float easily. In a way, kōrari are better than balsa, which has to be cut down, stacked and dried before use; in contrast, kōrari stay on the flax plant long after they died off and dry naturally. Easily snapped off among thick groves of riverside flax, the flower stalks could be easily collected by Māori and bundled together, before being tied with the broad, spear-like, fibrous leaves of the same plant. A simple formula every Māori traveller knew was that around waru tekau (80) kōrari were required to float an average man – although more, of course, if he was carrying valuable pounamu (greenstone). Bound together in multiples of 80, these bundles of kōrari could carry as many people as required. Māori did not risk swimming like the schedule-driven Pākehā would later do, which is exactly why river fatalities were barely an issue among tangata whenua (indigenous people).

Of the European colonists, the entrepreneurs were the earliest arrivals. Richard (Dickie) Barrett bravely sailed his working cutter, the *Harriet*, into the 'harbour' of Big River during a sealing voyage along the Kahurangi coast in 1836. At high tide this lagoon resembles a large lake, and Barrett would have eyed up any potential opportunities on his brief visit, in particular the tall stands of kahikatea and rimu luxuriantly growing right down to its lower reaches. Anything was open slather, including the thousands of fur seals that once bred in sizeable rookeries south of the Kahurangi River, and that were virtually wiped out by entrepreneurial sealers like Barrett. Seal Bay, south of the Kahurangi River, was even the site of a sealing station, abandoned some ten years before explorers Charles Heaphy and Thomas Brunner passed by in 1846. By then seal numbers had plummeted and only small groups were commented on by Heaphy. Luckily, substantial populations have built up here again today.

When I have tramped along this precipitous coast, I have tried to imagine the hardships faced by the earliest sealers. In around 1830, a sealing boat was staved in here on rocks, and the crew, with the exception of two, perished. Some Māori from Whanganui Inlet who were in the area collecting karaka berries killed the hapless survivors in revenge for the loss of their chief's son, who had gone to sea in the ship to which the sealing boat belonged and never returned.

Another story recorded by Heaphy and Brunner on their 1846 trip concerned the fate of the *Rifleman*, a wool ship of 400 tons that left Hobart in 1835 and

Scows line up to load timber from Gilberts Wharf at Karamea Harbour in around 1910. The Karamea Sawmilling Company (managed by the Gilbert brothers) built a wooden rail track from its sawmill near the Oparara River to the company wharf, where large quantities of excellent heart timber were sent off to Wellington and Australia. The Government Wharf is in the background. Photo: Karamea Historical Society

was never seen again. After spying evidence of a wreck of a ship of similar tonnage near Cape Foulwind, the explorers learned from local Māori that, after it was wrecked, scores of bales of wool had washed up along the coast. Allegedly, the crew members – who had all survived and made it to shore – were hunted down along the coast and 'captured and eaten by local Maori'. Can you imagine their ordeal, first shipwrecked and then hunted down like wild animals, to be killed and almost certainly eaten?

Barrett would not have been overly concerned about these stories, for he was considered a Pākehā Māori and was entirely comfortable living among the iwi of Cook Strait and New Plymouth, which he had done since 1828. With a good command of pidgin Māori, Barrett acted as interpreter and negotiator between Māori and New Zealand Company officials during their Port Nicholson (Wellington) and Taranaki purchases. Later, he went on to build and establish Wellington's first hotel, Barrett's Hotel, at the southern end of Lambton Quay.

After the sealers came scouts sent out by the provincial government.

James Mackay arrived with his parents in Nelson in 1845 as a 14-year-old lad, and just ten years later commenced his explorations of the mountainous country at the headwaters of the Karamea. Two years later, accompanied by two Māori guides, he travelled down the sea coast from Karamea to cross the Buller River in a canoe. The day was calm, so he sounded the river as he went, declaring it navigable for coastal vessels. Then he carried on to the Grey River/Mawheranui, where he paid £10 to be taken by canoe 'as far as Ahaura', his guide being Chief Tarapuhi. After exploring all the sources of the upper Grey, Mackay returned downriver, and at the mouth it was once again calm enough to take soundings from the canoe. There, too, he declaring the entrance navigable for smaller vessels.

At Karamea, early Māori used the estuary as a summer camp along the pounamu trading route, which started up in around AD 1500. The huge shell middens here are the largest found on the whole West Coast, in places so thick that the deposits were collected and ground up for fertiliser by local farmers between 1920 and 1950 – remains of the shell crusher are still visible along the estuary walkway.

In 1874, 30 European immigrants moved in to form the new settlement of Karamea. Shipping along the Kahurangi coast soon became essential, and the business was even subsidised by the provincial government. Before the first road went in, Karamea's settlers relied heavily on the sea for getting in supplies, and getting in and out themselves. With the pounding seas and dangerous, ever-changing river bars along this stretch of coast, it could be a fraught business for passing sea captains. More often than not, if it looked at all dicey they just sailed on. And that would be the end of that until the next vessel came along, which might not be for several months.

This far from satisfactory situation lasted until 1893, when 23 Karamea settlers got together to form their own shipping company, the Karamea Steam Ship Company. Because the inherent risk of entering the Karamea River was great compared with other more accessible rivers along the coast, subsidies were paid to shipping companies to set up there in order to make it more attractive for them to operate. Unlike today, the Karamea River at the time was highly navigable, a situation that changed after the Murchison earthquake of 1929, when damage in the interior caused it to silt up irrevocably.

The first vessel purchased by the Karamea Steam Ship Company – incidentally, from just down the coast at Little Wanganui – was the *Picton*, a 41.7-foot open launch with a beam of 9.4 feet and a draught of 5.2 feet. Powered by two 8-horsepower steam engines, it had been built in 1880 by Robertson Co. shipbuilders of Wellington. The vessel was put under the command of Captain Robert Johnson, a Shetland Islander with sea water in his veins who, it would be fair to say, had a hint of buccaneer in him. His new vessel proved to be badly balanced and far too short for some of the bundles of timber – particularly the long telegraph poles – it was required to ship. So the captain and his brother William took it upon themselves to lengthen the *Picton* by 15 feet.

An early newspaper account describes how this was done, comparing the lengthening to a woman being cut in half in a stage magician act, just much more difficult. First, the two brothers dug out a sloping cutting on the bank about 3 kilometres up the Karamea River, took the *Picton* there on a high spring tide and then crab-winched the boat up out of the river on long timber skids, which they constructed from logs. After chocking the boat all round with blocks, they simply used a crosscut saw to cut it in half. One hundred and fifty pounds of copper nails and bolts were used in the remake, extra knees were inserted, and sister keelsons running fore and aft were provided. Seasoned 'black birch' (beech) and yellow pine were the timbers used, and the ship was raised 2 feet 6 inches for a length of 20 feet. When the job was finished, she was 63 feet overall and had a 61-foot inside measurement.

To carry out this modification in such an isolated place was a real achievement. It was recorded that the settler shareholders who paid a visit to the ship after she was moored up again below Captain Johnson's house were all well impressed. Almost immediately, the little shipping company took on a regular run, transporting sawn railway sleepers from Karamea to Westport, and winning the contract to carry the mail back and forth as well.

Things were looking up for the shareholders, but unfortunately the life of the *Picton* was short. On the stormy winter's day of 9 June 1896, a length of badly coiled rope washed overboard and fouled the propeller as the vessel was crossing the Karamea bar, stopping the engines at the most critical moment. Unable to do anything, Captain Johnson and his two-man crew watched helplessly as their ship was driven onto the beach by North Spit. With no way to hold her there, she was soon wrecked by the pounding seas.

There is little doubt from reading the eyewitness accounts that Captain Johnson took responsibility for losing 'his ship' very personally. He was, after

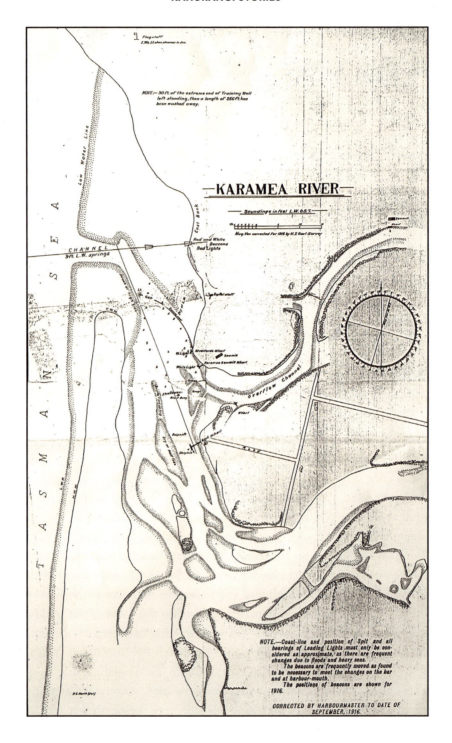

all, representing 23 local shareholders, fellow Karameans. They all stuck behind him, however, and made enquiries up and down the country for a replacement vessel. When none could be found, Captain Johnson took it upon himself on 12 November 1896 to travel to Sydney to buy a replacement. As he was departing, Johnson hugged his young son, George, saying, 'Be a good boy and help your mother, and when I return I will take you on a trip to Westport in the new boat I will buy in Sydney.'

The ship-less captain then picked up his heavy portmanteau to walk the 19 kilometres down the beach to Little Wanganui. He stayed the night there before fording the river the next morning and walking a further 23 kilometres along the rocky coast to Mokihinui, where he waited for the train to Westport. From there, he sailed on the next ship bound for Sydney.

It could be said that Captain Johnson hit the ground running in Australia. Exactly nine weeks after leaving Westport, he sailed back into that river port proudly in charge of the SS *Admiral*, which he had purchased in Sydney. After berthing at the Top Wharf, he consigned a letter overland to his wife in Karamea informing her of his safe arrival and stating that he would be returning home on 20 January along with distinguished settlers of Westport. He asked his wife to inform the company's settler shareholders and citizens of the town of the event. It was a bold marketing ploy, and Johnson's offer to transport Westport notables to and from Karamea was picked up by no less than 35 'leading townsmen'. It was reported that many more would have jumped at the opportunity had their business arrangements allowed it.

When the day of departure arrived, the weather turned nasty. The sea beyond the Westport bar was rising after a stiff nor'wester had come up out of nowhere after midnight. To make matters worse, just as the passengers started to turn up at 4AM – their reporting time – torrential rain began bucketing down from the sky, soaking everyone. Captain Johnson must have been asking himself that age-old sailor's question: 'Should I risk leaving or not?' A growing apprehension had already begun gripping his passengers,

A snapshot of an ever-changing waterway. The footnotes to this September 1916 Karamea River chart warn of 'frequent changes due to floods and heavy seas' and states that 'beacons are frequently moved as found to be necessary to meet the changes on the bar and at harbour-mouth'. The Murchison earthquake of 1929 caused Karamea Harbour to silt up eventually and become unusable. Photo: Karamea Historical Society

who had little alternative but to huddle below deck in the small cabin and nervously discuss the matter among themselves.

Just before 5AM, Johnson settled the matter, pulling the cord of his steam whistle and calling out, 'Let's go!' The ropes were cast off and the *Admiral* slipped downstream on its maiden voyage to Karamea. Crossing the big rollers that were crashing in over the Westport bar at dawn was hard enough, but being out on the exposed Tasman Sea was even worse and the little ship was fair buffeted by the waves. Having just beaten his way across nearly 2,000 kilometres of the open Tasman Sea, Captain Johnson showed little concern and exhibited full control of his seaworthy boat. As for his passengers, however, many became violently seasick and retired below deck to wait out the voyage.

After an extremely turbulent four hours and ten minutes, the *Admiral* was off Karamea, only for Captain Johnson to spy through his telescope the harbourmaster's 'Wait for tide' signal flying from the flagstaff. The only place to anchor offshore at Karamea is beyond the wave zone, roughly 3 kilometres out in 10 metres of water. But that's comfortable only in relatively calm conditions, which certainly wasn't the case that day. Johnson and his charges wallowed uncomfortably for another two hours, waiting for the crashing waves to calm down and the incoming tide to surge up the river. Fortunately, the weather suddenly improved, and at 11AM the signalman of Port Karamea hoisted the signal for 'Take the bar'.

Strict navigation rules applied to all river ports in New Zealand, Karamea included. Notices to mariners defined exactly what each flag meant, which lantern beacons were used and where at night, and which markers could be relied on for safe negotiation up and down each channel. As with all busy navigable river mouths, no vessel was permitted to enter the tricky Karamea unless the 'Take the bar' signal was up on the harbour flagstaff. At night, this was indicated by a green lantern positioned 20 feet vertically below a white light. Other signals for the Karamea River indicated 'Bar dangerous', 'Bar safe for 7 feet' and 'Bar safe for 5 feet'. Ships that visited regularly had their own flags, which recognised their individual draughts. At Karamea, the 'A' flag was for the scow *Echo*, 'F' was for the *Defender*, 'M' was for the *Nile* and 'W' was for the *Wairau*. The harbourmaster's decision was always final and not to be argued with.

If anyone knew how to get into the Karamea River, with its ever-changing labyrinth of muddy channels, it was Captain Johnson. In relatively clear

Captain Robert Johnson, from a solid Shetland seafaring family, skippered a succession of Karamea Steam Ship Company ships – namely the Picton, Admiral *and* Nautilus, *operating mainly between Karamea and Westport, Nelson and Wellington.*
Photo: Karamea Historical Society

conditions, he would start his approach by doing what all Karamea mariners were told to do, which was to bring his boat around so that the north end of Mt Stormy, a conspicuous 1,084-metre flat-topped mountain 10 kilometres inland, was bearing east. Staying a direct course for the bar opening was a matter of keeping the 'White Cliffs' near Little Wanganui (16 kilometres to the south) and Kohaihai Bluff (14 kilometres to the north) equidistant off each bow. The bar crossing itself was indicated by beacon posts painted white with a red band across the centre, after which two sets of white beacons led up the river.

The Karamea River is best described in its lower reaches as a shifting set of channels that change after every flood and churn up from the tides. The 1916 chart for the river warns, 'The beacons are frequently moved as found to be necessary to meet the changes on the bar and at harbour-mouth.'

In the case of the *Admiral*, and despite the atrocious conditions, everything went like clockwork. Captain Johnson proudly brought his ship up past the beacons and along the big row of piles of the Training Wall, slipping the ship into its new berth at Stafford's Wharf. A great concourse of settlers waited on the little wharf and adjoining bank to welcome the captain and his new command, not to mention the passengers. Never before had so many distinguished guests turned up at one time in the little pioneer settlement. Much surprise was expressed about the most adequate size of the vessel and the speeches flowed, congratulating Johnson on finding such a fine vessel to ply the Karamea–Westport run.

With the welcoming formalities over, the guests were all invited to Simpson's Hotel for a fine lunch, after which they were shown around the little town and its environs. Much preparation had been put into the occasion in a short space of time, and at 6PM everyone congregated back at the schoolhouse, where a huge banquet was laid on in honour of the visitors. With the exception of the top-shelf liquid refreshments, everything served up that night was locally produced. Three sittings were needed, and the young women of the town who attended the tables were kept busy all evening as the guests raised their glasses time and time again, the myriad of toasts knocked back to musical accompaniment. The visitors were well celebrated, 'so that they would take a great interest in Karamea after visiting us,' one of the townsfolk candidly admitted afterwards. The bottom line was that this organised visit was a marketing exercise, matching prominent buyers and suppliers with farmers and mining interests in a most provincial way. After the final toast to 'Our Entertainment', the schoolhouse was cleared and the dancing started, lasting right through until daybreak.

How many suffered hangovers the following morning is not known, but crack on schedule at 10AM Captain Johnson told his son George to pull the departure whistle, and called out to all the distinguished visitors to board. As the two crewmen cast off the ropes, three resounding cheers rang out from the settlers taking up the wharf. It was an occasion the likes of which Karamea had never seen before. Quite a few friendships had been made over the previous 24 hours, but mostly it was the new business partnerships and new associations that would irrevocably change the course of Karamea and its vast hinterland of natural resources. Not only could extractive industries like timber and mining be extended, but investors could also support farming and produce ventures, all safe in the knowledge that markets were reliably guaranteed and a full marine transport service was available. Without a doubt, the promise of economic advancement was about to be fulfilled, and all because of the new boat.

The return voyage to Westport in sunny weather aboard the *Admiral* went splendidly for the visitors. And no one was happier than little George Johnson, who stood with one hand on the wheel as his father brought the ship over the Westport bar and up into the Buller River. After tying up, the boy was even happier when his father gave him five shillings to spend in the shops of Westport.

The departing passengers, many with first-hand and veteran maritime knowledge, complimented both Captain Johnson and engineer Mr Hunter on a job well done. There was no doubt in any of their minds that the *Admiral* was the fastest and best-kept little ship on the coast.

For nearly two years, the *Admiral* plied the Westport–Karamea run, bringing essential supplies to Karamea from Westport merchants like Baillies, Taylor and Enright, and Greens. Farm implements, dynamite, low-weight livestock – anything was transportable. And on the return journey, timber, flax and delicious Karamea produce was carried – even fresh flowers for the fruit shop in Westport. Passengers, too, began making good use of the service. For anyone or anything that needed to travel between Westport and Karamea, *Admiral* was the boat to use.

However, the punishing route and ever-changing conditions proved tremendously hard on the little ship. Not only were the broadside swells off the Tasman Sea unrelenting, but two exceedingly hot, dry summers served to open up the *Admiral*'s upper hull. Drawing nearly six feet, she would often scrape the muddy bottom in the ever-changing river channels, adding to the workout. Karamea Shipping Company's decision to include pick-ups and deliveries from the problematic river mouths of the Little Wanganui and Mokihinui rivers was almost certainly a big factor in the *Admiral*'s decline into a leaky old tub. In the end, even the boat's twin bilge pumps could barely keep up with the intrusion of the sea.

The writing was on the wall for the *Admiral*, and on his last voyage aboard her Captain Johnson sailed her to Wellington. There, after much due diligence and negotiation, he swapped her for the *Nautilus*, a sleeker vessel with a slightly shallower draught. This new ship immediately proved superior to its predecessor. George Johnson recalled being aboard the *Nautilus* as an older lad when it worked up from Westport, calling up the Little Wanganui River to discharge cargo before sailing on to Karamea, all on the same tide.

Taking sightseers along the Kahurangi coast and up its inland waterways was something the boat was gainfully put to use to fill its schedule. On 15 June 1897, Captain Johnson took 40 curious Karameans, each paying five shillings, to investigate the Heaphy River at high tide. They spent much of the morning being buffeted up the coast into a heavy running sea, and when they did finally get there, Captain Johnson was unwilling to risk his boat or his passengers on the big breakers crashing over the bar. He returned to Karamea with all the disappointed passengers sheltering below, only to find the 'Do not enter' signal flying from the flagstaff. The boat hove to beyond the breakers, and a thoroughly restless night was had by all. By the following morning, it was finally deemed safe to enter and the signal was changed to 'Take the bar'.

Only 28 passengers took the next *Nautilus* charter up the Heaphy. This time conditions were fine and calm. Captain Johnson pushed his little ship through the easy swells at the river mouth to enter the lagoon, dropping anchor at the head of it. One of the exploring party later wrote, 'We discovered a limestone cave with stalactites and stalagmites, rudely augmented by two Maori skeletons.'

The fortunes of the Karamea Steam Ship Company proved mixed, but it battled on. In September 1908, the 80-ton wooden screw steamer *Ngungura* became the company's second vessel to strand on the Karamea bar after her rudder broke off in heavy seas. The steamer, captained by Frederick Fletcher, drifted ashore. Her anxious crew spent hours jettisoning the timber cargo in an attempt to refloat her, but all was in vain and she ended up a total wreck off Karamea. The dangers of the bar were well appreciated by this time. Karamea's Holy Trinity Church (now Karamea Memorial Community Church) was built after four local men drowned when their scow *Rangi* overturned while taking soundings on the bar on 19 July 1906.

Karamea sawmilling companies dramatically expanded their operations through the early 1900s to meet the exceptional demand from rapid house-building in the cities, including those in Australia. Some investigated having their own boats to cart out their timber. The Karamea Sawmilling Company, headed by William T. Gilbert, was the first to do so, chartering the *Wangaroa*, which at the time was the biggest ship to enter Karamea. In 1909, she made six trips to the lucrative Sydney market laden with timber. Karamea had become an international port.

Butter was produced commercially in Karamea from 1909, and the fledgling industry needed regular deliveries to its markets as a necessity. The Karamea Co-operative Dairy Company started up in 1911, initially coordinating with timber boats to transport its produce. Boats on the Karamea Harbour Board 'Arrivals' register around this time include the *Holmdale*, *Whakatai*, *Coronation* and *Aratapu*. One of the mainstays of the trade was the *Mangapapa*, a 106.8-foot wooden twin-screw steamer that had been built in Sydney in 1902. She plied out of Karamea laden with butter, timber and passengers, mostly to other West Coast ports and Wellington. But her end came on 12 October 1914, after she left the Government Wharf at Karamea on a full tide and in a stiff westerly. With a full manifest of butter and timber, the ship promptly became stranded on the North Spit of the Karamea bar. Within two days, the relentless waves had turned her broadside and the sea began breaking over her. She became a total wreck, her cargo of butter and timber strewn all along the beach right up to Kohaihai. Locals flocked to retrieve the big boxes of butter, which proved edible after the sand and salt had been washed off. The steamer now lies buried just beyond the town's golf course.

The worst disaster for local shipping occurred in 1931, two years after the newly formed Oparara Shipping Company purchased the *Kotiti*, a motor vessel of 61 tons, with a length of 71.4 feet, a beam of 16.3 feet and a draught of 6.4 feet. Originally built in 1898, the *Kotiti* was designed specifically for the Warkworth trade up the Mahurangi River. Initially, she was owned by the Coastal Steamship Company (which became the Settlers Company in 1905), before being taken over by the Northern Steam Ship Company in 1908. She shifted to the South Island in 1926, when she was sold to the Kotiti Shipping Company in Lyttelton, and three years later she was bought by the Oparara Shipping Company.

In May 1930, the *Kotiti* was fitted with a 175-horsepower direct reversible full diesel Fairbanks Morse motor, which gave her the ability to run on a diverse range of fuel, from wood powder and sawdust to low-grade fuel oil.

The channels and bar of the Karamea River have claimed their fair share of ships. Departing on the 2PM high tide on 12 October 1914 from the Government Wharf with a load of butter, timber and passengers, the 164-ton wooden twin-screw steamer Mangapapa *promptly found herself blown aground on North Spit by a stiff westerly. After attempts to reverse off the beach were unsuccessful, passengers were helped ashore at low tide and left to walk home along the beach with all their belongings. The plan to refloat the ship that night on the high tide proved unsuccessful.* Photo: Karamea Historical Society

The motor was started by detonating a blank .22 cartridge shell directly into the piston head, which got the piston going. Back in its day, this engine was nothing short of revolutionary.

The Oparara Shipping Company owners worked out that the *Kotiti* had to pull off 35 trips a year out of Karamea to make her profitable. The company had four shareholders: Hector Soares, the boat's engineer, who had 32 of the 64 shares; McLean, Karamea's shopkeeper, who had 10; Simpson, the town's hotel keeper, who had 10½; and Svendson, the post master, who had 11½. In addition to the revenue from freight, the four shareholders became eligible for government subsidies totalling £200 a month, a big incentive to starting the business.

By far the main freight carted was timber, and the company set its prices accordingly:

Further attempts to refloat the Mangapapa *turned to failure when strong seas sprang up and she was pounded by heavy waves. By morning, the beach was littered with the ship's wheelhouse and deck cargo, including 56-pound boxes of butter, which locals were quick to pick up. Today, the remains of the ship are buried under sand beyond Karamea's golf course.*
Photo: Karamea Historical Society

Karamea to Wellington 180 miles 5/- per 100 feet
Karamea to Nelson 102 miles 4/9d per 100 feet
Karamea to Motueka 98 miles 4/9d per 100 feet
Karamea to Westport 40 miles 3/6d per 100 feet
Iron Girders for Bridges £2 each

Under the capable command of Captain Christian Johansen, the *Kotiti* left Westport at 4AM on 10 October 1931 bound for Foxton, on its 30th or so trip out of Karamea that year. The five crew on board that day were the captain; engineer Hector Soares and his assistant, 15-year-old James Clarke of Millerton; a man named Hughes, who had no known relatives in the district; and a cook by the name of Davies, who was married and hailed from Reefton. In addition, the ship carried two passengers that day, both single men. The first was 'Ham' Matthews, a radio operator with the New Zealand Post Office.

Originally from Picton, Matthews had been sent to Westport following the 1929 Murchison earthquake to re-establish communications there after the telephone and telegraph network was totally destroyed. After disembarking from the *Kotiti* in Levin, Matthews was planning to take a ship to Picton from Wellington. He hadn't seen his parents for nine years and was keen to use the opportunity to catch up with them. The other passenger was Stanley (Stan) Cumming, a 24-year-old Westport taxi driver from a well-regarded local family. Cumming was along for the ride because he was particularly interested in the *Kotiti*'s new engine, an attraction that had seen him go on two previous trips. The ship had room for up to 20 passengers and routinely carried a few, despite not being licensed to do so at the time. It seems a blind eye had been turned to the practice – it was a small town after all.

After departing Karamea on 10 October with seven on board, the *Kotiti* failed to turn up at its destination and was never seen again. Then, on 19 October, the ship's lifeboat dinghy was found washed ashore a couple of kilometres north of Grey Cliff near the entrance to Whanganui Inlet. (Incidentally, this dinghy was used on the inlet for many years by its finder.) The following day, a lifebuoy with the ship's name written across it was found at Makara Beach near Wellington. Then a body washed up at Cape Farewell, which was soon identified as 'Ham' Matthews, one of the *Kotiti*'s passengers. Disturbingly, his autopsy revealed that he had come ashore alive, but later died of exposure, indicating that the ship had foundered close to shore. Empty barrels, spars and other deck material from the *Kotiti* began washing up at other beaches between Whanganui Inlet and Farewell Spit. But the biggest piece of evidence that the ship had been wrecked didn't wash up for some time. Found at Scotts Camp on the north side of Kohaihai Bluff in December 1934 and measuring around 10 metres long, the section was possibly part of the ship's keel, although some locals disagreed, saying it was off an earlier wreck that kept shifting along the beach.

The main immediate source of information about why the ship may have foundered came from local man Harry Soares. His father, Hector Soares, was half-owner of the boat and its engineer when it went missing. Much conjecture has been aired over the years about the *Kotiti* tragedy, but everything points to the ship foundering in heavy weather somewhere between Kahurangi Point and Farewell Spit, an infamous stretch of water. One mariner around this time described how his little ship, laden with coal, had battled north along here

The worst disaster for local Karamea shipping occurred in October 1931, when the 61-ton, 71.4-foot Kotiti *left the harbour with five crew and two passengers bound for Foxton, and was never seen again. Wreckage later found washed up indicated she had foundered somewhere north of Kahurangi Lighthouse, probably going down close to shore. A post-mortem carried out on the only body found, that of 'Ham' Matthews, determined that his cause of death was not drowning but exposure, indicating he had made it to shore alive that night. Although blame was never laid in this tragedy, many locals believed that loading issues, along with the raising of the ship's superstructure, had made the* Kotiti *unseaworthy.*
Photo: Karamea Historical Society

into a howling nor'easter for 2½ days. When the wind finally settled down, the skipper took his position and found he was just 2 kilometres from where he'd started! Soon after the *Kotiti* left Karamea, the weather did indeed deteriorate.

Of particular interest to investigators was Harry Soares' recollection of a disgruntled conversation between Captain Johansen and Hector the day before they sailed. The captain had clearly been condemning the loading procedures as a large quantity of oil drums and barrels were being stored on the deck, going so far as to declare angrily that this was going to be his last trip. How prophetic that would be. Evidently, Captain Johansen and Hector Soares had had previous altercations about deck loading, a classic owner versus operator conflict.

Playing around in the old Little Wanganui Harbour Board boat, just below Little Wanganui wharf, New Year 1948. Local cousins, from left to right: Wiggs (Bill) Hennessy, Athol Robbins, Bernard Robbins and Doug Simpson. Photo: Karamea Historical Society

Another rumour put forward by more than one eyewitness was that the *Kotiti* looked overloaded when she left the port that day, but no manifests were ever found to verify this. Some local fishermen speculated that the hull was sound, but that the wheelhouse and superstructure, which had both been added to, were not as sturdy as they should have been, and exposed the boat significantly. Some recounted their own experiences travelling on the *Kotiti*, claiming that the vibration from the new engine was terrific and the chief engineer too fearful to throw open the throttle in case it tore out the bottom of the boat.

But by far the most startling piece of evidence to wash up was a corked bottle, found among some of the debris near Cape Farewell. Inside was a short message on a torn piece of paper purporting to outline the disaster. However, this 'evidence' was immediately seized by Marine Department inspectors, who regarded it as a hoax that was not worth examining any further. The New Zealand Seamen's Union intervened on behalf of the families, and after long and protracted discussions a rudimentary photostat of the letter was finally produced.

When this copy was shown to the Cumming family in Westport, they immediately identified the handwriting as that of their son Stan, a passenger on the *Kotiti*, who always printed everything he wrote. They produced examples of his writing, including his meticulous taxi chits, all of which matched the note perfectly. But before anything more could be said, the Marine Department inspectors snatched back the copy, not even giving the family time to write down the words. Interviewed later by a newspaper, they recalled them like this:

HELP. CAN'T KEEP AFLOAT MUCH LONGER. JOHANSEN WASHED OVERBOARD HALF AN HOUR AGO, SHIP IS DISMASTED AND WHEEL HOUSE AND CABINS GONE, ENGINE ROOM MAKING WATER

After the publication of this remembered note, conspiracy theories abounded as to why the Marine Department was so keen to close the case. But one fishermen, who knew the coast from Westport to Farewell Spit intimately, explained it more pragmatically to the newspaper:

Along the whole West Coast of the South Island there is a tidal rip running in a northerly direction. This rip has peculiarities, in some areas it is fast and in others slow, with the faster action around bays. The first wreckage washed up was Kotiti's dinghy at Whanganui Inlet which suggested the ship foundered just south of here. Around the time of the disaster a northerly storm had sprung up which tended to curb the rip. The appearance of all the drum and deck cargo along just one stretch of coast indicates she wasn't that far offshore, certainly within sight of land.

Considering the rip and weather, the fisherman concluded that the ship had most likely foundered somewhere between Kahurangi Point and Whanganui Inlet, but no more than 5 kilometres from shore. Coastal vessels always pass between Kahurangi Lighthouse and the offshore reef of Kahurangi Shoals, so it all fitted together. What more could be said, especially as the note in the bottle was never seen again.

The Murchison earthquake of 1929 dealt the port of Karamea a savage blow. It not only ruptured apart the main Government Wharf, but also served to

The crew aboard Te Aroha *have a quick break before leaving Little Wanganui harbour. Left to right: chief engineer (name unknown), assistant engineer Jim Pepper, Chook Finnerty (from Westport), deckhand Gil Jacobs, date unknown.* Photo: Karamea Historical Society

send a never-ending flow of silt and debris down from the massive destruction in the headwaters of the Karamea River and its tributaries. The lower channels started silting up and it became more and more difficult for any of the bigger boats to enter the river. This resulted in the port at nearby Little Wanganui being used far more frequently, until eventually it had to be extended. This little river port gained its first wharf in 1900, its forerunner just a single pile in the river that ships could tie up to and from there transfer their cargo to a tender. Local man Christen Rasmussen, who ran the hotel at the mouth and a small farm adjacent to it, acted as the signalman until 1903, when that job was taken over by Harry Simpson, the new owner of the hotel and farm. With just the odd bale of wool, hides and small consignments of timber, freight in and out of Little Wanganui largely dwindled until around 1920, when the timber trade really picked up here. The big catalyst was the opening of the big Caliari and Havill Mill, along with other smaller sawmills, all trying to satisfy the incessant demand from other districts for new telephone poles, sleepers and sawn timber.

RIVER PORTS

The 1929 earthquake had looked like it would silt up the Little Wanganui River as well, but the harbour was kept open by building a tide-deflector wall upstream, which had the effect of clearing the channel back down to the wharf. Similar Victorian river technology was applied to the Buller River to ensure that Westport stayed open, except at Little Wanganui it was on a far smaller scale. Little Wanganui was declared a Marine Department port soon after the earthquake, and Captain Williamson was appointed the first harbourmaster in 1932. Later that same year, 'Nip' Simpson took over his position, one he held for 30 years until the wharf was closed.

From around 1930, another big timber mill, Granite Creek Sawmilling, used the wharf for sending out its timber. On one occasion the mill owners protested to the Marine Department with a formal letter after another timber company stacked all its timber across the wharf, making it near impossible for Granite Creek to load their boat. This was in the days of big scow shipments, with full loads of 50,000 super feet or even more. Granite Creek, Simpson Bros. (North Beach), Harris and Duncan, Stewart's, Caliari and Havill, and, later, Te Namu were the sawmills that shipped timber out of Little Wanganui. It was Kahurangi's bounty, and the supply of big trees seemed limitless.

In January 1929, the large three-masted scow *Zingara* was wrecked on Hokitika Beach after her steering chain broke. The salvaged ship's wheel was purchased in 1936 from the Hokitika harbourmaster for the princely sum of £10 and fitted to the Karamea Shipping Company's *Te Aroha*. This vessel had just been purchased as a replacement for the loss of the *Fairburn*, wrecked earlier that year against the Western Wall of Westport Harbour as she was leaving for Little Wanganui to load timber. Being slightly larger than the *Fairburn*, *Te Aroha* was easier to turn when negotiating tricky bar entrances.

That didn't stop the near misses though. *Te Aroha* nearly ran aground on the Little Wanganui bar on 29 January 1943, but luckily a swell lifted her off. The following year, on 1 March, she ran aground properly there and two Public Works bulldozers worked in tracks-deep water to gouge out a channel from the ship to the main river channel so she could be refloated. Karamea Shipping Company was charged £32 10s for the hire of the bulldozers, to which they protested, claiming no dredging work had been undertaken since the river had started silting up. *Te Aroha* also ran aground at the entrance to Port Mapua, and one notable fatality associated with the ship occurred at Little Wanganui wharf when she was tied up on the night of 22 May 1942.

While climbing back on board, seaman George Sim Mouat fell into the river, which was fresh after rain, and drowned. With these vessels it was standard practice not to bother with a gangway or safety net at such locations, but instead use a ladder and a lamp, which were in place that night. Once again, excessive timber stacked on the wharf was cited as an impediment to using the ladder, along with the fact that Mouat came back to the boat 'having imbibed more freely than benefited him'.

Crews regularly gorged themselves on whitebait if they were running up Little Wanganui, one oral history report recording that 1946 was the best run ever on the river. Boxes of butter were also routinely shipped out from Little Wanganui wharf until 1937, when the Karamea Dairy Company started trucking its produce along the new road put in over Karamea Bluffs. The serious shipment of timber from Little Wanganui, much of it for export, lasted right up until 1946, when silting issues started appearing in that river too. *Te Aroha* carried on working the river until she was shifted by her directors to run a dedicated Karamea–Tasman Bay–Wellington route in 1949. Another ship often associated with *Te Aroha* at Little Wanganui was the *Motu*, which met its end in 1961 when the inter-islander ferry *Maori* crushed her against the wharf while berthing in Lyttelton. *Te Aroha* had the distinction of being the last of the little coasters to ply Cook Strait.

In 1952, Little Wanganui's port was officially closed and much of the wharf was dismantled. It was partially rebuilt in 1963, when the scow *Kohi* sailed in to pick up three big loads of native timber from Te Namu Sawmill for buyers in New Plymouth – the first time Little Wanganui had seen a ship cross its bar in 16 years. Those last timber trips by the *Kohi* largely signified the end of Kahurangi coastal shipping.

The flat-bottomed *Kohi* was near identical to its sister ship, the *Echo*, equally well known as one of our last coastal traders. The two ships saw active service in the Pacific during the Second World War, carrying supplies to various island outposts, the *Kohi* affectionately becoming known as the 'ice cream ship' in the process. But her end was not that flash. Collingwood farmer Bruce James remembers the day in 1964 when the scow arrived at Takaka's Waitapu Wharf laden with another cargo of West Coast timber. On the way up, she had run into very rough seas off Farewell Spit, which had opened up some of her timber seams, allowing excess water to enter. The true damage to her hull was revealed when her cargo of timber was unloaded, and she had to be

Her deck stacked with sawn timber and empty beer kegs, Te Aroha *is ready to depart Little Wanganui for Wellington, date unknown.* Photo: Karamea Historical Society

continuously pumped just to keep her from sinking at the wharf. A proper marine inspection determined that the old girl was a write-off, and she was dragged ashore and stripped of most of her working gear. This included the on-deck 1956 Fordson diesel that operated the boat's overhead loading derrick, which was purchased by James to replace the petrol engine in his old farm tractor. Another local, Jim Pearson, used his old Aspen power saw to cut a big hole in the ship's side so he could extract the newly fitted diesel engine.

Around 1966, the *Kohi* was bought by Mangarakau-based cray fisherman Jack Emms, who patched her up and fitted her with a large refrigeration unit before towing her around Farewell Spit and into Whanganui Inlet, where she became a refrigeration hulk. This remarkable coaster still lies beside the wharf there today, slowly rotting into the mudflats.

As for the Karamea Shipping Company, a small notice in a Nelson newspaper in April 1978 announced that it was being voluntarily wound up by its directors. It was an ignominious end to a company that had given 52 years of service. Together with the Karamea Steam Ship Company and the Oparara Shipping Company, it had served the sea freight and passenger demands of the town and district of Karamea admirably. It could even be said that the three were linchpins in the upper West Coast's economic development. Over just a few generations, however, coastal shipping completely died out, and the little ships that once faithfully served the people are now all but forgotten.

Karamea's shipping history occupied a window of only 50 years. Attempts were made to save the port after the 1929 Murchison earthquake and protect the town from flooding. This included building a tramline around the edge of the old port site to carry rock from a quarry at Oparara. This rock was tipped into the river to create a river training wall, the idea being to confine the river to prevent flooding and sustain channel water levels for shipping. However, the huge effort had little effect against the forces of nature, notably the astounding quantities of debris coming down from the mountains for decades after the earthquake. The rows of railway irons, reconstructed bogey and granite rocks are all remnants of that time. Flagstaff is the name still given to the point where the navigation flagstaff once stood, but no boat of any size now enters this once illustrious estuary. They say that every place has a belle époque, and Karamea Harbour certainly had hers. As with all things, it is now being reclaimed by nature and another cycle is complete.

CHAPTER 8

MINING MAGNESITE

IT WAS A SIGN OF THE TIMES when DOC quietly changed its slogan in 2009, from 'Conservation for posterity' to 'Conservation for prosperity', under direction from its new bureaucratic masters, John Key's National Government. As the new Minister of Tourism, Key saw no conflict in applying his neoliberal economics over our public lands, opening up the possibility of utilising them to generate profit. Many saw irony, too, when that same government in 2015 commissioned a broad stocktake of New Zealand's estimated $140 billion mineral wealth, 70 per cent of which lay under land classified as conservation estate.

Of particular interest was Kahurangi, easily the most geologically diverse of any region in the country, which the report said contained fully more than a third of all our available mineral wealth, estimated to be worth around $50 billion. Deposits of coal, zinc, lead, copper, chromium, molybdenum, nickel, tin, tungsten, platinum, gold, silver, ilmentite, rare earth elements and even uranium can all be found within the boundaries of this national park or on adjoining conservation land. In advice to the Cabinet, the Ministry of Economic Development identified many of these minerals as 'highly prospective', saying they could be exploited if protection for conservation land under Schedule 4 of the Crown Minerals Act 1991 was relaxed. Oil in Fiordland National Park was cited as another commodity for which it was worth changing the rule banning mining in national parks.

It was a new challenge to national parks, and one to which the public of New Zealand reacted extremely badly. The Royal Forest and Bird Protection Society of New Zealand (Forest & Bird) Nelson–Tasman chairwoman, Helen Campbell, said Kahurangi's mineral wealth had been fully taken into account when the national park was designated, continuing, 'So what's changed? How poor are we that mineral values have overtaken our conservation values?'

The Tourism Industry Association New Zealand pitched in, too, saying that opening up the national parks to mining could give the country a bad look and put the $20 billion-a-year tourism industry at risk. The Green Party co-leader Metiria Turei was more hard-hitting, saying the advice from the Ministry of Economic Development had exposed the government's real agenda: 'They already know what they want, and they're preparing to steal it from the public. Far from not wanting to mine in national parks and only being interested in low value areas, the officials' advice shows they are keen to mine our most precious parks.'

This all said, the search for mineral wealth in Kahurangi has been relentless ever since the coming of the Europeans. By the latter half of the nineteenth century, prospectors had scoured much of the northwest Nelson wilderness looking for gold. The area stretching from the Cobb all the way over to the Roaring Lion and Crow catchments, and in particular the Mt Arthur Tableland, had been prospected, and where there was any sign of a 'colour', the land was well worked over.

The search for minerals wasn't entirely random, and the government was also heavily involved in geological research. Today, GNS Science (the Institute of Geological and Nuclear Sciences), a Crown Research Institute, is custodian of the 9,000 maps and field sheets produced in this country in the late nineteenth century. Two years after his appointment as director of the newly re-formed New Zealand Geological Survey (NZGS) in 1905, James Mackintosh Bell had his 'Whakaopai House' built at the mouth of the Heaphy River as a base for his planned investigation of the great wilderness that lay between the Karamea and Aorere catchments. That hut, which burnt down in 1926, was a forerunner to the modern Heaphy Hut on the same site.

However, it took until 1920 for the first real scientific minerals survey of the eastern Kahurangi area around the Cobb Valley to be carried out. This was when the NZGS sent in a highly capable mining geologist named John Henderson. Born in 1880 in Dunedin, Henderson had graduated from Otago University in 1902 with a Bachelor of Science and Diploma in Mining with a Certificate of Metallurgical Chemist and Assayer, before going on to get his Master of Science from Victoria University College in 1906 and his Doctor of Science two years later. He wasn't slow starting work either, taking over as director of Reefton's School of Mines in 1903 soon after receiving his initial degree.

Henderson kept his School of Mines job until 1911, when he joined the NZGS. He was eventually assigned to the Cobb area, where one of his projects was recording the presence of magnesite as outcrops – more correctly termed lenses – bulging from the landscape. Associated with this magnesite were considerable deposits of soapstone or steatite.

The geologist's instructions to look for magnesite were precise, as the establishment of a reliable supply of the mineral was of considerable national interest at this time. Its biggest and most important use was as a refractory mineral agent in the steel-making process, where it was crushed and added to the kiln with lime, causing the slag to separate from the steel. When soapstone is cut – something that can be done easily, as the rock is porous and retains heat – it makes a perfect lining for blast furnaces, kilns and incinerators. Pulverised into a powder, it was also used to make excellent fertiliser, rich in magnesium, and farmers just couldn't get enough of the stuff.

Henderson proved himself a most brilliant geologist, even if his search for magnesite in the field was never acted on in the short term. In 1928, he was promoted to the top geology position in the country, taking over the directorship of the NZGS from retiring Percy Morgan. Henderson held this position until he himself retired in 1945.

When problems surfaced in the late 1930s about the foundations of the proposed Cobb Dam, Henderson sent his most promising young geologist, Harold William Wellman, to sort things out. The Cobb Hydro Dam was about to become the most ambitious civil engineering project undertaken in the country at that time. The plan first involved building a huge dam, then flooding the lush tussock grazing flats of the Cobb Valley for 8 kilometres upstream. Not only was the reservoir's water level going to be the highest in the country at an altitude of 808 metres, but the dam was going to be the

The construction of the Cobb Dam, begun by the Hume Pipe in 1937 and finished by the government in 1955, was the biggest civil engineering project in the country at that time. But problems with the foundation in its early stages necessitated bringing in government geologist Harold Wellman, who also made it his job to identify deposits of magnesite around the dam site. Photo: Department of Conservation

first in the country built using modern soil-control methods and the first to incorporate instruments for measuring water pressure internally, all leading-edge technology at the time.

However, the project had not had a smooth start. Early excavations for the sprawling footings of the dam revealed that the base of the valley, previously thought to be solid rock, was in fact just massive, house-sized boulders suspended in glacial moraine. It was a tricky situation, as there were few alternative sites for the dam, which had already been moved a few hundred metres up the valley anyway. Wellman threw himself into the project from 1939, moving into a single man's hut there from November 1940 until June the following year. In his spare time he investigated and mapped the local geology, tying it into fieldwork that took him on many trips to coastal Golden Bay and over to the Flora Valley.

It was primarily because of Wellman's investigations that the Cobb Dam design was radically altered to a rock and earth construction after the original solid-concrete proposal proved out of the question on the glacial base of the valley. What resulted was the biggest dam of its type constructed in the country, 221 metres across and 35 metres from its foundation to the access road across the top. Although the dam's protective exterior is all chunky chert rocks, its interior is silty gravel and its shoulders are constructed of a far sandier gravel. It was pioneering genius. Wellman returned many times to study other features exposed over the dam's 5½-year construction period.

Government scientists back then were all pro-industry and very supportive of using their knowledge to create economic advantage. It was just the catch cry of those pioneering days and Wellman was no exception. With the bulk of his Cobb Dam investigations over, he turned his focus to investigating the conspicuous magnesite lenses his predecessor and now boss John Henderson had first identified back in the early 1920s.

Narrowing his attention to the four biggest lenses, Wellman went about producing detailed mapping of their extremities and estimating their likely tonnages if mined. His No. 4 site, nearest the Cobb Dam, came out as by far the most promising, bursting as it was with over half of the total available magnesite. Next, the geologist analysed compositions right across each of the separate outcrops – after all, there was no point in mining the No. 4 site if, say, No. 2 was richer in a mineral sense. For this job, mineralogist Colin Hutton was brought in to help Wellman make sense of the differing and intricate chemical makeups of the mineral across the fields.

Together, the pair set up a small laboratory in a rough hut not far from the dam and subjected their small mountain of samples, mostly all humped out on their backs, to a barrage of tests. After six months, they concluded that there was a continuum from ordinary soapstone (serpentine or steatite) through to talc magnesite and then to quartz magnesite, with increasing water content and increasing carbon monoxide along the transition. The result was not that surprising, of course, but it had to be established exactly. Geology is not like zoology or botany, which define distinct species; rather, it's more often a study of the gradual continuum of mineralisation through an area, a merging matrix, and this is what Wellman and Hutton came up with.

Their findings would set the pace for magnesite prospecting in New Zealand, Wellman's 1942 paper on the subject also suggesting accurate industrial uses for all the grades of the mineral. Wellman was a visionary geologist who was not afraid to think outside the square and question current views. He would become best known for his later groundbreaking work and extensive theories about huge movements along the Alpine Fault, all of which we accept as given today. Quite rightly, he has been dubbed 'the geologist who moved New Zealand'.

The story of the quest for magnesite up the Cobb would become intertwined with that of the miners who sought the long-fibred asbestos over in the adjoining catchment of the upper Takaka River. When Wellman started his magnesite investigation, the Cobb Dam Road had already been pushed well past the power house and dam construction area. A side road that branched off to the south 3 kilometres beyond the power house led to the asbestos mine, which was just getting up and running. Like the magnesite, the asbestos here is associated with a belt of ultramafic rocks called the Cobb Igneous Complex, which extends from just north of the Cobb Reservoir to Lower Junction in the headwaters of Takaka River.

Long fibres of green and greyish asbestos were first spotted up the Cobb in 1882. At the time, the world couldn't get enough of the new miracle mineral, which was fireproof, offered fabulous insulation and made an amazingly versatile new building material. Because of the sheer isolation of the Cobb, only about 100 tons were taken out by 1917, all hauled down in sacks on hard-working packhorses. It was mighty hard work being an asbestos miner up there, too, walking two days in, digging the mineral out with a pickaxe and shovel, and then bagging it up and bringing it out.

Just up the hillside from the most promising asbestos outcrops and overlooking the upper Takaka River is Asbestos Cottage, built in 1897 by one of the original miners. More famously now, this 6-metre-long hut was later used for 46 years as the home of Henry and Annie Chaffey. In 1915, Annie ran away from her loveless marriage and two adolescent sons in Timaru to live with prospector Henry up in the mountains of the Cobb. Asbestos Cottage became their home until the winter of 1951, when Henry had a heart attack tramping home in the snow. Annie subsequently moved back to Timaru, but committed suicide a short time later. The 'exiles of Asbestos Cottage', as Jim Henderson portrayed them in his eponymous 1981 book, were suddenly no more.

It is true that the Cobb Dam would never have got off the ground if it wasn't for the decades of rain readings Henry took. The Cobb River has a similar flow to the Avon River in Christchurch, and everything would have been mere speculation had it not been for Henry. A bronze plaque on the side of the Cobb Power Station acknowledges his work maintaining rainfall readings for 28 years, from 26 March 1923. Those readings were always taken daily at 9AM, and Annie religiously took them in Henry's absence. The average rainfall at Asbestos Cottage during this period was around 2,380 millimetres a year, and the wettest year was 1944, when 3,008 millimetres fell. As the years progressed, Henry's asbestos prospecting began earning the couple a comfortable living, at least comparable to his gold fossicking. He was like a human packhorse, and even when he was well into his mid-60s, he would carry sacks full of asbestos down the long track to the road end.

Henry was a strong advocate for an asbestos mine in the area. He sent off many a sample to prominent business people, eventually attracting strong interest from Australian pipe magnate Walter R. Hume, known as 'W.R.' The mine W.R. set up ran until 1963, when it had an output of around 40 tons a month, all trucked to Waitapu Wharf near Takaka and then shipped out. Reports had long been filtering out of Europe about the decayed lungs of Polish and Yugoslavian asbestos miners, who were dying early at the rate of around one in five, all gasping for breath in the process. But the dozen or so Cobb miners, who became covered in dust as they worked, were never told much about such 'spurious' information, nor would they have cared, for they had a job to do. Anyway, the miners suspected it was blue asbestos that killed people, not the green stuff they were mining at the Cobb.

After the asbestos mine shut down in 1963, Tasman (Tas) McKee of the Mapua-based Lime and Marble took over. Exercising new mineral rights, he arranged a joint venture with Broken Hill South of Australia to prospect the asbestos deposit with a diamond drill to find out exactly what reserves of fibre still existed. Back in 1932, the entrepreneurial McKee, with his father Arthur and brother Guy, had established the now infamous Fruitgrowers Chemical Company at Mapua, which later gained the reputation as the most toxic waste site in the country. That site has now been cleansed and detoxified to a depth of 2 metres below the surface. It was in 1938, after the McKees got the chemical factory up and running, that they set up Lime and Marble to mine the marble deposits at Ngarua atop the Takaka Hill.

Jock Braithwaite, who joined the company as a geologist in 1957 and became its general manager in 1980, said that in the 1960s the company established that around 30,000 tons of cement-grade asbestos fibre still existed under the ground at the Cobb, enough to satisfy New Zealand's demand for around ten years at most. However, the fact that the mineral had to be extracted from beneath significant quantities of overburden, along with the presence of huge quantities of less desirable short fibre and serpentine, made the mine too marginally economic to reopen. Recovery could be as low as 3 per cent of the total volume that had to be mined, and the numbers just didn't stack up. Pick-wielding prospectors like Chaffey and his earlier counterparts has taken all the easy outcrop pickings. There were only lower grades and hard yards left.

Undeterred, McKee became very keen to locate and extract minerals that New Zealand was importing, even becoming involved later in uranium, oil and other mineral explorations around the margins of Kahurangi. It was said that he frequently consulted the work of Wellman to give him clues, and no doubt would have talked to him too. All in all, McKee's findings spurred him on to instigate the establishment of the first magnesite mine in the Cobb in the late 1940s, reached via the road that runs between the reservoir and Cobb Ridge. You can still make out the blocked-off access track, which branches off the second U-bend as you travel up the Cobb Dam Road from the reservoir.

The magnesite from that first mine was all trucked out to Lime and Marble's Ngarua works. Here, it was crushed and bagged, and sold mainly to tobacco farmers in the Motueka Valley, who appreciated its high magnesium content, essential to growing high-grade tobacco. Extraction from this first quarry lasted until around 1965, but the mining remained difficult throughout that time thanks to the steepness of the site and the patchy deposits of magnesite. Some attempt to extract talc was made around this time also.

Geologist Peter Riley joined Lime and Marble that year, and his first big job was to shift the mine to a new site. He helped move two huts from the recently closed asbestos mine to the company's new quarry just across and slightly over from the dam. These relocated huts were joined together, and a cookhouse added at one end. This was the No. 4 outcrop initially favoured by Wellman, but poor access had prevented anyone working it on a large scale until the road was properly extended across the dam. Often with industry, it's best to wait for an adjoining industry – or, even better, a government agency – to put in a facility, then negotiate to use it. In the case of the new road, which petered out into an access track up the hill to Lake Sylvester, Lime and Marble only had to branch off it from a bend at the bottom and put in a little over a kilometre of access road to their quarry.

MINING MAGNESITE

After the asbestos mine off the Cobb Dam Road shut down, Lime and Marble shifted the single men's huts to their new magnesite quarry just beyond the Cobb Dam, joining them up in a row and adding a cookhouse at one end. The quarry employed a team of five or six men who worked straight 15-day shifts. Photo: Garner Teale

A jack of all trades, Alfred (Alf) Teale was head quarryman at Lime and Marble's magnesite quarry up the Cobb. In the photo above he can be seen helping the bulldozer driver by pushing down the larger overburden rocks with a steel rod, while in the photo on the right he turns his hand to after-work cooking duties.
Photo: Garner Teale

MINING MAGNESITE

Blasting kicked off in a big way at the relocated operation, and removal of the magnesite got into full swing. The head quarryman was Alfred Teale, who lived at Ferntown near Collingwood but was indispensable at all of Lime and Marble's quarries, shifting around from job to job as required. Whenever McKee had a prospecting mission, Teale was his first choice to take along because of his huge practical knowledge working with rock. Teale's son Garner recalls how he particularly loved working and living up at the isolated magnesite mine, but he would chop and change depending on where he was required. 'Mr Teale – Quarryman' was a story about Alfred that appeared in the *School Journal* in 1976, and outlines a typical day at the company's Ngarua quarry on Takaka Hill. First, Teale would drill the back and bottom of a rock face with holes, which he would then 'pop' or fill with explosives, linking them all up and finally measuring out enough fuse to give him plenty of time to get clear. The explosion would shatter the rock into manageable blocks that could then be carted off. The story outlines how Teale had worked in coal mines in his early days, which left him covered in 'black dirt', while working in the marble quarry would leave him covered in 'white dirt'. "'Black or white, it's all clean dirt," Mr Teale says. "It washes off easily, I worked on the clay benches making drain pipes, before the war. I've worked with the earth all my life – it's all clean dirt."'

Interestingly, anyone working with magnesite always ends up with soft, almost soapy-feeling hands, explained by the high talc content of the rock, just as Teale and all his workmates would have experienced up the Cobb. There was nothing soft in the truck drivers' work, though, as they now had to travel further to get their loads to Ngarua for processing. Initially, the last section of gnarly road to the quarry, which bulged with moraine boulders, proved so bad that only 7-ton gross loads could be carried at most. Right from the very start, the truck drivers were wary of the steep drop-offs along the route down into the Takaka Valley, especially on the narrow, winding section below the power house. As a result, some insisted that their cab door be removed to make for an easy escape in case they plummeted off the edge. There were no seatbelts or hard hats back then of course. The progress of every truck proved incredibly slow, and only two round trips a day at most could be completed. But that all changed in the early 1970s, when the road to the power house was sealed, and in 1979, when the bridges were upgraded to Class 1, or an

18-ton limit. All these improvements translated to heavier loads and a faster turnaround, making for a more economic operation.

Three huts and a cookhouse were constructed on the little flat above the new magnesite quarry, used by the six men who worked shifts there for a couple of weeks at a time. Barry Simkin, who took over as manager of Lime and Marble after McKee died in 1973, said the company originally had a mining permit for the annual extraction of 300 tons of magnesite, which was taken out in two lots: 150 tons in early summer and a further 150 tons in late summer, periods when the men were required to work two separate two-week shifts in a row. In 1974, the company was allowed to increase its take to 500 tons per annum, which was further increased to 600 tons in 1979. This production increase necessitated more drilling and quarrying, including bringing in the company's big Air Track drill from the Ngarua quarry. This increased extraction rate allowed Lime and Marble to stockpile more than 1,200 tons of magnesite, which was used to fulfil the company's orders until the quarry closed down in 1981. Simkin conservatively estimated that around 8,000 tons was extracted from the site, but including the previous operation and unaccounted production, the overall figure is probably more than 20,000 tons. Nearly all of the magnesite extracted from both operations was sold to tobacco farms for fertiliser, while some was subsequently added to poultry feed as a health supplement.

After extraction ceased and the quarry was abandoned, things went quiet in the area for nearly 30 years. Then, out of the blue in 2008, a start-up company called Steatite Ltd, with an address in rural Ngatimoti, just inland from Motueka, obtained a mining permit for the 50-hectare magnesite quarry block that had been left out of Kahurangi National Park because of its extraction history and high mineral values. Steatite Ltd director Gion Deplazes made it well known that his intention was to process and potentially export the highly heat-retentive steatite soapstone for use as stove liners and even entire stoves.

Deplazes' application outlined how he wanted to work and expand the old quarry site, then move onto two outcrops further up the hillside, just to the south and southwest. Approval was being sought for the removal of around 15,000 tonnes per annum, to be trucked out in 9-tonne loads up to 32 times per week. Extrapolated, this could mean ten truckloads a day in summer when conditions were most favourable for extraction. Doing the calculations, up to 600,000 tonnes might be removed over the 40-year lifespan of the operation.

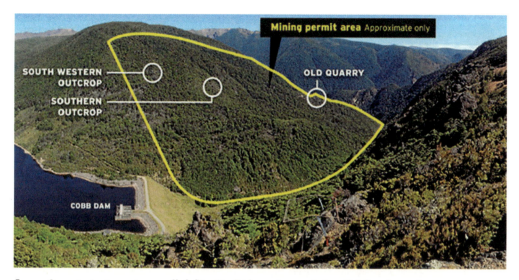

In 2008, a start-up company called Steatite Ltd put in a mining bid for the 50-hectare magnesite quarry block left out of Kahurangi National Park because of its potential economic value. Director Gion Deplazes said he wanted to remine the original quarry and then move up to two other outcrops originally surveyed by government geologist Harold Wellman.
Photo: Nelson Mail

To open up the two new quarry sites (marked above), 650 metres of new and highly visible roading would have to be put in, with many trees felled and pushed aside. This was going to be nothing like the way Lime and Marble operated in the area. It looked far more ambitious, and some people in the Golden Bay and Motueka communities were starting to get worried. Crown Minerals had already given approval for the operation, and it was now up to DOC and the Tasman District Council to grant the application. Deplazes had got over the first big bureaucratic hurdle, but he still had two to go.

Opposition to the mining proposal mounted, led by Forest & Bird, Friends of the Cobb, and several other groups and individuals. They argued that the already tricky winding road to the Cobb would become even more dangerous with so many truck movements. The view from the shelter and information kiosk on Cobb Ridge, a major entry point to Kahurangi National Park, would be ruined by the scene of sheer devastation on the opposite side of the valley. What's more, the peace and quiet of the area would be shattered, and a stay at the former construction workers' houses, now referred to as the Cobb Cottages, a community-run refuge for many local families and visitors, would not be compatible with round-the-clock mining activity, lights and truck movements.

The case against the mining application grew on all fronts. The areas of past and potential mining were cited as home to an unusual range of 'at risk' plants, which many conservationists thought should be left undisturbed. Ultramafic rocks, of which the Cobb Igneous Complex is one of several in the upper South Island, have a high concentration of minerals, especially magnesium and iron, which inhibit and even change many plant species that grow on them. This has led to a highly distinct mineral belt flora. While most of the Cobb quarry block is covered in mature mountain beech trees (*Fuscospora* spp.), the areas with magnesite outcrops contain many of these unusual plants. They include 11 species that are considered at risk nationally, notably *Pittosporum dallii*, a large shrub that eventually develops into a small tree and bears sweet-scented flowers. The plant has a very limited distribution, restricted to ultramafic outcrops in northwest Nelson, and is easiest seen planted alongside the kiosk on Cobb Ridge and in the garden of the Cobb Cottages. A few more of these shrubs have now also been planted in cages in the dam area. One of the biggest specimens is on the right along the track leading from the Sylvester carpark to the Alpine Garden, and another is in the garden itself. Also found here are two rare sedges and a forget-me-not, *Myosotis brockiei*, plus another gorgeous flowerer, *Notothlaspi australe*, which is related to the alpine penwiper (*N. rosulatum*). Growing on many of the mānuka (*Leptospermum scoparium*) near the old quarry are specimens of a dwarf and cryptic mistletoe. The closer you look, the more plant magic you are liable to see.

Months turned into two years as Steatite Ltd waited to see if DOC would grant access to the former mine. After that, the company would still have to go through the torturous resource consent process with Tasman District Council. Deplazes was obviously aware of the growing opposition, and went all out to sell his idea to the public. In a submitted article in the local *Guardian* newspaper of 13 September 2012 headed 'Cobb Valley Soapstone – Lives and Gives Forever', Deplazes pushed the near-magical properties of the stone, describing its composition of minerals as nothing short of miraculous:

> It has amazing heat conduction and storage capacity. A stove made from this stone will radiate out for many hours after a fire has gone out,

therefore reducing a family's wood, coal or chip consumption considerably. The radiant heat stored by the stone makes for a dry, comfortable and healthy environment. These beautiful soapstone fireplaces will easily last over 100 years, and produce a fraction of the carbon footprint and environmental footprint of a conventional steel burner.

In the article, Deplazes revealed that he and his family had lived in the area for 22 years, residing on a small farm where they strove for self-sufficiency, feeding themselves from their organic orchard and vegetable garden, as well as raising cattle and sheep. In the school holidays they would take their young children tramping, often to the Cobb. Their business was in architectural design, which fitted in perfectly with the stove idea. And perhaps more importantly, Gion Deplazes belonged to a family that had been extracting soapstone from a small quarry in Switzerland for more than a hundred years. His pitch was all about producing the stoves, which he said would not only help the environment but could also be exported to Europe, where the demand for them was high.

Deplazes was definitely correct about the near-miraculous qualities of soapstone. To give an idea of its heat-retentive properties, if you take a fist-sized piece of rock that is at room temperature and put it into boiling water, after just two minutes it will have absorbed enough heat to be close to 100° Celsius. After 40 minutes out of the water, it will still be too hot to hold without wearing heat-resistant gloves, and only after 60 minutes will you be able to begin touching it with your bare hands. Translate this to larger slabs encasing a burner, and the hot soapstone will continue to disperse heat long after the fire inside goes out. Deplazes was also correct in his claim that versatile soapstone could be used in gas and electric heaters, for pizza ovens and benchtops, and even as stone grill slabs at restaurants. He'd already negotiated with a New Zealand manufacturer that had shown interest in using the material in its wood burners. In addition, there was potential for the rock to be made available to local builders and craftspeople.

But all these benefits aside, the tide had turned for Deplazes, and he must have felt the growing opposition to his grand plan. In his Crown Minerals application, he had been legally required to give a worst-case scenario for the effects of his mining, and that was now being used against him. In effect, he was actually asking for the removal of not much more than 5,000 tonnes a month – about the volume of a two-storey house – and to be realistic, that was about as much extraction a small company could possibly expect to carry out in such a remote place. Lime and Marble, who were experts in the game, had clearly shown the limitations of working up the Cobb. In the end, all the stories claiming the mining would ruin the view and create an endless procession of trucks went against Deplazes.

Almost out of the blue, in September 2014 Steatite Ltd withdrew its mining application, much to the gleeful applause of conservationists. So was that the end of the matter? Not at all. The high-profile case, which had attracted far more negative attention than Deplazes would have liked, had the effect of starting a concerted push to give the area increased protection and include it in Kahurangi National Park. DOC started this slow bureaucratic process, and in July 2016 the 50 hectares surrounding the old magnesite mine were finally added to the park.

Today, it's an easy and pleasant 20-minute walk through beech forest to the quarry along the old access road that swings right from Sylvester carpark. A little over a kilometre in length, the track is even enough to push a wheelchair along or for kids to negotiate on their bikes. The quarry itself is quite spectacular, with views down the lower Cobb Valley and up to the Lockett Range. Continuing a short way up on the left, you reach the elevated grassy flat where the huts once stood. On the right, a marked track leads to Diamond Lake Stream, a three-hour route onto the tops that is suitable for trampers only, although if you head down it for 80 metres you will come to a lovely dappled section of the stream that is a perfect place to sit on a hot day. Most notable is the big mossy slab of flat rock that sits midstream here. You have to keep your wits about you here though, because there are steep drop-offs, especially around the rim of the quarry.

Back at Sylvester carpark, a path (rather overgrown these days) leads down to the Alpine Garden. This subalpine arboretum was established by Forest Service ranger George Lord and his wife Edith in the 1960s, and was later added to by the Given family. The Lords in particular acquired a vast knowledge of local plants during their time at the Cobb. Hundreds of different hebes grow there, and it is said that Edith could identify every one of them. She was most instrumental in putting in the Alpine Garden, and particularly liked the idea that less mobile people could drive in to see the plants together in one place. The couple eventually moved down to Takaka, where Edith became a Guide leader, kept up her gardening and tramping, and also became an avid Forest & Bird member. Her old friend June Clark said that their great tramping partnership began in 1975 and continued in all weathers, for varying lengths of time. They enjoyed botanising for small treasures, surrounded by magnificent scenery and enjoying the simple pleasure of being alive: 'These were always special times wherever we tramped, but it was always in the Cobb or Sylvester that we made our spiritual home. Myttons and Bushline huts were our huts.'

Today at the Alpine Garden, a variety of birds can be spotted, including a very friendly robin. Better still, great spotted kiwi (*Apteryx haastii*) have made their way back into the Cobb, and have even been spotted around the Cobb Cottages just across the dam. Kahurangi is considered one of the remaining strongholds of the species, with the highest numbers along the park's western edge, particularly the tussock grasslands of Gouland, Mackay and Gunner downs. Credit for kiwi moving back into the Cobb Valley can be put down to the work of Friends of the Cobb, who now maintain and check some 460 stoat traps in the area, including around 300 in the valley itself.

Perhaps as a suitable aside to this essentially soapstone story, the rock's relative softness and lack of grain make it an excellent carving medium, although many sculptors come to the Cobb seeking harder and more colourful varieties of steatite to carve. In 1979, Ligar Bay artist Campbell Ewing spent six weeks ensconced in the fishing lodge that used to exist just up from the Cobb Dam to carve a chest-high hunk of the stuff into a creation that resembled a saddle or wave. All smooth and gorgeous, it was something kids could even climb and play upon. To Ewing, it reflected the shape of the deep-cut glacial valley against which it was silhouetted: 'Its function was to mediate between us and our perception of the undifferentiated vastness of nature.' He compared looking through the wave as being like looking through the viewfinder of a rifle or camera. For Ewing, this effort was also a symbolic gesture of thanks, a giving back to the area for the soapstone he had sourced there for his carvings. With help from then Cobb Valley ranger Bob Dickson, the sculpture was mounted in the middle of a splendid clearing between Myttons and Trilobite huts at the top of the Cobb Reservoir, along a rough track that used to exist between the two huts but has since become overgrown.

For more than 25 years, the sculpture stood *in situ* in its expansive hillside clearing, admired by the odd passer-by and collecting a fine patina of fungi in a few places. Then it just disappeared sometime around late 2006, cut off its steel reinforcing-rod base and carted away, never to be seen again. Someone had gone to a lot of trouble, needing at least a wheelbarrow to cart it off, although around here even a small helicopter could have been used on the raiding mission and no one would have noticed. In the big scheme of things, up there in the Cobb mountains, a missing statue isn't a huge issue I guess, but it still fills in another interesting chink in the amazing story of Cobb soapstone.

The postscript here, though, must go to quarryman Alfred Teale. After he died in 1989, his son Garner was sorting through his possessions and came across a sheet of song lyrics his father had written, based on his working experience at the dolomite quarry at Mt Burnett above Ferntown, where he would often be required to work as part of Lime and Marble's regional operation. Garner never recalls hearing it sung or recited. A real working man's song, Teale's lyrics record the everyday life of a Kahurangi quarryman in the 1960s and 1970s.

The Dolomite Lament
A.L. Teale

Working on the Dolomite is anybody's fun,
Especially the beer when the day's work is done,
Lots of them start and go the other way,
When it's rush another shipment up to Whangarei.[1]

Chorus
Boom goes the cross man, bang goes the King,[2]
Use up the jelly and let the echoes ring,
Kahu[3] lifts the brake and everything is fine
With a thousand tons of glass stone, coming jigging down the line.

Up in the quarry everything is swell,
Wet to the waist and working like hell,
Gorden comes around with a message to pass,
Westrupp's[4] on the phone for another lot of glass.

MINING MAGNESITE

Chorus
Boom goes etc...

Round at the plant where the wind whistles thru,
Awashing of the glass stone. When there's nothing else to do,
Fast as they wash it and shove it out the door,
Ted[5] is on the crusher and is munching up some more.

Chorus
Boom goes etc...

Everything's at the pad from plum bob to a rule,
Back at the Plant, we can't find a tool,
Start to do a job – there's nothing to be had,
They've even taken Jack Mangoes[6] down to the pad!

Chorus
Boom goes etc...

---

1. Shipments 'up to Whangarei' were to the glass factory there, the dolomite being used for fluxing glass.
2. The 'cross man' Teale refers to is Tom Cross, and the 'King' is Tom King; the turn-off to Mt Burnett just before the quarry is now known locally as Kings Cross.
3. 'Kahu' is Bruce Kahu, a man 'who couldn't say two words without swearing' according to Garner Teale.
4. 'Westrupp' was Gordon Westrupp, the manager of the works.
5. 'Ted' is Ted Rae, Teale's good mate who lived in a hut down below the quarry.
6. 'Jack Mangoes' was a general rouseabout.

CHAPTER 9

RANGER'S DIARY

WHEN DOC WAS CREATED IN 1988, essentially through the amalgamation of the Forest Service, Wildlife Service and Department of Lands and Survey, a whole new departmental culture came into being. The transition was hard for many of the traditional Forest Service rangers, who were used to more autonomy and to doing things their own way. They knew the mountains and they knew what was best for them from working among them. A lot of rangers successfully made the change, but a lot left too.

Max Polglaze, ranger for the Cobb and Leslie/upper Karamea for some 18 years, was one of those who found the changeover to DOC hard. He stayed on for a while, until he had had enough of it all, then quit. Polglaze first joined the Forest Service when he was 18, deer-culling in Canterbury after training at the Blue Glen hunter training camp in the Golden Downs forest behind Motueka. After six years of that, he ended up in Australia, working for a New South Wales topdressing firm and earning his private pilot's licence along the way. On his return to New Zealand, he enrolled in the Wanganui Commercial Pilot School and went back to deer-culling to pay for the 200 hours of flight time he needed to pass his commercial licence.

Although Polglaze loved flying, it wasn't the direction he eventually took.

Keeping tracks dry by draining water tables and digging ditches was an essential part of a ranger's work. Here on the Mt Arthur Tableland, formerly known as Salisbury's Open, in 1981, Max Polglaze (top) works with Dave Schubert (left) and Russell (Russ) Griebel (right) to dig out a new drain. Griebel and his goat-culling colleague Bob Waldie would later die when Bush Edge Hut (on the left branch of the Motueka River) was swept away in a flash flood in February 1995. Hunters Hut was built in 1997 to replace it and named in memory of the pair. Photo: Max Polglaze

Lower Gridiron Shelter became one of Max Polglaze's quirkiest creations, sporting bunks, a running water supply, a basin, a fireplace and a swinging chair hanging off the rock. From left: Elize Baas, Colin Baas, Snow Meyer and Max Polglaze. Photo: Max Polglaze

While working as a loader driver carrying out venison recovery for Nelson helicopter pilot John Reid, he met Helen, who would become his wife, and they shifted to Australia. The couple of years they spent there didn't work out as well as they had expected, and they came back to New Zealand in around 1970, when Max was offered the Cobb Valley ranger's job by Nelson Forest Service boss Snow Corboy. The job description understated the actual role, and Max found himself not only looking after the Cobb, but the whole of the Golden Bay backcountry and the top half of the Heaphy Track. He recalls, 'The Heaphy at that time was really overgrown. You wouldn't know it today. We never had chainsaws. It was all crosscut-saw, axe and slasher work. Four was an average work party.'

When the Polglazes' two daughters, Julie and Tracey, came along, the couple faced the extra challenges of bringing them up in the remote location of the Cobb. There was no Plunket support, no friends, and no female company for Helen either. It was a hard few years. Helen was pregnant with their son Daniel when Max took the job as the Ngatimoti-based Forest Service ranger covering the Mt Arthur Tableland and the Leslie/Karamea and Baton valleys.

It was here that Polglaze found his true vocation, directing his small work teams into projects that would enhance the experience trampers had when visiting this 'magic' place, even if it meant bending the odd rule. Some of his most painstaking work was done on the massive rock shelters that still exist along the track between Flora Hut and Salisbury Lodge on the tableland.

In a tight area of Gridiron Creek that Polglaze called Gridiron Gulch, he transformed an overhanging rock shelter long used by passing trampers into a more comfortable resting place now known as Gridiron Shelter. Today, you'll still find a running water supply, basin, concrete fireplace and swinging chair hung off the rock, all of which Polglaze put in. And it was all constructed without Forest Service permission. Polglaze admitted in an interview once that 'building that shelter was a bit naughty', especially given that a ban had been passed on building unauthorised huts in the North-West Nelson Forest Park.

'At the time, we were working in the area and we needed a base. The materials were in there and we did it quite nicely,' Polglaze says. He told his Forest Service bosses that he would cheerfully pull it down, but they never asked him to. 'They had to growl officially, but privately they quite liked it.'

Two larger rock shelters can be found nearby, one along the gulch and another off the track leading to the tableland. While they don't have huts built into them like Gridiron, they were tastefully improved with the addition of bunks and fireplaces to offer an almost Neolithic experience.

Now retired in Upper Takaka, Polglaze looks back on his experiences in the park as 'a helluva nice period of my life'. In particular, he felt uplifted by the spiritual tranquillity of the mountains, a place where he could imbibe the peacefulness of it all. On the long maintenance stints away from home, he forged strong friendships with workmates like Mark Donovan, Dave Shubart, Wayne Elia and Snow Meyer. Reminders of the work these men carried out also remain, like the stained-glass etchings of plants and native birds Elia cut into some of the hut windows in his spare time.

Those who worked under Polglaze reckoned he was the best boss anyone could have. He didn't say much, but what he did say was worth listening to, and no worker seemed to annoy him, no matter what mistakes they made. All in all, he epitomised what was best about the Forest Service.

It should be said that Polglaze's dissatisfaction with his job started to creep in before DOC came into being:

> *I guess I'd been dying inside for the last few years before the changeover. There was just too much bureaucracy creeping in, just too many people wanting a bit of the action. And I can't stand committees. We Forest Service rangers became like dinosaurs. A new breed of manager had arrived, and we just didn't fit in anymore. When DOC offered severance pay to cut down their staff, I took that option.*

I was lucky enough to get hold of one of Polglaze's monthly work diaries a few years back. It outlined everything he and his workmates Ralph Stringer and Snow Meyer did for 12 straight days when they were flown into the Leslie/upper Karamea area in August 1981. Polglaze always recorded his work meticulously – it was part of the job – and his writing makes for inspiring reading. His accounts are informative, too, about the effort and initiative that went into setting up our backcountry facilities.

The mission that August was principally to repair two walkway bridges that had proved defective, one across the upper Karamea River just upstream of Saturn Creek, and the other across Slippery Creek, a 30-minute walk up the valley from Karamea Bend. Polglaze and Stringer drove to the Flora carpark on the morning of Wednesday, 5 August. On board their truck was a load of tucker and bridge gear, including a 1,800-kilogram concrete anchor block, various lengths of wire rope, rock anchors, rock drills 'and other necessary paraphernalia for the job'. A complete C10 suspension bridge tower had already been taken up to the carpark and assembled there, ready to fly in. Pilot Les Maas arrived at 10AM, first flying the big tower and other gear in two loads to the upper Karamea bridge, where a landing site had been specially cleared. On his third trip that day, he flew Polglaze, Stringer and their supplies to Karamea Bend Hut. Polglaze recounted events in his diary:

> *Left most of the grub there, picked up a few things, radio, chainsaw etc and flew on to Crow Hut. Ralph and I unloaded the machine and laid out a long length of ¼' wire rope while Les flew off to the Bend and picked up Snow Meyer, who was keen to help us on the job.*
>
> *Returning to Crow, Les hooked his chopper onto one end of the*

wire rope we had laid out and flew it around the head branches of the enormous leaning red beech tree which had been a potential threat to Crow Hut ever since it was built. This went off as planned, the cable passing through the top of the tree a good hundred feet up on both sides, reaching down to the ground.

They left the ropes hanging down like that, ready to tie back later when they felled the tree, which had been deemed a problem. Maas then flew Meyer and Polglaze up to the bridge site before flying out. Stringer stayed back at Crow Hut and 'laid in the week's supply of dry firewood' the team would need while staying there.

Up at the bridge, still on day 1 but now in the early afternoon, the first job for the two men was to string up a tarp and lay out all their gear beneath it. Polglaze's plan was to lift the bridge in one piece and secure it to new concrete anchorages, which they had to build. Three times in the previous decade this substantial footbridge had been damaged by flooding, and it was time to raise it above the flood zone. On the true right bank of the Karamea River, this would involve blasting out and exposing a suitable rock face in which to set the anchor bolts, while on the true left bank the existing tower would be replaced by the new, larger one Maas had flown in that morning. After string-lining the areas for the new tower footpads, the pair excavated and boxed them up, then concreted them using gravel mixed on the river beach and carried up in buckets. A small bonus was the discovery that one of the old footpads lined up perfectly.

Said Polglaze, 'Snow, we only have to cast three new ones – someone up there is looking after us for sure.'

Replied Meyer with a wry grin, 'Yeah well, I don't know, Max. He hasn't done much for me these past three years.'

It was half an hour's fast walk back to Crow Hut, and dusk was gathering when they arrived. Stringer had the hut warm and a billy of tea on the boil. They'd gotten off to a damn good start

On day 2, the 30-minute fast-paced walk back to the bridge warmed the men up nicely in time to start work. It was going to be a fine day once the heavy frost lifted, and Polglaze 'indulged' himself in a little rock drilling and blasting on the true right bank to expose a clean, near-vertical face to take the new anchorages. He was relieved when the four bolt holes in the rock drilled easily, not jamming the drill steels or fracturing the rock as could sometimes happen. And, just as satisfying, the new expansion bolts 'slipped in like they were going home'.

Over on the other side of the river, Meyer and Stringer were digging out a new slot for the anchor block, when they exposed the top of a huge granite boulder 60 centimetres down. This was 'the best kind of anchor,' reckoned Polglaze. They drilled into the hard-as-hell boulder and screwed in the four spare expansion bolts they had luckily brought along. End result: an extremely good anchorage for a minimum of time and effort. At the end of day 2, things were looking good.

Day 3 proved to be the challenging one, as the trio contemplated how they would kedge the bridge across to its new anchorage in one piece using a block and tackle. The whole bridge weighed at least half a tonne, had six cables and spanned 25 metres overall between anchors. If it dropped into the water, the current would add another half a tonne to the weight, making it virtually impossible to get out.

They started by casting off the cables from the true left bank, barring the top one, which they tied off with a calculated 1.2 metres of slack – the same distance as that between the old and new true right anchors. It was a matter of logistics, and every step was thought through in advance. The men started by straining the bridge towards its new position using a block and tackle placed some distance into the span. The final two top ropes were cast off their true left bank shackles, and the bridge went across with a rush, brought up short just a metre above the river. They hoisted the bridge up a bit, raising it higher above the river, then cast off the old anchors and slowly swung it across to its new position, finishing the job off with wire strainers. With one side clamped, they crossed the river on a service line and pulley, then took out the old A1 tower and set up the new one on its footpads. Polglaze was obviously relieved when the shifting part was over, writing, 'There is no more challenge, the rest is purely mechanical.'

Day 4 turned into a dawn-to-dusk epic. Work included resecuring all the main cables of the bridge, replacing flood-damaged tread netting and fixing broken hangers. Polglaze took measurements, calculating that the bridge sagged by an acceptable 4 per cent, and the three men lock-wired off the turn-buckles before wrapping them in tar tape. This day of wrap-up jobs gave Polglaze – clearly a philosopher ranger – an opportunity to take:

RANGER'S DIARY

If he wasn't writing up his detailed work diary in a hut at the end of a busy day, Max Polglaze would dedicate himself to increasing his knowledge of his surroundings. Many a Forest Service employee who worked under him reckoned he was the best boss anyone could hope to have. Photo: Max Polglaze

> *a couple of nice smokos sitting in the sun watching the river run, listening to my two evolutionist friends postulate on how the valley would look in 500 years, while a small voice in me cries, it has been demonstratively shown life forms evolve, shape, adapt, but don't discount divine ordinance either, for where is the meaning and purpose of life – any sort of life – without it.*

Day 5 saw the trio back up at the bridge after breakfast for a final tidy up. Then everything was packed up and stowed ready for the flight out. They were back at Crow Hut by 5PM, their earliest finish yet by far.

On Monday morning, day 6, Stringer and Meyer carried out routine maintenance on the nearby Crow Bridge, 'resagging' it and opening up drainage channels. Polglaze now had time to turn his attention back to the massive red beech overhanging the hut that they had tied back on day 1. In particular, he didn't like how the enormous buttress of the tree facing the hut had rotted away. For Polglaze, a highly practical man, the answer was immediately obvious:

> *I wanted to attend to that tree personally, because if anything went wrong, if the hut or bridge was smashed* [by the falling tree] – *then the fault would be mine. There has been a lot of hoo-ha over the years about this tree. The old bushman* [Meyer] *himself backed away from the job once, a few years back, when I asked him to fell it, but to be fair the wire rope that Les flew around the head of it was an important form of insurance that the old bushman never had.*

The men tied back both ends of the wire rope that was strung through the tree to a nylon rope. This was then taken back hundreds of feet from the hut and pulled extremely taught with two wire strainers. Polglaze wrote about the deed in a matter-of-fact tone:

> *Next a stage or landing on poles 10 or 12 feet above the ground put us above the buttress into solid wood above the rot. A good deep scarf with the 051 Stihl, a modest backcut and it was all over. Half a day to set it up, half an hour to fell it. There'll be five years of firewood in the tree I reckon.*

Pragmatic for sure, but Polglaze couldn't help but add a few personal thoughts:

> *But consider: for maybe hundreds of years this tree has flourished here, growing with the perfect light, a venerable host of the forest to a host of birds and insects. It would be there yet if man had not come and built a hut in its shade. Even then a peaceful co-existence might have been possible had it leaned away from the man-made device, but it didn't. The decks were stacked, the outcome inevitable. Sheer size is no defence against an animal gifted with the power of reason.*

In the ranger's diary there is a photo him atop the platform in the process of sawing through the massive trunk, the caption besides reading, 'Max Polglaze puts another tree to the saw. In the next life, as a penance, he will probably be a tree and some unfeeling logger will truncate him so.'

Perched atop a 3.5-metre-high landing made of saplings, Max Polglaze begins the cut to fell the 30-metre-high red beech that used to lean over Crow Hut. Photo: Max Polglaze

The next photo is of Meyer leaning against the cut-off stump, which is twice his height. He looks slightly uncomfortable, hands clasped in front of him, like men who live in the bush can be when you try to take a photo of them. The caption records the interchange just before the photo was taken: "'Stand up against the stump, Snow, and let's get a picture of you.'"

"All right, but make it a good one. It's the last you'll get of this old riverman…'"

After this comes a photo showing some huge fossilised animal footprints that Polglaze had spied in a layer of Tertiary mudstone half an hour downstream from Crow Hut. In the caption, he asks as if he has an audience, 'Does anybody know what form of life made these footprints in the sands of time… the largest would be 24–30" long?' Kahurangi is full of such wonders, and those who venture there cannot help but come across them – if they are observant, that is.

Pilot Les Maas touched down at Crow Hut at 3PM on the Monday, just like he said he would. Stringer went with him to Karamea Bridge to hook on the two loads for their next job at Slippery Creek. Stringer accompanied Maas to Slippery with the second load to clear the net, then all three men were flown to Karamea Bend Hut. Polglaze spent the last hour or two of daylight unpacking and stowing the new tucker Maas had brought in, while Stringer laid into cutting and chopping another load of firewood. Meyer pottered around doing his own thing. That night, they celebrated being back at Karamea Bend and the six days of fine weather they had had. Polglaze even had the luxury of his first hot shower, in the little annex of the hut.

On day 7, there were rain showers all day until the weather cleared up around 4PM, but they were nothing the men couldn't work in without a coat. In fact, they surprised themselves, and the Slippery Creek Bridge job kicked off surprisingly well. They knocked off late in the afternoon, by which time the big anchor was dug in and buried, the A1 tower stood up on its pads, and the span had been freed from a leaning tree and swung across into its new position. Rather than use concrete footpads in this instance, they saved time by digging big rock slabs into the root mass, making sure they were on solid load-bearing soil.

Slippery Creek was a 'bitzer' bridge, which had been built by Meyer from all the materials left over when the other bridges up here were put in in 1974. At one end it was secured to a live tree, 'so the job here was to tidy it and make it engineeringly acceptable'. Polglaze and his team checked the rock anchors on the other side and deemed them still strong. Even though they had smaller, 14-inch bolts, these were at an angle to the strain and so could never be pulled out like a cork from a bottle. Today, all this work would require an engineer's certificate, but back then Meyer and Polglaze conferred and decided that the set-up was safe enough. Common sense was every ranger's attribute.

The trio carried the hefty rock drill back to Karamea Bend that night, and before it was completely dark Polglaze blew some big rock 'floaters' off the new track they had cut down to the river on their previous trip.

Day 8 started early, and the men were away by first light. It was the best day yet, sparklingly bright after the valley fog lifted. Later that day, Polglaze wrote about how good it felt to be in the company of men and free from the demands of civilisation, able to give one's all to a particular line of action. Stringer seemed amused that his two workmates raced out of bed at 5AM, and Polglaze commented, 'It must not be easy to live with a couple of prima donnas who run things too efficiently for comfort.'

They finished the work on Slippery Bridge that day, putting in extra tread ropes under the netting, resagging it, and lock-wiring, taping and stabilising it. Then they packed up all their working gear ready for collection by helicopter, and were back at Karamea Bend by 2PM, just as the sun was leaving the hut.

To fill in the rest of the afternoon, Polglaze helped Stringer and Meyer build a decent bridge across the swampy creek just below Karamea Bend Hut, at the foot of their new track. The piles had to be driven down 2 metres before they found bedding in the gravel. They completed the job just on nightfall, and were satisfied with the results. The new track now gave good wheelbarrow access from the driftwood and gravel beds of the Leslie River back up to the hut.

That night, Polglaze wrote up the new Slippery Bridge statistics for Forest Service records:

Tr.l. bank: 4,000lb anchor block and A1 tower
Tr.r. bank: rock anchor screws
Span: 78 ft 6 inches, tower to rock anchor
Height above water: 20 ft
Tr.r. side: 3' 6" higher than tr. left
Sag: 5%

Days 9, 10 and 11 were all spent at Leslie Clearing, working around the rebuilt Leslie Clearing Hut – they walked there from Karamea Bend on the Thursday (day 9) and returned on the Saturday (day 11). On the way there, they called into the camp of possumer Ken Ryley, wondering if he might have a spare packet of tobacco. Polglaze took a photo of Ryley's tent camp, complete with its stone and corrugated-iron chimney, which was tucked away in Toitoi Creek just up the Leslie Valley from Karamea Bend, and stuck it in his diary. He had visited the man in his camp before on a cold, frosty morning, and was surprised by how warm the tent was, with its double-skinned construction – polythene outside and scrim inside. Fur prices were down this year, Ryley told him. For the 130 skins he was pictured next to in another photo in Polglaze's diary, he received an average of $7.04 per skin – the best price offered by six buyers.

At Leslie Clearing, Meyer pottered around, mostly doing inside jobs, while Stringer burnt off and reoiled some weatherboards. Polglaze spent the time with a chainsaw and slasher, underscrubbing around the hut and its environs, taking out the 'barbwiresceae' but leaving all the trees, both big and small. Common among these were lowland ribbonwood (*Plagianthus regius*), which has apple-blossom-like flowers in season, and kaikōmako, or firestick tree (*Pennantia corymbosa*), along with the occasional small beech. The result after this tidy-up was impressive: a lovely little hut in a beautiful park-like setting. Clearly pleased with the result, Polglaze wrote, 'I think perhaps this is the nicest place I have seen. As I said to Snow, "If I was a tramper walking down the clearing I would be bloody well enchanted – it reminds me strongly of the gingerbread house in the Hansel and Gretel story." And so it did, good enough to eat!' He hazarded a guess that, in time, the hut would become the most loved and photographed in the whole of North-West Nelson Forest Park. The ranger may well have been right, but sadly Leslie Clearing Hut burnt down in around 2001.

Polglaze would have liked to have spent a day tidying up the Wilkinson Track while he was in the vicinity, but Saturday turned wet. It wasn't too wet to potter outside the hut though, and before they left, the trio planted some mint and watercress in the small creek that runs through the clearing, and a few raspberry canes alongside the wood shed.

Interestingly, the Forest Service hut at Leslie Clearing attended to by Polglaze was the fourth to stand here. The first was Salisbury's Log Cabin,

Working for the Forest Service, Max Polglaze had his fair share of helicopter rides over the years. But he also relied heavily on his faithful packhorse Roddy to carry in supplies and tools for many of his wilderness jobs. Photo: Max Polglaze

built by John Salisbury in the 1890s for use during cattle musters. It never had a chimney, the smoke from the fire inside just escaping through an open gable end. A photo taken by Dick Beatson in 1931 shows it to be fairly derelict by then. The second hut here, called Collins Hut, was built by a gold prospector named Collins, who originally came from Napier. He worked under the auspices of the Gold Prospecting Subsidy Scheme, set up by the government during the Great Depression. Then came Scout Hut, built in 1953 by Graham Keen and Jock Stocker with a troop of Takaka Scouts. That shelter was enlarged by Snow Meyer and the Holmes brothers earlier in 1981.

The men arrived back at Karamea Bend on the Saturday afternoon, in time to listen to the All Blacks test match against the Springboks live on Meyer's radio. They all stayed in the big hut that night, leaving the fireplace of the little staff hut cold, but only because 'the old bushman [Meyer] had taken it upon himself to box up that fireplace so that we could pour a higher hearth'. Polglaze fetched some rough filling, gravel and sand in a wheelbarrow from the riverbed up the new track, while Stringer once again attended to the wood heap.

Sunday, 16 August, day 12, was their last in the bush. It was also their first quiet, relaxed day since flying in. Meyer and Stringer poured the hearth using a spare bag of cement left over from the Slippery Creek job, while Polglaze pottered away with the barrow, gravelling a bit of the track to the firewood trees 'and so the day passed in a pleasant haze'. Des Whiting walked in about 1PM from the Roaring Lion, having spent two days hunting without sighting a single deer. For their part, the three men had seen only one deer over the 12 days, spotted on the riverbed opposite Slippery Creek at first light.

Snow Meyer became famous for living up the Karamea Valley, where he mostly based himself at Crow Hut. Polglaze reflected at the end of this trip how remarkable 'Herr von Meyer' actually was. He never found out his true age, although he thought it to be about 62 or 63. In fact, Meyer was only 57, so Polglaze found out later. Meyer had undergone major surgery just a couple of years before, had worn a pacemaker ever since, and for the whole job with Polglaze and Stringer had been sporting a hernia in his groin – although it didn't seem to affect him a bit over the 12 days. And what's more, he had helped Polglaze and Stringer out of sheer love for the area, putting younger men to shame in the process. You see, after he had finished working for the Forest Service, Meyer just stayed in the forest park, working for nothing and doing his own thing. He and Polglaze had a marvellous rapport, with never a cross word or thought passing between them – in itself remarkable considering how different they were. Polglaze found Meyer stimulating company, and quite different from the sad, lonely man who had written him a letter a few months previously, complaining of his plight. Meyer was like that – up and down. Said Polglaze in his diary:

> *I am presently playing him like a Leslie River trout and I think I have him hooked on the thought of acting as an expert guide on the payroll of a tourist fishing venture which is due to start in the Karamea/Leslie this summer. It would be an ideal vocation for him at this stage of his life and I just hope it works out all round.*

Les Maas flew his chopper into Karamea Bend at 3pm on the Sunday, just like he said he would. He uplifted the gear from Slippery Creek, then flew Ralph, Max and Helen (who had come along for the ride) back out to the Graham Valley, diverting to the Flora carpark and hovering briefly so Max could jump out and pick up the truck they had left there. As it was a Sunday afternoon, the carpark was loaded with people who weren't prepared for the big rotor blast, which blew over their cups of tea and sandwiches. 'Like lambs to the slaughter. But they all took it in good heart,' Polglaze wrote, later hearing that Maas had chuckled all the way back. The work trip was over, and it was time to go home and have a few days' break.

CHAPTER 10

HERITAGE HUTS

ROUGHLY HALFWAY UP THE TRACK leading from the road end at Trilobite Hut to Fenella Hut in the upper Cobb Valley, you suddenly come across Chaffey Hut, perched on big boulder piles in a sloping clearing overlooking the river near where Hannah Creek flows in, and just a few minutes' walk short of Chaffey Stream. This split-slab hut was considered derelict and beyond repair in 2009, deteriorated to such a degree that it was even taken off the Topo50 map. Then three years later, thanks to a massive effort, it was wonderfully restored to all its former hand-split and hand-hewn glory by the local branch of the New Zealand Deerstalkers' Association (NZDA), with input from DOC.

Spending time at Chaffey Hut makes you realise how well situated it is, overlooking Fenceline Flat on the other side of the Cobb River and up to Mt Benson in the Lockett Range. In summer, the magnificent mountain meadows break out in a riot of vivid displays of yellow Māori onion (*Bulbinella hookeri*) and delicate mauve-striped Cobb Valley gentian (*Gentianella patula*), which grow between the red tussocks (*Chionochloa rubra*).

Chaffey Hut was originally built over the summer of 1952/53 by Jack McBurney, the first Forest Service ranger appointed to the Cobb. The hut is named after nearby Chaffey Stream, which remembers Henry and Annie Chaffey, who lived in Asbestos Cottage to the southeast of the Cobb Dam. Despite the hut's name, however, the couple had nothing to do with it, and it was built after Henry died.

Unlike DOC rangers today, with their quarters and staff huts, McBurney had to live in a hut near the single-man's camp built for the Cobb Dam workers. The siting of Chaffey Hut was no accident, exactly halfway between the road end at the top of the lake and Cobb Hut, where every fortnight McBurney was required to take rain readings. The spot was always his lunch stop on the way, and he often stayed overnight there on the way back. It became his place of respite from all the hurly-burly at the dam.

Excerpts from McBurney's reports – effectively his work diary – reveal every step he took in building Chaffey Hut. He was often assisted by Jack Cowie, a surveyor on the Cobb Dam project who shared McBurney's need to escape the incessant noise of the construction site.

In his '6th Report, Cobb Valley Catchment Area, period 28 April to 25 May 1952', one of the work diaries McBurney kept, he wrote:

> *I have started packing materials and tools for which to repair Myttons Hut. I have pegged out a site for the new hut on a terrace south of Hannah Creek. I have also packed in some iron for the roof part of the way. Also noticed vandals were busy on the hut at Chaffey's Cottage [Asbestos Hut] and torn part of the roof off. Also a few sheets of iron have been taken off Myttons Hut roof and put in the fireplace where a fire was lighted on them. There seems to be a number of undesirable visitors to this area… Deer seen 3, deer destroyed 2* [part of a forest ranger's job back then was to take out every deer he saw].

Later on, in his 13th report, dated December 1952, McBurney wrote: 'The hut at Hannah Creek is slowly taking shape. The concrete for the fireplace is now completed and all the iron for the roof is on the site, but I cannot put it up until I put the walls up, or strong winds will blow the roof off. Deer seen 32, deer killed 16.'

He begins to refer to his new hut around this time as Hannah Creek Hut; it is not known when it was renamed Chaffey Hut.

In his next report, covering the period 8 December 1952 to 4 January 1953,

McBurney details how he went about selecting the trees from which to make the slabs for the hut: 'I cut a large red beech tree down and am readying it for a crosscut saw to cut it up, ready for splitting into weatherboards for the Hannah Creek Hut. Deer seen 39. Deer destroyed 18.'

His final mention of the hut is in May 1953: 'Hannah Creek Hut suitable for camping in although not quite completed. The bivvy at Chaffey Stream has collapsed and does not keep the rain out. Deer seen 4, deer destroyed 1.'

Later that year, in a brief comment in his 24th report covering the period 9 November to 6 December 1953, McBurney casually mentions that the hut is complete: 'I have removed some tools from the new hut to Myttons Hut on which I will now be working. The new hut has three bunks, one bunk is in the porch.'

McBurney was born in 1919 at Te Awamutu. His Scottish-born father was a wounded Gallipoli veteran who ended up marrying the Welsh nurse who tended to his injuries. After first settling on a farm near Te Awamutu, they moved to New Brighton in Christchurch. Jack's mother would take the children walking all over the Port Hills when they were young, and encouraged them to ride their bicycles from an early age. Every school holidays, the family would camp out at Mt Grey/Maukatere in the Ashley Forest, where they would explore. That outdoor emphasis inspired all the children to live their lives thus.

Young Jack took up an apprenticeship as a fitter and turner, finishing it in the RNZAF. He was stationed in the Pacific for a time during the Second World War, maintaining fighter aircraft. It was while he was a corporal gunnery instructor at the RNZAF Delta training camp near Blenheim that he met Edmund Hillary. Prior to their meeting, each was climbing independently in his own spare time. Sharing their mutual passion, they started climbing together. The pair went on many a trip, cycling up the Wairau and stashing their bikes in the scrub, before climbing up Branch River to Scotts Knob, and even scaling Kaikoura's mighty Tapuae-o-Uenuku, Footprint of the Rainbow.

Chaffey Hut (upper photo) was in a totally dilapidated condition before it was restored to its former glory in 2012 (lower photo) by Golden Bay branch members of the New Zealand Deerstalkers' Association (NZDA) with assistance from DOC. The horizontal-slab hut was originally built over the summer of 1952/53 by Jack McBurney, the first Forest Service ranger appointed to the Cobb. Photo: Paul Lenz

After the war, McBurney got in touch with Hillary again, and they went off climbing various peaks of the Southern Alps. The two men would discuss their work prospects. Being a beekeeper, Hillary always had his bees to turn to for a living, but McBurney had nothing like that. He had gone off the idea of being a fitter or turner, as the grease and grime – not to mention having to be in a noisy workshop all the time – just didn't suit him anymore. He thought about farming. He was a bit of a loner after all – not a very social sort of person – and he recognised that in himself. But with no money he had little chance of ever buying a farm. Initially he became a deer-culler on the West Coast, but then joined the Forest Service as a trainee ranger.

Ranger training in the Forest Service involved a basic induction into everything practical – building, engineering and tool maintenance – as well as a rough guide to the finer aspects of the great outdoors, including all the flora and fauna. It was a time when one prevalent instruction in how to distinguish birch (beech) species went like this:

> *It's not easy to distinguish between the different birch* [beech] *species, but leaf shape and size, bark, wood colour, aspect and position all give clues. You've got three main types of birches* [beeches] *– red, brown* [silver] *and black. The bark of the red is silver and the wood of the red is pink, but only when it's green. The brown* [silver] *quite often has the black bark but the green timber is red. Sometimes the bark of the black is white, but the timber is yellow and sometimes brown when it is green.*

McBurney was soon assigned as the first ranger in the Cobb Valley, taking along his fairly deaf yet faithful Alsatian dog for company. Part of the ranger's responsibilities included hosting a variety of government wildlife scientists, all keen to investigate the mountain ecosystem that had been opened up by the new dam access road. With his mountain and bush experience, McBurney was a natural observer. The scientists shared their knowledge with McBurney as he went about with them, and he became keenly interested in the micro-ecology around him, especially the insects, which enthralled him.

Heritage always mattered to McBurney, too. After Henry Chaffey was found frozen to death on the track leading up from Motueka and his wife Annie was convinced to come down off her now lonely mountain, McBurney became instrumental in the preservation of Asbestos Cottage. He advocated

First wall frame up: ranger Jack McBurney starts construction of the Chaffey Hut in 1952. Over the course of the job, he was often assisted by Jack Cowie, a surveyor at the Cobb Dam.
Photo: Shirley McBurney

that the 1897-built asbestos prospector's hut be restored as it was when it was abandoned by Annie, so that trampers could use it. The alternative was to let it go to rack and ruin in the extreme weather conditions or at the hands of vandals. When McBurney first visited the hut after it was abandoned, he found that it had already been broken into and many valuables stolen, including Henry's binoculars, a collection of signed books by such renowned authors as H. Guthrie Smith and Thomas F. Cheeseman, and Henry's large selection of mining and prospecting books. The empty hut also looked as if it had been charred by fire – even the jars of preserves under the bed had a black coating. Examining the contents of a box beside the bed, McBurney found a neatly folded pile of Annie's Edwardian clothing. He carefully packaged these and other personal effects, and took them back to the Nelson Forest Service office for safekeeping. He decided to leave behind the few dozen jars of good jam for trampers, who well appreciated them over the next year or two.

McBurney met his wife-to-be Shirley at the Cobb in 1956, towards the end of his posting there, and they married the following year. She had come to visit her sister Pat Beattie, the district nurse in Takaka, who would come up the Cobb once a month to hold a clinic for the dam workers, attending to any minor medical conditions and injuries. Jack knew Pat through skiing trips they had been on together to Mt Robert.

McBurney wanted to move on from the Cobb, as he had largely outgrown his Forest Service job and wanted to specialise in what he loved: entomology. He applied for, and got, a field research job in the Biological Services Unit of the Forest Research Institute in Rotorua. He worked in the Southland and Nelson conservancies, then in Rotorua as senior observer for the Forest Biology Survey for five years, before moving to the Entomology Division in Nelson. McBurney was an enthusiastic member of the Entomological Society of New Zealand, developing a broad knowledge of both invertebrates and vertebrates, acquired during his years of outdoor life, forestry experience and working in the Systematics Section of the Entomology Division. It is a credit to the man that he became so renowned for his natural ability, even though he was academically unqualified and lacked a university degree. So well regarded was McBurney that he was eventually promoted to lead the Biological Services Unit team, a position he held for four years. The entomologist's passion for insects developed even more over time. During his final years he began seriously writing up the results of his field studies and completed several publications, one a paper on *Anagotus helmsi*, a beech weevil in the family Curculionidae, something Shirley remembers took a lot of work on his part. He also had many more papers at draft stage. Jack died of coronary failure in Nelson in 1978, long before he should have. He was only 59. May the work and life of this unassuming ranger of the Cobb never be forgotten. Chaffey Hut is his memorial there.

It is a great pity then that the bureaucratic powers that be stopped all further maintenance on Chaffey Hut in January 1994, and it became marked as 'derelict' on maps. DOC's 2004 Recreational Opportunities Review tagged the structure for removal, but public opposition prevented that from happening. Still, DOC could not afford to restore the hut and said that as there were enough huts along the track already, it didn't warrant an allocation of public money.

Enter the Golden Bay branch of the NZDA. This proactive outdoors club was formed in 1964 at an inaugural meeting in the Anglican Hall in Takaka,

HERITAGE HUTS

The tent camp set up by members of the Golden Bay branch of the NZDA when building the new Anatoki Forks Hut in the summer of 1975. Photo: Roger Price

with Lawrence (Skeet) Barnett elected as president and Brian Reilly as secretary and treasurer. In the mid-1970s the club had its biggest membership, totalling 140, compared to its current 75 or so. In 1971, the members started opening up the old mining track leading to Anatoki Forks, re-forming and clearing it. It was a mammoth effort that took around 800 man hours, but it reduced the walk-in time from 14 hours to 6½ hours. After that, club members rebuilt Anatoki Forks Hut (complete with a wetback-heated shower), a project they completed in 1975.

In January 1988, the branch entered into discussions with DOC to take over the old Lake Keeper's Hut (now called the NZDA Hut) near the top of the Cobb Reservoir, a deal they signed off three years later. After endless working bees, this hut now stands as a testament to the innovation of club members. It even has a hot shower (just like the club's Anatoki Forks Hut) and a small hydro plant out the back that generates electricity for lighting and for a small heater that keeps the chill off in winter. Members also check stoat trap-lines up the valley, so it's no wonder that their interest would eventually focus on the dilapidated Chaffey Hut.

The club began lobbying DOC in December 2008 to be allowed to restore the hut. The department agreed to the proposal in September 2009, and planning and fundraising began in 2010. The following year, NZDA members began splitting slabs, with restoration work starting in earnest in April and finishing in July 2012. It had been member Wayne Sixtus who initially came up with the idea for the project, his interest having been sparked when he checked out the restoration of the 1926 Riordans Hut up the Kill Devil Track: 'Seeing that rebuild got me going. My family has been involved with the Cobb for four generations. I have a great fondness for the area. Chaffey Hut was a job that needed doing. Golden Bay Deerstalkers became very motivated to get this project off the ground and see it through to fruition.'

Around 1,500 hours of volunteer labour and $12,000 of costs ended up going into the Chaffey Hut restoration, with monetary assistance coming from Tasman District Council, Pub Charity, the Pupu Hydro Society and DOC itself. With the horizontal-slab hut initially in a very dilapidated condition, it was no small job. Virtually all of the internal beech pole framing had to be replaced, along with nearly all of the 1.3-metre-long horizontal slabs or billets that make up the external cladding. The new billets were made from wind-felled red beech trees around 800 metres down the track, which were sawn into suitable lengths and then split radially from the pith of the trunk towards the sap or outer wood, using a maul and large steel wedges.

As to be expected, many of the split slabs had to be rejected on the grounds of quality, due to knots and spiral grain. Usable slabs were dressed with an axe or adze into reasonably regular, parallel planks before being stacked and left to season. During the reconstruction, each slab had to be individually scribed and altered to fit with the previous one, again by axe or adze, and also scribed to the framing to achieve a snug fit. Sections of original slabs that were retained were all numbered so they could be put back in their original positions.

The original gable roof was also reinstated, as was the 350-millimetre drop in the floor along the length of the 5-metre structure. This was exactly how McBurney built it – you walk noticeably uphill towards the open fireplace on the back wall. The whole 11.5-square-metre structure used to sit on just 15 huge rock piles, but in the rebuild the bearers were bolted to the rocks. The hut's wooden safe and storage box are the originals, as are the sheets of three-ply that line the walls. A new steel open fireplace was prefabricated in Takaka and flown up by helicopter. Heavy beech poles make up the framework for

DOC's John Taylor has become an expert in heritage hut restorations. He joined the Chaffey Hut restoration for four weeks in April 2012, when much of the cladding and finishing work took place. The rebuild was kept as faithful as possible to the original horizontal-slab construction.
Photo: Gerard Hindmarsh

the three bunks, with an extra mattress thrown in that can be used on the floor. Any of the original slabs that weren't quite up to scratch were used to build a wood shed out the back.

The club also provided most of the labour for the 18-month job. During the main part of the rebuild, at least seven members from the 75-strong club came up most weeks to help. Wayne Sixtus and Paul Lenz played a big part, as did Tony Hitchcock from DOC, who spent many hours helping to split the horizontal billets. Non-club volunteers also helped out, like builder Andy Cole, who was on site for two weeks, and ace DOC hut restorer John Taylor, who joined the men for four weeks during the busiest patch in April. Taylor says that Chaffey Hut is a great example of a traditional horizontal-slab hut:

> *Slabs were often fixed vertically like with Cecil Kings Hut [1935] up the Wangapeka and Riordans Hut up the Kill Devil, but the advantage*

Unlike many older slab huts, which are constructed with vertical slabs, Chaffey Hut utilised 1.3-metre-long radially split slabs called billets, which are fitted horizontally. During the reconstruction, each new slab had to be scribed and altered by axe or adze to match the previous one, and also the framing, to ensure a snug fit. Photo: Gerard Hindmarsh

> of doing them horizontal like on Chaffey Hut is that they are able to be a lot shorter, which gives a big advantage to the woodsmen splitting and carrying them to the site. We kept as faithful to the original hut as we possibly could.

Taylor cut his teeth restoring huts using entirely traditional materials and methods. Projects he has worked on include Riordans Hut, Waingaro Forks Hut (late 1930s), Tin Hut Shelter (pre-1926) and the Ministry of Works Historic Hut (1970). More recently, he joined a hut conservation team that worked on Shackleton's Hut (1908) in Antarctica.

Taylor's efforts were well appreciated again in 2014, when he restored the Cobb Tent Camp. Dating from the late 1970s and situated between the Chaffey and Cobb huts, this is quite possibly the last remaining original tent camp in the whole country. These basic pole and stretched-canvas shelters were introduced by the Department of Internal Affairs in the late 1930s for their deer-cullers. In the 1960s, the Forest Service operated a hunter training camp at Dip Flat in Marlborough's Wairau Valley, in which 500 men went through a gruelling programme under the watchful eye of Harry Ferris. After a few days they were put into tent camps, which they were required to completely dismantle and then rebuild, becoming experts in the process.

Many older New Zealanders developed a real affection for tent camps, either through their work or just tramping by them. The shelters were even more highly regarded when they sported a corrugated-iron chimney inside a chunky wooden frame, making them particularly cosy affairs. But as the use of helicopters increased and the network of backcountry huts expanded, so the use of tent camps began to decline. A few hung around fairly intact in the Ruahine Ranges until the 1980s, but by 2015 only the Cobb Tent Camp was left. Taylor put out the word that he was planning its restoration, and couldn't believe the support that flooded in – including from an upholstery shop that offered to supply all the canvas free of charge. The work had to be historically accurate, using materials sourced from nearby, including beech and mānuka poles for the superstructure, cedar for the fireplace, and red beech fashioned with an axe and adze for the bench, stools and platforms. At the opening of the restored camp, DOC was rightfully acknowledged for its work in preserving the heritage of our deer-culling era.

The Cobb Tent Camp restoration proved an inspiration, as it brought about the creation of a new tent camp called Soper Shelter at the head of remote Lake Stanley (altitude 770 metres). This re-created camp was built in three stints in early 2016 through the combined efforts of members of the Golden Bay Alpine and Tramping Club (GBATC) and DOC, notably again Taylor and his offside, Tony Hitchcock. Its official opening on Saturday, 16 April 2016 felt like a significant wilderness occasion – indeed, this remote place had probably never seen so many people (39, to be exact) gathered in one spot. Twenty-four guests were shuttled in by helicopter for the day, the rest bravely walking in up the aptly named Kill Devil Track from Uruwhenua near Upper Takaka, a hard two-day slog.

The site of this new tent camp is to die for: a delightfully dry, *Dracophyllum*-dappled knoll just a stone's throw from the point where the south branch of the Stanley River flows into the head of the lake. There's even an inviting

Seen here in dilapidated condition just before it was restored in 2015 by DOC's John Taylor, Cobb Tent Camp is situated halfway between Chaffey Hut and Cobb Hut, and was quite possibly the last original tent camp left in the country. These basic pole and stretched-canvas structures were introduced by the Department of Internal Affairs in the 1930s as a low-cost solution to providing backcountry shelters for their deer-cullers. Photo: Paul Lenz

swimming hole close by and, amazingly, there are no sandflies. Great spotted kiwi, whio (blue ducks, *Hymenolaimus malacorhynchos*), kākāriki (yellow-crowned parakeets, *Cyanoramphus auriceps*) and bush robins (*Petroica australis*) can all be heard and spotted around here, and a few amateur ornithologists even believe South Island kōkako (*Callaeas cinerea*; declared extinct in 2007 but now classed as 'Data Deficient') still live in the area. Onekaka resident Alec Milne reckons he heard the unmistakable melodious, organ-like call of the bird in the upper reaches of the Stanley River in response to a recorded call he was playing. The birds may well live on up here, in what is essentially unexplored country.

For the opening of Soper Shelter, there was billy tea and bacon soup, prepared for all on the big rock campfire, along with ample sandwiches slapped together on the newly hewn benches. A few speeches from all the right people completed the proceedings and the obligatory ribbon was cut.

The restoration of the Cobb Tent Camp inspired the Golden Bay Alpine and Tramping Club to team up with staff at DOC's Golden Bay office, notably John Taylor and his offside Tony Hitchcock, to build Soper Shelter (pictured) at the head of remote Lake Stanley. The work was undertaken over three stints in 2016. Photo: Gerard Hindmarsh

The camp clearing that day was full of local legends – seemingly anyone who'd had much to do with the place was there. Retired Forest Service ranger Max Polglaze looked suitably impressed, and there was even a descendant of the first grazier who drove cattle through here in the late nineteenth century.

A historic tent camp Soper Shelter may be, but a petrol-powered rock drill was needed to break up a massive boulder embedded in the site before it could be levelled off at the start of the project. Long labouring hours were spent harvesting and notching the sapling spars of red beech into a solid framework anchored into mountain cedar posts, the impressive structure supporting an expansive custom-made canvas awning over the more modest 6-metre by 3-metre inner tent sanctum itself. It's the chainsaw-milled and adze-hewn details that catch the eye, right down to the furniture and the impressive corrugated-iron chimney, accurately framed with log sections of mountain cedar. Even the rustic weatherboard-clad long-drop is a masterpiece.

The well-built Soper Shelter will improve access to this outstanding area of backcountry, even if Lake Stanley itself can be rather spooky. Stumps of drowned beech trees protrude from the surface of the 3-kilometre-long lake like tombstones from a black marble surface, while wisps of mist tangle among the towering, sun-bleached spires of more durable mountain cedar. Kahurangi's largest natural lake didn't even exist until 1929, when the Murchison earthquake sent the whole side of nearby Mt Snowden (1,859 metres) down into the valley, creating a massive rubble dam. The still-raw catastrophic cleavage stretches almost 2 kilometres up to the top of the mountain. The mind boggles to imagine the hillside coming down, collapsing with such force that it surged up the slope on the other side of the valley, bulldozing the beech forest as it went.

There used to be a rough little hut here right beside the dam, appropriately called Smokey Drip Hut. Built by five local hunters in 1971, it was demolished by DOC in 1988 after two independent geologists reported that its site on the unstable slip meant that anyone staying here was in dire danger in the event of another earthquake. To their credit, DOC's Golden Bay staff did develop a number of plans for replacing Smokey Drip, an essential midway hut on the four-day Kill Devil–Waingaro–Lake Stanley–Anatoki route, but none of these came to fruition because of budget restrictions.

It took John Pemberton, president of the GBATC, to get plans for a new shelter up at Lake Stanley underway. Working with DOC, the GBATC developed the idea of constructing a replica historic tent camp, in keeping with the nature of the restored huts along this circuit. Tent camps were erected for deer-cullers right into the 1970s, and building shelters like these is akin to going back to the future.

Soper Shelter is named after Golden Bay locals Frank and Berna Soper. In 1960, along with Keith Marshall, the couple formed the GBATC, with Berna becoming the club's first secretary. Frank led the building of three huts at Boulder Lake, Adelaide Tarn and Lonely Lake, and together with Stan Northcote-Bade the couple were instrumental in persuading the government to form the North-West Nelson Forest Park in 1970, which eventually became Kahurangi National Park. It was fitting that Frank, now 91, attended the opening with his son and two daughters, giving a speech that was complemented by the reading by Piers Maclaren of one of Frank's poems, 'Lines from Lonely Lake'. Also present at the opening was Skeet Barnett, Frank's 87-year-old tramping mate.

This area has a rich, if sparse, history. From 1875 to the 1930s, the Salisbury family from the Graham Valley grazed sheep and cattle through the Cobb area and up into the Stanley Valley, sowing exotic grass seed as they went. Mustering was fraught with difficulties thanks to the challenging weather and aberrant stock, but became easier following the construction of a rudimentary whare (hut) on the Stanley River. Other events in the area included the arrival of goldminers from the nearby Anatoki catchment in the 1880s and, in the 1930s, the establishment of a camp of around three dozen miners at Waingaro Forks, who were put to work there under the government's Gold Prospecting Subsidy Scheme. The last of these men left in around 1937. Even more recently, Lake Stanley was fished commercially for its big eels by a succession of anglers, first John Leckie in around 1981 and then Hamish Black. The last person to fly out slingloads of live eels for export was Jim Pacey in around 1991. The few eels that still remain in these tannin-stained waters can often be seen patrolling the edges of the lake.

Soper Shelter provides a genuine adventure in earthquake country, unlike Te Papa's simulated Earthquake House theme room. With the construction of the new tent camp, more people will now be able to stop off at Lake Stanley. Sure, there will be wear and tear, and risks to cope with, but any downside will be more than made up for by the fostering of an appreciation for true wilderness in our national consciousness. How good that will be!

CHAPTER 11

TRACTS OF IRON

MANY WILL APPRECIATE THAT ONEKAKA, on State Highway 60 between Takaka and Collingwood, has a truly glorious past, being no less than the illustrious birthplace of New Zealand's iron and steel industry. It signified a promise to a fledgling country that real industrial wealth lay just around the corner. After all, if a country could make its own steel, it could make anything.

This remarkable boom came about here because the foothills behind Onekaka, stretching over to Parapara and now included in Kahurangi National Park, are essentially ground zero for a huge deposit of high-grade limonite, a complex but extremely pure form of iron ore thought to have formed through the erosion of laterites laid down in the Tertiary period. Back in 1907, James Mackintosh Bell of the Geological Survey of New Zealand estimated in his *Geology of the Parapara Subdivision* that 50 million tons of top-grade limonitic ore was literally rusting out of the hillsides above Onekaka, saying, 'It is remarkable that the great deposit of iron ore at Parapara, so well known for so many years, should have remained practically untouched to the present day.' Later, the geologist would make the claim that it was the largest iron ore deposit in the whole world. The *Nelson Evening Mail* enthusiastically ran with that hope, speculating that there would soon be 'a populous industrial centre on the shores of Golden Bay'.

Utilising the vast reserves of limonite (iron ore) in the hills directly behind its works, the Onakaka Iron and Steel Company became the basis of New Zealand's fledgling iron and steel industry. Over 12 years from 1923, the plant produced more than 41,000 tons of pig iron, but Depression economics, combined with intense competition from cheap imports, finally forced its closure in 1935. From left to right: main office, cookhouse and single men's quarters, with the towering blast furnace rising behind the boiler and engine rooms.
Photo: Alexander Turnbull Library, F29121.

Today, all of New Zealand's steel is produced at Glenbrook, southwest of Auckland, the rapacious furnaces fed a mix of Huntly coal and ironsand from the mouth of the Waikato. But back in the early twentieth century, Onekaka ore was the best source from which to extract iron. Black ironsands were still causing problems for steelmakers, whereas limonitic rock – with near 80 per cent iron purity – could be relied on to cast precision steel items. This still largely holds true today, with New Zealand having to import all its high-precision steel needs.

I first 'discovered' the ruins of Onekaka's ironworks back in 1977, not long after I shifted to Golden Bay. An advertisement for cheap fire bricks had led me almost to the end of Ironworks Road, where the owner of the land at that time, Bruce King, simply proclaimed, 'Follow me!' Within a few minutes I was overcome with utter astonishment at the rambling scale of the derelict industrial works, bristling with regenerating ferns and scrub.

Pushing aside the gorse and barberry, we finally arrived at the amazing beehive coking ovens, and it became obvious to me that these were the source of the tapered bricks I had come to buy. King had my small order of 120 bricks stacked for me – just enough, I had calculated, to line the back and sides of my wood range. And they were only 20¢ each! But when I saw where King was taking the bricks from, my heart sank. Those ovens were just too magnificent, too grand even, to be dismantled. The farmer couldn't be blamed, though, for selling the last salvageable commodities from a glorious past – after all, no one else cared, so why should he? It was just a microcosm of our national industrial heritage. Besides, as he'd already taken the bricks out, I bought them.

Initial attempts to extract iron in New Zealand, from titaniferous ironsands near New Plymouth, were largely unsuccessful. Fine sand and impurities fouled the smelting process, and the end result was a hugely inferior iron. Attention soon turned to more conventional and far purer ore: the limonite at Onekaka. Predictions that New Zealand would produce the world's cheapest pig iron were promising, and in 1920 the Onakaka (*sic*) Iron and Steel Company was incorporated. Strangely, the new company chose a phonetic spelling of the common mispronunciation of the more proper Onekaka, which translates as 'burning sands'. If you walk along the iron-tainted beach by the old Onekaka Wharf on a hot summer's day, you will certainly appreciate the origin of this name!

Much credit for New Zealand's early steel industry, and for the whole Onekaka Ironworks story, goes to John Ambrose Heskett. This industrial pioneer had both vision and perseverance, first in Taranaki experimenting with the problematic ironsands, and then at Onekaka, where he was finally rewarded with management of New Zealand's first iron and steel plant. The prospect of this major industry was regarded as heralding a new era of opportunity and wealth for the area, not to mention bringing great benefits to the whole country. Capital of £80,000 was raised and the pig iron price of £14 per ton was highly encouraging. A flurry of construction followed. Heavy plant and machinery were barged into the nearby inlet, including sections for the 16.8-metre-high blast furnace shipped over from Taranaki, and a petition to the county council resulted in the upgrade of the road that would become the main service access between the plant and wharf.

Good-quality pig iron was produced in early trials, and the government – keen to see less dependence on imported iron – promised a production bounty. The future looked bright, and the Anchor Shipping and Foundry

To feed the blast furnace, coal was brought up from the Liverpool Colliery in Greymouth and converted to two grades of coke in 24 beehive ovens of two different sizes. The eight ovens measuring 4 metres in diameter and 2.3 metres in height produced coke in 36 hours, while the 16 smaller ovens measuring 3.7 metres across by 2 metres high required a 56-hour process. Teams of stokers worked around the clock, in such intense heat that they required new boots every two weeks. Photo: Alexander Turnbull Library, F147659.

Company of Port Nelson was commissioned to begin making castings. A steel support still visible in Marsden House on Nelson's Nile Street carries the words 'First casting from Onakaka [*sic*], A, S. and F., 1922'.

Ore bins, overhead cableways, beehive coke ovens, a dam and flumes were all constructed in a massive flurry of activity that employed hundreds of men. Pile-driving for the 370-metre-long wharf adjacent the mouth of Onekaka Inlet began in 1923, and a narrow tramway with a gauge of 2 foot 6 inches was constructed to connect the wharf via the little inlet and up a gentle gradient to the works, 2.4 kilometres away. When all these separate projects came together later that year, and the damage from a 'mysterious fire' was repaired, production began in earnest from early 1924. It would have been a proud moment for works manager Heskett, even if the price of pig iron had begun slipping to a low of £9. The reality of the seesawing price of pig iron was that the first 100 tons produced by the works came in at a loss.

But hopes stayed high and the company capital had already been raised to £150,000 in anticipation of increased production. Iron ore and limestone were carried down from adjacent quarries high in the hills above Onekaka by means of bins on an aerial cableway. Coal was shipped in from the Liverpool Colliery at Greymouth, then towed up in the company's little loco to the works, where it was offloaded into big bins. There, the coal was converted to coke in the beehive ovens. In their unenviable job, the workers manning the ovens were subjected to such intense heat that they required new boots every fortnight.

Hydraulic feeders supported on a sloping ramp held up by huge metal trestles lifted the measured quantities of ore, limestone and coke into overhead bins, which then deposited directly into the top of the blast furnace. Under extreme heat in the furnace, the liquefied limestone would form a cap over the molten ore, collecting impurities and cooling as slag. This was then tapped or let go from the furnace, and poured into a wide ditch that led down into a gully.

Tapping the slag was a big event in the community, especially among the families of the workers, as it was a regular fireworks show. Any tappings after dark could be depended on to give the best effect. Blankets and picnics were laid out, and the families would settle in for the visual extravaganza. In her book of early recollections of the area, *Courage and Camp Ovens*, Enga Washbourn describes one such occasion:

> *Dazzling white-hot molten iron poured out of a hole into the molten pig beds. The tall black building behind became illuminated with orange red light which reflected on the damp shiny faces of the men as they worked in the heat. At more frequent intervals slag was drawn off and poured in a brilliant luminous waterfall over a cliff into a valley, turning into a hard glassy substance.*

The pig iron was poured directly into moulds, and once cooled, the ingots were loaded onto little rail trucks for transfer to the wharf, where they were stockpiled for shipping. An average loading would involve 17 hours of continuous labour for a team of 20 men. Mittens made from the cut sections of truck inner tubes were worn for protection as the men stacked the awkward 56-kilogram ingots.

A works community of school, post office, single men's accommodation and cookhouse evolved, and a state-of-the-art hydroelectric plant was installed to make use of the company dam in the Onekaka Gorge. Interestingly, the

As construction of the Onekaka Ironworks got into full swing, single men's huts sprang up beside the site along Ironworks Road. Photo: William Logan

community petitioned the government in around 1924 to change the incorrect spelling of Onakaka Post Office to Onekaka, a move that would standardise the use of the name, including that of the works.

The Great Depression brought a dramatic drop in iron and steel prices, and the company – with its reliance on raw ingots – began to suffer. The directors conferred and agreed with manager Heskett that diversification was the key to survival, and in 1927 gave their approval to move into pipe manufacture. The traditional vertical casting method was chosen, and lucrative contracts such as the new Wellington gas pipeline resulted in acres upon acres of stockpiled pipes at Onekaka.

But the optimism was short-lived, for the decision to cast pipes proved disastrous. Newly developed and cheaper centrifugally spun pipes flooded the market, mainly from Humes in Australia, and Onekaka's sales plummeted. Worse still, cheaper imported iron, mainly from India, had affected sales of Onekaka's raw ingots, and the plant was forced to shut down in 1931. That initial closure was a bitter blow to Heskett, who tirelessly tried to persuade the directors that new avenues should be explored to keep the plant open. Recommissioned two years later, it faltered on until May 1935, when defeat was finally admitted. The company was liquidated after producing 41,194 tons over its 13 years of operation. It was a terrible shame, for the relatively soft iron produced at Onekaka made it a versatile product, particularly for such things as stoves – two highly satisfied stove manufacturer customers of the works were Metters (NZ) and the Sunshine Harvester Co. of Australia.

The outbreak of the Second World War saw extensive prospecting and development in the area at the hands of the State Iron and Steel Department. And in 1941, heavy machinery and equipment were once again unloaded at Onekaka to upgrade the works, with more than £100,000 spent on just relining the blast furnace and beehive coking ovens. The rationale was that the works needed to be kept in a state of immediate readiness in case supply lines were cut by the Pacific War with Japan.

Despite all this effort and expenditure, however, the plant was never fired up, and after the war it was simply abandoned. Tenders were put out for some of the equipment, and the magnificent blast furnace was toppled by explosives so that the never-used fire bricks could be extracted. Fossickers, souvenir hunters, and brick and scrap gatherers have all exacted their toll under a succession of private owners ever since.

Today, it is hard to imagine the hive of industry that must have existed up this now tranquil valley. Gorse and blackberry regrowth protect what is left of the 24 coking ovens, the largest of which are 4 metres in diameter and 2.3 metres high.

The toppled blast furnace sports large, gaping rectangular holes where its cooling blocks were removed, but its 16.8-metre length is still intact. Six water-cooled bronze tuyères once blew air into the furnace to create the blast effect. Unfortunately, however, the excessive regrowth of vegetation does not allow an overview of this industrial wonderland today. Entry into the smelting complex is along an impressively narrow path between the huge concrete ore bins and a moss-covered bank studded with slender trees reaching up to the light. Surrounded by a necklace of ferns, a huge square concrete shaft with embedded steel rungs disappears into half-flooded horizontal tunnels. Crossing a concrete wall, you clamber down among the mānuka, now towering over four big plinth-like concrete structures. Nearby is an arching tunnel with a brick-lined roof and walls, surely once the support for the big boiler room, although it's hard to make it all out these days. The brickwork is wonderful, especially in the arches.

Further up the valley, Onekaka Dam can be reached on a pleasant half-day excursion into Kahurangi National Park, beginning in the Washbourn Reserve or through private property from the end of Ironworks Road. A small hydroelectric scheme has been built at the old works dam, its shareholders selling their excess power to the national grid. Objections from local residents led to the modification of the original power proposal to allow for the downstream passage of native fish, notably the endemic shortjaw kōkopu (*Galaxias postvectis*), and to preserve access and avoid visual degeneration.

High in the hills and protected by their isolation, the limonite and limestone quarries are perhaps the best-preserved reminders of the past, littered as they are with industrial scrap – including the odd hanging ore bin. Sadly, little remains of the old wharf at the end of Washbourn Road aside from a few jagged steel uprights. Originally built entirely from locally milled native timber, the wharf deteriorated quickly and within two or three years of completion had to be strengthened by driving ex-Wellington tram rails in alongside every pile and adding bracing – a massive job. At low tide, remnants of the tramline supports can still be seen running back through the middle of the inlet, their trail these days as much marked by the odd ingot that rattled and fell off the little train.

'The Future of Onekaka', an article by F.J. St Just in a 1947 edition of *Better Business* magazine, laments New Zealand's lethargy in exploiting Onekaka's vast iron ore reserves and the lack of effort to save the failing industry:

> *When the hills are shrouded in mist, Onekaka appears lonely and in lachrymose mood. It will not always be thus, the time will come when man will urgently need the treasure in this mineral store. Then the wheels will begin to revolve again and the buckets will creep along the aerial tramway from the quarries bringing ore for perhaps dozens of blast furnaces.*

Only a humble line of hills separates the Onekaka ore reserves from the ones in the Parapara catchment, but it may as well be a different world. The more colourful ore on the Parapara side was not utilised for steel production, but as pigments for making paint.

Since 2012, local resident Dick Nicholls has gone about uncovering the fascinating layers of history connected with the limonite deposits of the lower eastern Parapara Valley. Previously the caretaker of nearby Milnthorpe Park for 38 years, Nicholls 'retired' from that job in early 2012, but shifting up the Parapara Valley only seemed to get him going again. Most days, the 74-year-old hits the hills near his home, in hand his trademark super-sharp slasher, which he uses to remove regrowth and uncover the efforts of a splendid past. He's not employed by anyone – it's just how he likes to spend his time, making tracks and planting trees.

Nicholls' research into the past endeavours in the vicinity has been meticulous. He has even dug out old government survey maps and prospecting geologists' drilling records, using them to uncover a rich labyrinth of benched tracks and workings, water races, adits and shafts. He's also discovered two deep gulches – an American mining term for a gully incised by sluicing – down the steep hillside that were created by hydraulic sluicers in an earlier goldmining era. It's nothing short of a remarkable piece of detection work, and significantly for Nicholls, a rewarding insight into the pioneering Washbourn family, notably patriarch William and his two sons Henry (Harry) and Arthur (Arty).

Explains Nicholls: 'The big story for me has come from uncovering their monumental work. When they shifted to Onekaka they built a benched track all the way to their paintworks, across the hills behind Tukurua and over a saddle to Parapara, an amazing achievement alone to cut that in over 3 kilometres of rugged country.' All these tracks now lie within Kahurangi National Park, whose boundary comes closest to the sea in coastal Golden Bay. They can be accessed from either the ridge line of Gates' Mill Road in Tukurua, or up the Parapara Valley Road.

William Washbourn emigrated from England to Nelson in 1852 with his wife Susannah and five children. He became highly regarded as one of the most entrepreneurial diggers of his time, excelling in surveying, building tracks and water races, and prospecting. It is said he was almost intuitive in his appreciation of what lay beneath the ground. As a goldfield warden, he was responsible for enforcing the newly formed goldmining regulations. He also became a shopkeeper, and as an engineer he developed new methods of gold extraction, notably hydraulic sluicing. He is credited with 'discovering' new goldfields in the Quartz Ranges near Bainham and at Richmond Flat up the Parapara Valley, and lived at the latter for four years before moving to Onekaka. At the Quartz Ranges, Pākehā miners clashed with Māori miners who had come from the North Island over claims, and Washbourn tried his hardest to keep the peace. His son later reminisced about that particular incident, in which the Pākehā miners were spoiling for a fight and would have come '500 strong' if necessary. In 1873, William moved to Richmond Hill, just beyond Richmond Flat, and with his two sons worked several gold claims and, later, a silver mine. Their ventures did not prove profitable, however, and in 1878 the three moved to Onekaka and turned their attention to the limonite, which they began to prospect.

By far the most colourful limonite comes from the Parapara side of the deposit. Well before the arrival of Europeans, Māori collected the concentrated reddish pigment from here, making it into their trademark kōkōwai, which they used to paint everything from their bodies to carvings, canoes and even meeting houses. Ochre from Parapara was regarded as some of the finest in all Aotearoa, and is said to have been traded up and down the country. The best raw kōkōwai has the texture and density of an oil crayon, and can be dabbed directly onto the skin, but usually it was heated in the coals of a fire to concentrate the colour even further, then pulverised for use. Not far up Parapara Valley is Maori Gully, where this pre-European industry was quite possibly centred. Large, flat stones on which the ochre may have been pounded are still evident up here. According to locals, early morning and late afternoon are the best times to look for kōkōwai, as the light accentuates the rich rust-red and umber hues of the deposits.

In the course of his archaeological sleuthing, Dick Nicholls initially focused his attention on uncovering and reinstating an old dammed lake halfway down the true right side of the Parapara Valley. Known locally as Washbourn's Dam, it was likely designed by William when his family still resided in Motueka and he was busy in the Collingwood goldfields. Explains Nicholls, 'My estimate is that this dam was built around 1859, to supply water for gold sluicing down the hill. Everyone thinks it supplied water to the paintworks that got built here but that's incorrect.'

Passing through the scrub here is the oddly named BNZ Road, a kilometre-long walkable track that has now been cleared thanks to Nicholls' efforts. Along it are the remains of another dam, entirely overgrown now, which was used as an additional reservoir for gold sluicing, and further along, the stone wall and fireplace remains of a miner's hut, near hidden among the vibrant regrowth. The BNZ Road got its name after the 640-acre leasehold of would-be ore smelters Howard Keep and John Chambers of Auckland was acquired

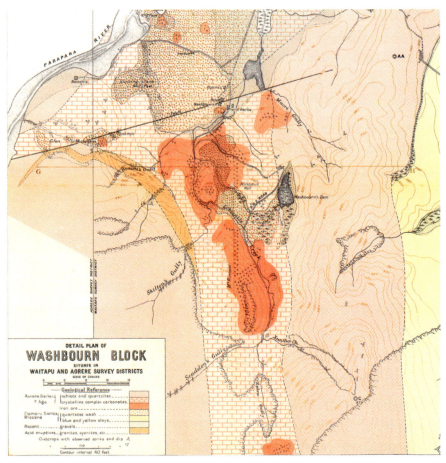

A detail from James Mackintosh Bell's 1907 geology map of the Parapara Subdivision. The New Zealand Geological Survey geologist would later claim that the iron ore reserves at Onekaka were the largest in the world. Photo: J.M. Bell, E.J.H. Webb and E. de C. Clarke, The Geology of the Parapara Subdivision, Government Printer, Wellington, 1907

by the Bank of New Zealand in around 1888 after the pair fell into financial strife. Keen to make the property saleable, the bank constructed the road and vainly gazetted it in its own name, then proceeded to stack some ore in an attempt to upgrade the block into a going concern with a higher resale value.

Southwards along the Parapara Valley, an overgrown bulldozed track cuts around a steep hillside. This was put in by the State Iron and Steel Department of Michael Joseph Savage's Labour Government. During the 1930s and 1940s, an 80-strong team of men constructed a comprehensive system of prospecting shafts and boreholes all around here. Dick can point to adit after adit leading into the hill, one not far from a much earlier goldmining-era gulch created that plummets deep into the gully. Just along the track, boreholes have been drilled at 30-metre intervals. This terrain has been seriously worked over, and the activity didn't finish that long ago either. The last extraction work took place as recently as the mid-1970s, when both the Golden Bay Cement Company and TNL operated two small quarries here. The latter extracted the limonite for use as a concrete-hardening additive, this material being used in many of the big dam projects down south, including the Clyde Dam.

However, it was turning some of the more colourful iron oxide seams into paint that showed the greatest economic promise. In the early 1870s, T.B. Louisson and Daniel Johnston began manufacturing paint in Nelson from ore brought in from Parapara. In 1879, they sold their interests to the New Zealand Paint Company, which five years later was bought by William Washbourn using a legacy he had been sent from England. He operated his renamed New Zealand Haematite Paint Company up the Parapara Valley Road with his sons Harry and Arty. They later inherited it when William died unexpectedly on 27 April 1888. His health had been failing steadily, and severe rheumatism meant he could only get around with a walking stick. It was suspected he had slipped or suffered a heart attack while crossing a small bridge over a water race through his garden, which he had designed many years before. Arty had come home to find his father slumped over the race, his head underwater, causing him to drown. The patriarch's death was a great shock to the family. The two Washbourn sons continued the operation until 1906, when they sold it to Messrs Cadman and Berry.

There is no doubt that William totally overhauled the paint operation when he took it over, and that he made it a successful business recognised throughout New Zealand and in many countries overseas. He understood chemistry and mineral composition, and to his mind the plant had simply not been turning out a satisfactory quality of paint under its previous owners. Improvements were made, and instead of taking 48 hours of constant firing to dry a ton of paint, it became possible to do it in eight. Previously, 4 tons of ironstone calcine produced only 3 tons of inferior paint. William worked out that by making the gratings smaller to keep the ore in the stamper boxes longer, he could get 12 tons of top-notch high-iron-content paint from 24 tons of ore. He was a thoroughly practical man who understood every aspect of

The paintworks at Parapara were operated by the Washbourn family. The large overshot waterwheel drove the machinery, the water being conveyed to it via a 3-kilometre-long race from the Parapara River not far from its junction with Glen Gyle Creek.
Photo: Nelson Provincial Museum, Tyree Studio Collection, 179839

the mining industry. Experimenting with different-coloured ironstone from all around Parapara, he had hoped to find a good seller, always sending off samples to Wellington to establish their iron content. One lot of ore, collected near the bridle track that dropped off into the Parapara Valley, produced a pleasing bright orange. Ever keen to try out new products, it was said William's house – including its roof – had more coats of paint lavished upon it than any other building in Golden Bay. 'Our front door is very grand, with three colours on it… the yellow is a fine bright colour,' he once wrote in a letter to his family.

The New Zealand Haematite Paint Company ended up producing high-quality paint pigments at a quarter of the cost of imported oxides. Considering how much paint was being used in the flourishing colony, it was a dramatic development, and no longer was the country dependent on imported products.

New Zealand Railways become their best customer, and virtually every wagon and railway shed in the country was painted with the reddish-brown line that became so familiar to generations of New Zealanders. A brighter colour ended up on hundreds of woolsheds around the country, but the paint company's attempts to make a red roof option for the domestic market was unsuccessful. At the height of production at the works, they exported around half of the paint they churned out to Australia.

A 30-foot overshot waterwheel drove all the machinery at the paintworks. The water that powered this was conveyed via a 3-kilometre-long race (more of a ditch, roughly 1.2 metres deep and wide) from the Parapara River, the intake near its confluence with Glen Gyle Creek. From the race, the water flowed along a ditch dug into the terrace above the works, and then poured over a bank in a flume that was directed onto the waterwheel below.

In the manufacture process, the colourful paint ore (which was mined from tunnels) first had to be calcined, or heated to reduce it to a powder, before going into a battery of six stampers, each of which weighed 340 kilograms. After crushing, the pulverised product was flowed through berdans (rotating grinders) to further reduce the ore to a finer powder, which was then passed over tanks of still water to trap any sediment. The paint pigment was then dried in a kiln, before being pulverised through rollers and bagged for market.

Reckons Nicholls, 'It's thoroughly fascinating, the ongoing interest poured into this area, but if I had to pick what stands out amongst everything that happened in this area, it would have to be the work of the Washbourns. Their trackwork in particular is a real tribute to them, and it's been a real privilege for me to be able to reveal it again.'

Nicholls' own story is amazing. He quit his librarian job in Wellington in 1974 and shifted to Golden Bay with the intention of organic gardening. But his sights soon shifted to an unoccupied 180-hectare block of coastal Crown land that no one seemed to know what to do with. His detailed proposal to plant native trees among the scrub was supported by Larry Russell, then Commissioner of Crown Lands in Nelson. Within a year, Nicholls had established a plant nursery while living in a caravan on the land.

He recalls those early days: 'It was relatively easy getting natives established in the sand dune country, but shocking fertility over the rest of the place meant I got pitiful success everywhere else. Even gorse wouldn't grow on most of it.'

Influence to change his ecological strategy came from the likes of Neil

Dick Nicholls has been responsible for reopening many of the historical tracks around the iron ore and ochre reserves in the eastern Parapara Valley. Here he pauses at the entrance to one of the prospecting tunnels, this one put in by the Parapara Iron and Coal Syndicate in around 1907 and later extended by prospectors from the State Iron and Steel Department.
Photo: Gerard Hindmarsh

Barr, best known for his regular column on trees in *Farmer* magazine and a passionate advocate of planting exotic eucalypts. It all sounded ideal to Nicholls, who says, 'They thrived in poor soils, broke up the iron pan with their roots, enhanced fertility, and attracted native birds to feed on them and disperse the seeds through their droppings.'

Consequently, more than 90 varieties of eucalypt – at least 50,000 trees – were planted at Milnthorpe over the next two decades. Most were propagated from seed on the property. The lush growth beneath the towering exotics gives botanical purists less cause to raise their eyebrows these days, and an ongoing native planting programme is currently underway. Financial assistance has come from many local families. Golden Bay residents and an increasing number of visitors make use of the rock causeway Nicholls built in the early 1980s to gain access to the foreshore at Milnthorpe, as well as the extensive track system that criss-crosses all parts of the property. Wooden boxes posted at the main entry points contain photocopied maps. For such a small block, it is remarkably easy to get lost in here.

Initially, Nicholls' revegetation scheme was called the Milnthorpe Vegetation Project, but that was changed to Milnthorpe Park in around 2000. This was more than a name change though, effectively signifying scenic reserve status for the block. Instead of being administered by DOC, however, the running of the property was handed over to an incorporated society. That unusual move had been proposed in 1997 by former Tasman Mayor Kerry Marshall as the best long-term regional solution for a community asset that has never properly fitted into any conservation estate classification. It has also enabled locals to do things like walk their dogs here, or to name remembrance tracks and put up art installations, none of which you can do in a scenic reserve or on conservation estate land. It was a case of ordinary people taking control of their public space, and it has worked.

For project manager Nicholls, the change of status gave the block of coastal land the protection and recognition it deserved. Even though he is not involved at Milnthorpe these days, the park remains a credit to his creative endurance. He is still a great believer in using hand tools only, especially his razor-sharp slasher, with which he has cut kilometres and kilometres of tracks all around Parapara and Milnthorpe. At all times he has maintained a philosophical approach: 'Walls, ditches, gold workings, the effort that has been put into this land over the years is a monument to heroic endeavour. But in the long term it's basically futile as well. Nature reclaims all as if it never existed. My efforts included. As Shakespeare wrote, "full of sound and fury, signifying nothing".'

CHAPTER 12

CARBON FOOTPRINTS

BY FAR MY BIGGEST FILE of archived material relating to Kahurangi National Park deals with fascinating Whanganui Inlet, and by far the most interesting document I have come across during my research into this area is W.H. Sherwood Roberts' *Nomenclature of Nelson and the West Coast*, published by the *Otago Daily Times* in 1912. The son of an officer in the East India Company, Roberts had emigrated from England to New Zealand in 1855, landing in Nelson on 6 May. Travelling overland to Invercargill, he became a squatter before losing his cattle run two years later under the Land Sales and Leases Ordinance 1856. Subsequent ventures brought him mixed fortunes and he finally settled in Oamaru in 1878, where he became heavily involved in local affairs. He also became well known as a 'literary man', writing his 500-page *History of Oamaru and North Otago* and, later, *Maori Nomenclature*. Drawing on a wide range of life skills, this man's works make top-shelf reference material. In his book *Southland in 1856–57, with a Journey from Nelson to Southland in 1856*, the section titled 'West Whanganui' starts with a general introduction:

> West Whanganui should be Whanganui (big bay or harbour). It is a fine inlet, about seven miles by three when the tide is in, but as most

of it is shallow a large extent is dry ground or mud flat when the tide is out. It has a harbour entrance between two high promontories, with a bar which has only 6ft of water on it at low spring tides.

The account goes on to give the old Māori name of the south headland as Raraha-taua (meaning 'to rumble like a war party'), and says that in the 1850s an old pā (fort) named Onawa-noa (literally, 'the time when the tapu would be removed from him') overlooked the entrance on the north head, which was called Muna-nui-hawata (meaning 'to mutter his great authority'). There is some doubt expressed by the author as to the correctness of this last name, and he refers to 'Halswell's map', which records the north head pā as Pa-raro-pa (meaning 'pā on the north head yonder'). 'Both names may be right,' he comments, 'the latter being the pa and Onawa-noa some other place on the Headland.'

Now comes the strangest observation from Roberts' visit to Whanganui Inlet, on 22 March 1856, when he was wandering along a bed of wave-worn sandstone left dry at low water:

I noticed the perfect impressions of eight naked feet, plainly embedded, like fossils, in the solid sandstone rock, which must have been soft when the humans walked over it. They were a short distance from the Maori Track up the Whanganui brook, and a few chains below high water mark. There are six adult footmarks with narrow heels and wide spread toes, and two child's footmarks, all equally perfect.

What?! Any footprints set in hard sandstone must surely be aeons old, and not something that could even have been achieved in the last few thousand years. My mind boggled when I read this, and I have never read about or spoken to anyone who has heard of these footprints since. Could they have been made in soft mud that later dried out and was mistaken by Roberts for stone bedrock? It seems these footprints might have to remain a mystery.

Footprints of another kind at Whanganui Inlet made the headlines in 2009, when geologist Greg Browne of GNS Science confirmed that he had found 70-million-year-old dinosaur footprints in Late Cretaceous sandstone along the coast here. It made big news as a 'hugely exciting' discovery that was reported both nationally and internationally. These were the very first dinosaur

When Greg Browne of GNS Science announced in 2009 that he had found 70-million-year-old dinosaur footprints in Late Cretaceous sandstone around the shores of Whanganui Inlet, the news was reported internationally as the first dinosaur footprints to be recognised in New Zealand and the first evidence of dinosaurs in the South Island. Some palaeontologists have, however, expressed doubts that the depressions are, in fact, dinosaur footprints.
Photo: Dr Greg Browne

footprints to be recognised in New Zealand, not to mention providing the first evidence of dinosaurs in the South Island.

Out of the find came a two-year touring exhibition, *Dinosaur Footprints: A Story of Discovery*, featuring four re-created footprints in two triangular display modules with in-built lighting and an audiovisual presentation. It visited around ten New Zealand museums, starting in Auckland, and included the Nelson Provincial Museum in July to September 2016. The thousands of local school pupils who went to see the display were no doubt inspired by their first interaction with a dinosaur.

The trouble for many was that these footprints – found at six locations spread over 10 kilometres, with the biggest site containing 20 footprints – don't exactly jump out at you. As anybody who has seen the re-created footprints will attest, they resemble anything but footprints, instead looking more like semi-circular depressions in the rock, up to 60 centimetres across but many measuring just 20 centimetres. Browne postulates that these markings were made by sauropods – long-necked, long-tailed, pillar-legged herbivorous dinosaurs – that were between 2 metres and 6 metres long, and loped around grazing the fringes of the tidal inlet. On the sauropod scale, these Whanganui individuals were small. Indeed, some sauropod species (family Titanosauridae) could reach 40 metres in length and weigh up to 100 tonnes, and were literally the largest animals ever to have roamed the Earth.

Browne is no stranger to Whanganui Inlet. As an oil and gas scientist, he has conducted geological surveys here over repeated visits for more than a decade and is well acquainted with its intricate shorelines. He came across the distinctive depressions in the mid- to late 1990s, and spent years carefully considering all the possible geological and biological explanations for the unusual features, gradually ruling them out one by one. His investigation also included comprehensive comparisons with dinosaur footprints in similar-aged rocks in other parts of the world.

The geologist has said that what made the discovery so special was the unique preservation of the footprints in an environment where they could have been easily destroyed by waves, tide or wind:

> *The footprints, made in soft intertidal beach sands, were preserved when the tide came in and quickly filled the footprints with soft muddy sediment… The preservation of these delicate structures allowed us to work out which way the dinosaurs were walking, which parts were their heel and toe portions, how soft the sediment was when they moved through the area, how fast they were travelling and how heavy they were.*

Browne's three-minute video on YouTube is certainly convincing. But that said, it would be fair to add that some of his own palaeontology colleagues at GNS Science have been guarded in expressing agreement that the depressions are actually dinosaur footprints. Off the record, one commented to me, 'Where are the toes? Why can't we see even slight impressions of the toes?' Browne argues that, based on overseas evidence, sauropods characteristically did not leave clear toe impressions. They were pentadactyls, with five toes, but these were arranged in a tight club-like foot to provide them support in the soft sand and mud environments they grazed in.

Browne's original paper, published in the *New Zealand Journal of Geology and Geophysics* in 2009, is titled 'First New Zealand Record of Probable Dinosaur Footprints from the Late Cretaceous North Cape Formation, Northwest Nelson'. The word *probable* here certainly leaves things a little open.

The abstract goes on to say that the research adds considerably to our knowledge of dinosaurs. Palaeontologists long suspected that dinosaurs were present in ancient New Zealand, but evidence has been slow to surface. Dinosaur bones, mostly vertebrae, have been found at only three locations, in northern Hawke's Bay, Port Waikato and the Chatham Islands. Englishwoman Mary Ann Mantell found the first complete bone recognised as that from a dinosaur, in Sussex, England, in 1822, while Joan Wiffen takes the credit for discovering New Zealand's first dinosaur fossils, 150 years later in 1974.

Many Whanganui Inlet residents found out about Browne's discovery only after being contacted by family members overseas who had read the story online. That the exact locations of the footprints remains a guarded secret, and the stated long-term intention to remove at least some of them for preservation, has possibly not helped make this a discovery that has solicited much local excitement. Rather, it has been treated more as an important national discovery that warrants wider attention – which it has certainly received, especially through the museum exhibition.

Some locals go further and remain positively sceptical about the footprints found on their land, even pointing to the fact that Browne is an oil and gas scientist and his original journal article was not widely peer reviewed by international palaeontologists.

However it all gets dissected, credit must go to Browne for coming up with this interesting and well-researched work. He has certainly enhanced my understanding of ancient Whanganui Inlet. Northwest Nelson was largely submerged under the sea between 70 million and 20 million years ago, and the footprints would have been covered by hundreds of metres of marine sediments. Through the action of plate tectonics about 25 million years ago, New Zealand was then uplifted and northwest Nelson emerged from the sea. During the past 20 million years, the soft overlying sedimentary rock has been eroded away, eventually exposing the footprints. Today, Whanganui Inlet – the second largest inlet in the South Island – largely resembles the landscape

An exposed coal seam at Kaihoka in Whanganui Inlet. Early Māori were known to utilise the bituminous deposits here, while early European mariners diverted into the inlet specially to replenish their coal supplies and fill up with extra to sell off in Wellington.
Photo: Gerard Hindmarsh

through which the dinosaurs wandered 70 million years ago, munching on vegetation very similar to that seen here now. What a stunning thought!

With its narrow entrance and obviously shallow bar, Whanganui Inlet was understandably bypassed by James Cook, who gave the name Cape Farewell to the headland 13 kilometres northwest when he departed New Zealand on 31 March 1770. The Māori name for Cape Farewell was Tau Mauka, which translates as 'dry hill ridge'. The French explorer Jules Dumont d'Urville passed the harbour, too, on 13 January 1827, naming it 'harbour-barred' thanks to its small entrance. His log records the event:

> *Towards 6PM we believed we could see on the coast a vast basin capable of offering a good anchorage, and I had great hope of being able to enter it next morning to examine that part of New Zealand. In consequence, I approached the coast closely, to reconnoitre the place. We*

passed at less than 2 miles; and at that moment M. Gressian mounted on the crosstrees to obtain a more exact view. He assured me that the basin was very extensive, but, unfortunately, communicated with the sea only by a narrow channel, completely barred by breakers. I was consequently obliged to renounce my hopes of entering. We gave it the name of 'harbour-barred'.

Frederick George Moore liked to boast that he was the first Pākehā to call into 'West Whanganui Harbour', a name used until 1910, when it was changed to West Haven or just Whanganui. Moore's was not a planned visit. Almost as soon as he arrived in Port Nicholson (Wellington) from England in 1840, the ambitious settler set off again, sailing out into Cook Strait with the intention of exploring land in Taranaki. Instead, he was blown across the strait and around the top of the South Island by a fierce gale, and desperate for shelter, went for the gap that suddenly appeared in the cliffs south of Farewell Spit. Here, he found himself in a 'good, smooth, landlocked harbour with sufficient water, reasonable holding ground and grand scenery'. Moore took a sample of 'the best coal found in New Zealand', whacking bits off the seams that stuck out of the mudflats like rows of black teeth. But it was his find near the end of a small peninsula jutting out into the inlet that would impress him most. Here he came across a small yet thriving group of Māori, living in one of three settlements in the inlet at that time. According to Moore, not only had they 'built and fortified a sort of pah', but also cultivated the most fantastic gardens, which filled whole clearings in the adjacent bush. This settlement was known as Onawa-noa back then but, as its later European name of Pah Point suggests, the sheer drop to the water here would have made it a perfect place to defend. Moore subsequently enthused that Whanganui Inlet was a place of fertile soils that will 'one day be deemed one of the best ports on the West Coast of the Middle [South] Island'. He later wrote in his journal:

In the waters of the harbour and on the shores of the adjacent coasts there was a plentiful supply of good fish – mussels, pipis, oysters, crayfish, etc. ducks of all sorts abounded while… the forest and bush was full of pigeons, wild pigs, kakas, woodhens and young birds, food everywhere for the simple catching… plenty of edible fern, raupo roots and nikau. With on all sides a charming fairylike landscape of hill and vale clothed in great beauty and profusion peculiar to the more fertile lands of New Zealand. Here Rewi and kind family were face to face with beautiful nature free at the winds, well housed and apparently happy and innocent of the crooked ways of civilization and its luxuries, they had already cultivated a garden and had Indian corn, potatoes, melons of various sorts and some taro.

Despite his claims, Moore was by no means the first Pākehā to come here. Whanganui Inlet was known to European sailors for its coal well before he arrived, and pre-European Māori regularly burnt the bituminous deposits they smacked off with rocks from the sloping seams exposed around the shores of the harbour. Even the earliest commercial coal extracted here was shipped out a good four years before Moore blew in. In 1836, opportunist sealer Richard (Dickie) Barrett sailed his cutter *Harriet* into the inlet, almost certainly during the same expedition on which he entered Big River (see Chapter 7), and got his crew to shovel out some 10 tons, which they loaded onto the little ship for resale in Wellington. A few years later, 50 tons was extracted, and passing steamers began to take coal regularly from Whanganui Inlet – they were literally coals for the taking!

After coal was discovered at Motupipi, residents there petitioned the provincial government to change the name of their Massacre Bay (inspired by the original name of Murderers Bay, given by Abel Tasman in 1642 following his unfortunate meeting with Māori off Wainui Bay) to Coal Bay, later changed again to Golden Bay after the precious metal that inspired the Aorere gold rushes of 1857. Altogether, around 6,900 tons of coal were extracted between 1842 and 1965 from the Motupipi coal seam.

However, by the start of the twentieth century the main extraction of coal in Golden Bay shifted to its western side, where the thicker seams correlated more to the coal measures of the Grey Valley, suggesting a similar classification to that at Brunner. Indeed, the coal found further west was ranked high volatile bituminous C, compared to the inferior sub-bituminous A deposits at Motupipi.

A significant 868,000 tons of coal would be removed from what is geologically known as the Collingwood Coal Field, most of it from three mines at Puponga, in the Onetahua Survey District. These were the main Puponga Mine, worked from 1896 to 1943 and 1953 to 1973; North Cape,

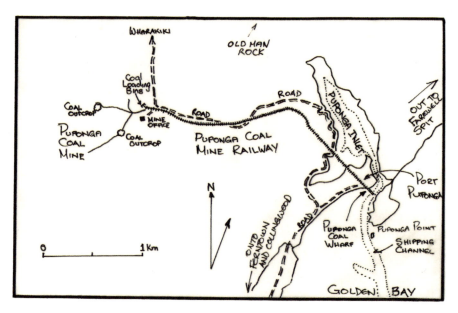

Map showing the second tramway route used by Puponga Coal and Goldmining Company Ltd from 1901. Donald the locomotive relentlessly ploughed the 2.5-kilometre route between the mine and the wharf, filling the settlement and valley with clouds of thick, acrid black smoke.

which operated from 1910 to 1930; and Wharariki, worked from 1947 to 1951. All these mines closed for the reason that they were worked out, but they played a huge part in the development of Puponga, the South Island's northernmost settlement.

In his 2003 book *Coal Mines of Puponga*, Peter Dyer describes the extremely difficult start to mining in this area. Joseph Taylor, strong-willed but unpractical, albeit trained in chemistry, mining and geology, discovered a sizeable outcrop of coal while out exploring at Puponga with his sons. He immediately discussed his find with James Walker, who managed the Ferntown Coal Mine, and together they applied for a 100-acre mining licence to cover all the area around the Puponga outcrop, this being granted in June 1895.

Taylor may have been a lay reader with a licence granted by the Bishop of Nelson, but by all accounts he was an opinionated man and had the knack of getting offside with nearly everyone he dealt with. Apparently, the Collingwood County Council and Collingwood Roads Board did not take kindly to being told what services they should provide, and ended up obstructing Taylor's coal-mining venture whenever they could. Through sheer persistence and stubborn hard-headedness, Taylor managed to overcome his many obstacles to triumph in the coal business.

Puponga's past is well recorded and even considered illustrious by some. Its heyday years were between 1904 and 1943, when the township of 350 – over a hundred families – had a hall, school, general store, bakery and butchery. The latter inspired a 1926 novel, *The Butcher Shop*, by Jean Devanny. Published in London and with a print run of 15,000 copies, it sold well but was banned in New Zealand, Australia, Germany and some states in the US. The reason for its ban in New Zealand was its supposed 'obscenity', in particular 'its frank portrayal of farming conditions which could be detrimental to the Dominion's immigration policy'. But many suspected it was banned in the belief that it might inspire communist worker ideals.

Devanny was born Jane Crook on 7 January 1894 at Ferntown, near Collingwood. She was number eight of the ten children born to Jane Appleyard and her husband, William Crook, a miner. The younger Jane had a distinctly working-class upbringing, and it was a schoolteacher who supported her in changing her name to Jean at an early age, a name she felt expressed her character better. Remembered as very intelligent, musical and always enquiring, she attended school only until age 13, when she had to leave to care for her ailing mother. Four years later, she met Francis Harold (Hal) Devanny at a dance in the Puponga Hall. Hal was also a miner and was already heavily active in union affairs. They married later the same year and went on to have three children, the eldest registered as Harold but always called Karl after Karl Marx, essentially the family hero.

Jean and Hal became increasingly involved in the miners' union and participated in Marxist study circles, the likes of which had strong support in mining communities like Puponga and down the West Coast in the early twentieth century. One firebrand was Donald Macrae, who worked at the Dobson Mine to save up enough to pay for himself to go through medical school. The young man was an inspiring debater and would command the floor at meetings, keeping everyone spellbound with his persuasive arguments for the application of communist ideals. He was only one of many who travelled to spread the cause. As a result, the Devannys came to know many of the leading labour activists of the time, including Bob Semple, Pat Hickey, future Prime Minister Peter Fraser and Harry Holland.

When the mine at Puponga temporarily closed in 1917, the Devannys moved so that Hal could take up another mining job in Fairfield, near Dunedin. Two more hard-working years later, he joined Semple's tunnelling gang, working in the isolated Orongorongo Valley east of Wellington. But while he was away, the youngest Devanny child died after suffering from peritonitis. It was said Jean was grief-stricken by the loss, giving up her music completely and never going back to it.

The family moved to be with Hal in Wellington, where he now earned good wages. Looking to the future, they purchased a boarding house, but neither of them had any business acumen and they made no profit. Jean tried to occupy herself by joining the women's branch of the New Zealand Labour Party, with Fraser, Holland and Walter Nash all encouraging her to become more involved in party politics. But that Labour Party was too right wing for her – she was a communist through and through.

Jean turned to writing in the early 1920s. Her best-known work, *The Butcher Shop*, was based on her experiences at Puponga, where the women would often congregate and chat as they waited to buy their meat at the local butchery. Later, she would describe the novel as 'a terribly confused and foolish book; its meagre merit sincerity, frankness and a certain power of phrasing'. There is little doubt that the theme of the novel reflected Jean's strong belief that married women in a capitalistic society were little more than the economic, social and sexual property of their husbands, and only in a socialist state could they ever find independence. Critics were tough on her work, one writing that the book 'suffered from rhetorical excesses, over-reliance on melodrama and inadequate characterisation'. But Devanny was way ahead of her time, describing contemporary social conditions entirely from a woman's perspective.

Between 1926 and 1932, Jean went on to publish a book of short stories and three more novels. The family shifted to Australia in 1929, and Jean soon became well known as a charismatic speaker at workers' rallies in Sydney. She also ended up having a long-term relationship with J.B. Miles, general secretary of the Communist Party of Australia. Her writing became more prolific in Australia too. She wrote another ten novels and four works of non-fiction, the most significant being *Sugar Heaven* (1936), which focuses on the role of women in a strike in the sugar-cane fields of northern Queensland.

Jean was expelled from the Communist Party in 1941, ostensibly for 'moral degeneracy and disobeying an order', even though the exact details were never made public. She was readmitted in 1944 but continued to be outspoken and controversial, finally resigning in 1950 when the party leadership criticised her portrayal of Australian race relations in her novel *Cindie*.

Jean and Hal eventually settled down in Townsville, where she died on 8 March 1962 of leukaemia. Her autobiography, *Point of Departure*, was finally published in 1986.

Along with Jean's butcher shop, Puponga's coal mines have now shut down. But the settlement's time has come again, albeit in a different sense. Farewell Spit is now recognised as a bird sanctuary of international importance, nothing less than the southern terminal of the East Asian–Australasian flyway, linking New Zealand to Mongolia and Russia as a flying corridor for migratory birds. Nearby Wharariki Beach has also become a star attraction, rated one of the world's top ten beaches and an obligatory bucket list attraction that in summer now pulls some 450 vehicles a day to the enlarged carpark at the end of the road.

There are few indicators of those heyday years now. A small sign on the Wharariki road indicates the blocked-up entrance to the Puponga Coal Mine, and the odd fenced grave marks a mine worker's unfortunate end. The first fatality at the mine happened on the afternoon of Thursday, 26 January 1905. James Muirhead, a 45-year-old native of Scotland, was employed as an underviewer at the mine and that day was working at the bottom of the dip haulage. Five loaded mining tubs were being hauled to the surface when the coupling link between the first and second tubs broke, sending the rear four bins hurtling back down the tunnel. After they smashed through the first of the timber pit props, they collected Muirhead, who simply had nowhere to run. His workmates frantically cleared the debris, only to find his left leg and lower body severely crushed. The mine manager and a doctor were urgently called for as they brought him to the surface. But all the doctor could do when he got there was ease Muirhead's pain. The man was a goner and everyone knew it.

Muirhead's funeral was held two days later. It was attended by more than a hundred miners and by others from all over the district. Some of the miner's last words included a request that he be buried immediately above the accident site. His grave can still be found today, surrounded by a small white picket fence, high above the mine.

Despite local tragedies such as this, there have also been things to celebrate. In 2016, a remarkable restoration put the spotlight on the settlement once again and involved a little train that was once the darling of the area. Forget Thomas the Tank Engine, it was Donald's turn to shine. The quaintly named 0-4-0 hauling loco saw 30 years of service with the Puponga Coal and Goldmining Company Ltd between 1901 and 1930, becoming a Golden Bay icon in the process. At the time of writing, it is in the final stages of restoration in the workshop of the Blenheim Riverside Railway Society (BRRS).

The task has been enormous, a part-by-part rebuild involving the advanced engineering skills of dozens of volunteers and a string of strategic funding and private donations to keep the process going. Until the late 1980s, the 6-ton, 2-foot-gauge tank engine had been in a dilapidated state, lying on its side half-buried in swampy ground outside the mine, where it had been shunted off the track and out of its shed to make way for two new locos. Several major parts were pillaged off it, including all its brass fittings and 64 steel boiler tubes.

In 1989, hearing that steam enthusiasts John Orchard, Cliff White and Murray Guthrie had travelled over from Blenheim to look at the engine, Collingwood Museum Society members dug it out with the intention of putting it on display at the Golden Bay Machinery and Early Settlers Museum in Rockville. But when the enormity of that task hit home, they decided instead that the loco should be given on permanent loan to the BRRS, on the condition that restoration start within two years. It was a pragmatic move, as such a complex rebuild would have been difficult in Golden Bay without access to heavy-duty railway workshops and the expertise that goes with such facilities. In 1990, Donald was loaded onto the truck of Ash Murdoch from the Renwick Lions Club and taken over to Blenheim.

At the time, no one was more chuffed with the restoration idea than Puponga resident Oscar Climo, who had owned the discarded loco for several decades after buying it from former mine owners, Neale and Haddow of Nelson, for £2 10s.

Climo's big childhood memory was riding the little loco down the 1-kilometre line from the mine to the end of the Puponga wharf, where a scow would be waiting to load the coal. Not long before he passed away in 1999, he recalled in

Donald at work. The top photo, taken at the Puponga Coal Mine in 1909, shows Donald about to leave from the overhead coal-loading facility. The loco's shed can be seen on the left and the miners' bathhouse on the right. Bottom photo: some of Donald's work involved transporting materials for the never-ending mine expansion from the Puponga wharf to the pit.
Photos: Nelson Provincial Museum, Tyree Studio Collection, 178138 and 178512.

CARBON FOOTPRINTS

Jeff Robary from the Blenheim Riverside Railway Society inspects the remains of Donald after the locomotive was transported to Blenheim in early 1991. Along with two others, he went on to spend the next two years working on the engine, the first of many dedicated volunteer task groups that have helped with the restoration. Photo: Gary Coburn

an interview with Don Grady that the engine was always everyone's favourite among the hauling locos that worked at Puponga: 'He had a throaty roar when he got going full steam. I can well remember how Donald used to blow big black smoke rings as he chuffed along the track… On a still day the rings just got bigger and bigger as they went into the upper air.'

The restoration of Donald has taken much longer than originally envisaged, mainly because some pretty heavy-duty work had to be completed first. This entailed entirely dismantling the remains and sandblasting every part. The chassis, broken in half at some stage of its working life, had to be rewelded and strengthened. The boiler, beyond repair, was replaced with one found in Greymouth, and a new tube plate was manufactured for it in Christchurch. Then came the massive job of drilling all the new rivet holes and riveting them in a blacksmith's forge. Fitting the 64 steel boiler tubes was another marathon job, as was turning and fitting the new axles, wheels, smoke box and funnel. Two big modifications included adapting the boiler to burn diesel instead of coal, and adding a third trailing axle (changing the loco from a 0-4-0 to a 0-4-2) to reduce track wear at Blenheim.

Donald after its 27-year restoration in Blenheim. It took a while but it was worth it!
Photo: Gary Coburn

Because Donald will soon be used for transporting the public around more than 5 kilometres of BRRS-laid line (Beaver Station–Brayshaw Park–Riverside Park, with a branch line off to the Omaka Heritage Aviation Centre and Omaka Classic Cars), air brakes and lights have had to be fitted too. The entire cab had to be mocked up in plywood so that this could be transported to Cuddon Engineering, where the new steel cab was fitted. In late 2016, John Orchard, general manager at BRRS, said:

> *This last push has been big, probably as much done to it in the last 12 months than the previous 25 years altogether. It's not the only project we are working on, of course. Most Saturdays we have around 22 volunteers turn up, but at least six of them have been working fairly consistently on Donald. Some say it's bad luck to make a finish date. The final paint job is going to cost $3,000 alone.*

Donald's relatively rare provenance alone makes the enormous effort of restoration worthwhile. The engine was originally transported from Glasgow to Wellington on the steamer *Machrihanish* in October 1901, before being reshipped to Port Puponga via Nelson. The grunty little loco was a throw-off from a line built for the Glasgow gasworks from 1896 by the Glasgow Railway Engineering Company. Workers at the Puponga Coal Mine immediately took a shine to it, and soon christened their new little engine Donald. The exact reason for that name may be long forgotten, but you can see why this compact, classic-looking loco has fostered affection over the years.

Donald was powered by two 7-inch bore cylinders, each with a 10-inch stroke, capable of delivering an impressive combined tractive effort of 2,140 pounds at 80 per cent capacity. Its four wheels, each measuring 1 foot 10 inches in diameter, rode along a narrow-gauge track set just 2 feet apart, although the loco was 4 feet 7 inches wide overall. The engine was 13 feet 2½ inches long, and to the top of the cab measured a tad under 8 feet 4 inches. The boiler carried the Marine Department's plate number 3412 and its first recorded inspection was carried out on 21 August 1902.

Donald's rolling stock consisted of two types: side-tipping wagons, each with a 1-ton capacity, for use on the main line between the mine and the wharf; and tippler discharge wagons or mine tubs, each with a 0.5-ton capacity, which brought coal from the working face to screens in the mine itself.

How wonderful it is that Donald will soon be seen chuffing around the BRRS track at Blenheim, not to mention being maintained in a fully equipped 1,500-square-metre workshop with four lines running through it. It's fair to say that there is no chance the engine will ever return to Golden Bay, and that Puponga's darling Donald has well and truly found a new home.

CHAPTER 13

CHASING THE KĀKAHI

MOST NEW ZEALANDERS are dimly aware of our freshwater mussel or kākahi, a dark brown to black bivalve around 60–80 millimetres long that inhabits the muddy margins of many of our watercourses and lakes, but few people know much more than that. The aptly named Sue Clearwater, an ecotoxicologist with the National Institute of Water and Atmospheric Research (NIWA) in Hamilton, has made it her job to wade around New Zealand searching out populations of our endemic mussel. Her passion for the creatures is nothing short of infectious, and my appreciation of kākahi and desire to know more about them has risen dramatically as a result of Clearwater's three research visits to Golden Bay in as many years.

I've long known about the colony of kākahi that exist just beyond the raupō (bulrush) beds at Kaihoka Lakes and at a few other dune lakes within the Puponga Farm Park, and always made a point of wading out and showing them to my kids whenever we visited. Some 12 years ago, Mark Fenwick from NIWA rang to ask me for a few location pointers to help him find some kākahi, so naturally I told him about the lakes. I also took him to a private pond at Onekaka, which I had more recently heard was chocka with mussels.

The freshwater mussels in that man-made pond ended up being a species

Being careful not to raise sediment that will obstruct her vision, Sue Clearwater from NIWA uses her viewing tube to check for kākahi, or freshwater mussels, in the Onekaka River.
Photo: Gerard Hindmarsh

entirely new to science – *Echyridella onekaka* – which was formally identified in a paper by Mark Fenwick and Bruce Marshall to the Malacological Society of Australasia in 2006. Big deal you may think, a new freshwater mussel. But until this point only two species had been identified in New Zealand: the common kākahi (*E. menziesii*), widely distributed through the North and South islands; and the scarcer *E. aucklandica*, restricted to the North Island from Northland to Whanganui. Weirdly, isolated populations of *E. aucklandica* are also found in Lake Wairarapa in southern North Island, and in Lake Hauroko in Fiordland – likely as a result of transplantation by Māori centuries ago.

Clearwater had been initially inspired by freshwater mussel research carried out in the central North Island by Mark James, Dave Roper and Chris Hickey, especially revelations that the bivalves lived for decades yet few juveniles could be found, implying that they might be in decline. But it was the relatively quiet 'discovery' of the Kahurangi kākahi that was the catalyst for Clearwater's

Two juvenile mussels (approximately 0.7 millimetres long) cultured in captivity by NIWA and Landcare Research. The original larval (glochidia) shell (0.23 millimetres long) is still clearly visible by the shell hinge. The cilia-covered foot is protruding from the shell, and the large gill is visible inside, shaped like half a fern leaf. Darker lines inside the shell are the animal's gut. Photo: Dr Sue Clearwater

visit to Golden Bay, and the establishment of her overall goal to understand how taonga (treasured) species such as this can be more effectively restored in our freshwater systems. In Golden Bay, the ecologist has been wading through creeks and lakes, in particular the Onekaka catchment, to establish the exact distribution of the new mussel species. Sophie Allen of the Working Waters Trust and others are pitching in now to add more knowledge.

To look for the bivalves, Clearwater dons her waders and carries an underwater viewer, lugging along notepad, GPS and sample bags. Meticulously, she scours selected creeks to find likely spots to investigate, often based on the observations of farmers and old-timers. She is excited that work carried out by local landowners and biodiversity restoration groups appears to have helped return some of Golden Bay's stream habitats to a condition that favours species such as the freshwater mussel.

*A magnified live common kākahi (*Echyridella menziesii*), looking past the tentacle-like orange papillae edging the inhalent siphon for a peek at the delicate white gill deep inside. A glimpse of the smooth exhalent siphon can be seen to the right, and the dark brown shell is decorated with green algal growths. Rejected algal food clings on to the mussel's mantle in a fuzzy green clump to the left.* Photo: Dr Sue Clearwater

Clearwater readily admits that little is really known about these long-lived creatures (the oldest freshwater mussel found in this country so far was 55 years of age) or what makes them decline or thrive. She explains:

> *It's of concern that only geriatric populations remain in many of our rivers and streams. In some of our shallow nutrient-laden lakes mussels have died out completely, whereas in Lake Taupo and some Rotorua lakes they are still well represented. Just last month, a NIWA team sampled a stream on the outskirts of Auckland that had patches of 2,000 mussels per square metre. I've seen dense populations in the Waikato hydro lakes too. But the younger ones are absent in many locations. Juvenile mussels are very sensitive to contaminants – copper and ammonia, for instance – and the inputs of those pollutants has increased in the past few decades.*

The ecologist is quick to point out that we can't jump to conclusions: 'Worldwide, there are around 850 species of freshwater mussels and we know from overseas research that populations are invariably skewed towards adults. What the juveniles get up to after their larvae stage is still a bit of a mystery, because freshwater mussels have the most an amazing reproduction strategy.'

Unlike marine mussels, which spray their eggs and sperm into the ocean currents for fertilisation, mother kākahi inhale passing sperm through their siphons and protect the fertilised eggs in specialised brood chambers in their gills. When the time comes for the sand-grain-sized larvae (called glochidia) to leave 'home', the mother mussel suddenly lurches to grab the snout of a passing small fish, which it clamps shut for nearly a minute until the fish is 'sedated' by partial suffocation. She then 'sneezes' over the fish, releasing the parasitic larvae while the fish gasps for breath. There is no struggle during the process, which lasts only a minute or so, and finally the dopey-looking fish swims off, with the larvae firmly attached to it.

Admittedly, this is one of the more spectacular methods kākahi use to infest fish with their larvae. The majority of species worldwide – including those in New Zealand – generally appear to broadcast their larvae, possibly using some kind of lure to bring a host fish in close enough for attachment. Clearwater continues:

> *We don't really know what happens to those delicate juvenile kākahi after they drop off their host fish because you never see any. Presumably they live in habitats yet to be discovered. We think they live below the surface of small patches of well-aerated sediments where conditions have to be exactly right – Goldilocks style! Too much silt or too little water flow will probably kill them. The smallest juveniles we come across in decent numbers are perfectly formed young mussels measuring around 15–20 millimetres, and that's not often.*

Also known to Māori as kāeo, ngāeo, waikākahi and ngūpara, freshwater mussels were a valuable food source, easily obtainable when many others were out of season, and were often fed to the infirm, infants and the elderly. Kākahi were also dried and chewed like gum, and some Māori still like to collect these particular mahinga kai (natural resources) to cook up a feed, a skill that requires considerable practice. An early Women's Division cookbook

The camouflaged beauty of decades-old freshwater mussels, embedded in shallow stream beds, is revealed. Freshwater mussels play a non-stop role, day and night, in filtering waterways.
Photo: Dr Sue Clearwater

features a recipe for the shellfish, but any further European culinary mention of them is virtually non-existent. Most reports state that they taste bland or bitter, which probably depends on when and where they are collected. This may have been fortunate for the species, however – being easy to collect and relatively long-lived, they would likely have been overharvested and driven to extinction.

The freshwater mussel's ability to filter-feed is impressive. A 1995 study in South Otago's 118-hectare Lake Tuakitoto, a relatively shallow water body with a mean summer depth of only 0.7 metres, calculated that the resident kākahi population filters the entire volume of water every 32 hours, leading to speculation that the mussels could be used to clean up water bodies polluted with algae and sediment. Other studies also mention turnover times relating to lake volume. Mark James (1987) examined Lake Rotokawau, a small lake in the Rotorua region whose depth reaches 74 metres. The mussels here form a 'bathtub ring' around the lake at a depth of 2–10 metres and are extremely dense in places, reaching around 800 per square metre. In his summary, James calculated that it would take the mussel population in Lake Rotokawau around six months to clear approximately half of the epilimnion (inshore water volume) where they are located. So the impact of mussels in larger, deeper lakes is quite different from those in shallower bodies of water, but the fact remains that they are likely to change water quality significantly in their local environment, especially when their densities are high and water movement is minimal. Another report, written by Ngaire Phillips in 2007, also gives a review of the idea of biomanipulation using mussels. The trouble is, anecdotal evidence is pointing to a gradual decline in freshwater mussel numbers, so finding enough of the bivalves to do the clean-up job may be difficult. Concludes Clearwater:

> *The important thing now is finding out more about kākahi so we can develop our conservation strategy. For example, we are already making good progress on growing thousands of juvenile mussels, which may soon make them available for restocking and restoration efforts without compromising source populations. They are an integral part of our freshwater ecosystems; it'd be a real tragedy to lose them.*

Water-clarifying freshwater mussels? Add them to the list of Kahurangi wonders.

CHAPTER 14

ROARING LION GOLD

BEFORE SETTING UP WAIWERA ESTATE winery at Clifton in Golden Bay, Dave Heraud was a successful sales adviser for a plastics extrusion company in Wellington. The end of his marriage in the early 1980s was the catalyst for the change, which he admits also gave him the perfect opportunity to focus on catching up on some wilderness adventures. One of his highlights was climbing Aoraki/Mt Cook, but a close second was when he spent six weeks with his good tramping mate Michael Clark in a well-equipped tent camp up the remote Roaring Lion River.

This 50-kilometre-long river drains slightly over 1,000 square kilometres of Kahurangi's remote interior. It starts as a trickle in the Tasman Mountains, to the east of Centre Mountain, gradually turning southwest before eventually tumbling into the mighty Karamea River at the Earthquakes Lakes. Fourteen sizeable tributaries flow into the Roaring Lion, each adding to the noisy torrent that gives the river its name.

It took two helicopter flights to ferry Heraud and Clark in with everything they needed for the duration of their trip. Along with their food, stashed into two 44-gallon drums, they brought all the gear and tools they needed to set up a spacious fly camp, including crosscut saw, axes, wedges, hammer and shovels. Heraud's .308 Mauser rifle was loaded, along with some extra ammo, and they had a fishing rod each and several books on trout angling. They also brought along a small alloy gold sluice and gold pans – after all, there's nothing quite like a bit of gold fossicking to fill out the long days.

In fact, one of the aims of the trip was to come back with some Roaring Lion gold. Heraud had done his homework, researching the history of the area and speaking to others who had gone up there. He'd also been through the entire text of Jim Henderson's book about Henry and Annie Chaffey, *The Exiles of Asbestos Cottage*, which had come out a few years before. In particular, he was interested in any mention of Henry's gold fossicking up the Roaring Lion, noting that he seemed to base his operation there around the point where Discovery Creek flows into the main river, but also spent time up Cavern Creek. Heraud noticed from the accounts that whenever Chaffey came back from the Roaring Lion he wasted no time getting down to Motueka to sell his gold and get drunk on some of the proceeds. For Heraud, it was a goldminer's giveaway – Chaffey had regularly found gold up the Roaring Lion, and now he and Clark were heading there four decades later to find some too.

Chaffey hadn't been the only miner up here of course. The first track into the Karamea catchment was put in around 1867, spurring a short-lived gold rush in the Roaring Lion Valley after good 'colours' were found up a tributary that was promptly called Discovery Creek. At its height, up to 200 miners were said to have tried their luck up here.

The two hopeful modern prospectors were deposited with all their gear on a wide gravel beach around three-quarters of the way down the river and about 600 metres from its confluence with Discovery Creek. After the chopper had gone, they hauled all their gear onto a lightly wooded terrace just above the flood zone on the eastern side of the river and set up their camp among the scattering of trees.

Having the luxury of weeks of camping in one place gave the pair plenty of time to explore. Each day they travelled further and further from their camp on specific missions, sluicing and panning as they went.

More exciting than finding a few colours in their pans was their rediscovery of Chaffey's permanent camp near Discovery Creek. What was left of his crude sapling-framed one-bunk hut had fallen over, but there was plenty of stuff scattered around outside to tell the story. Adjustable billy hooks still hung

In the 1980s, Dave Heraud and Michael Clark were flown with all their gear by helicopter into the catchment of the Roaring Lion, where they set up camp for six weeks. Ostensibly, the purpose of their trip was goldmining, and the pair are seen here fossicking in the main river a few days after their arrival. But the highlight of their trip turned out to be the discovery of Henry Chaffey's Roaring Lion camp near the river's confluence with Discovery Creek.
Photo: Dave Heraud

from the campfire, which had an oversize camp oven sitting on it, ready to go. Carrying the heavy cast-iron oven in all the way from the Cobb would have been nothing for Chaffey – he was a veritable human packhorse. Heraud and Clark also found stashed some lengths of tin drainpipe with glass at either end, an old miner's trick for looking into deeper parts of a river for signs of glittering gold. Nearby was some rolled-up cable, which they suspected Chaffey had used for a flying fox to get over the river to Cavern Creek, another of his favourite prospecting spots. Everything was covered in forest litter, but Heraud and Clark were certain the camp was Chaffey's. No one else had spent any great length of time up there in recent decades, and the pair would have heard about it if they had. Anyway, there were no plastic or polythene remains to be seen. The camp wasn't just a 'oncer'; it had a more permanent feel, as if someone had come and gone regularly.

Heraud and Clark hadn't packed a camp oven because of the weight factor, so they 'borrowed' Chaffey's, hauling it back down to their camp to cook everything from cherry pie to goat stew. It was the height of the helicopter hunting era in this great wilderness, and the two men never saw a deer the whole time they were there – not even on a three-day excursion they undertook from Discovery Creek to Centre Mountain. But there were plenty of goats, and Heraud would bag one every so often to supplement their supplies. The wilderness was heaven for the two men.

Without a doubt, Henry and Annie Chaffey also cherished their seclusion in the years they lived up the Cobb. One might think it was an idyllic life, but those who knew the pair describe their relationship as a good-natured bickering that went on every day they were together. Little wonder then that Henry would go off fossicking for gold up in the Roaring Lion catchment, a two-day grunt from the couple's Asbestos Cottage home.

Henry's longest stint mining by himself up the Roaring Lion lasted two months. He and Annie would keep in touch by writing notes to each other, putting them in a sock tied to their dog's collar, and telling it to 'Take it to Dad' or 'Take it to Mum' depending on whose turn it was to reply. The dog would run off in the morning and deliver the note the same day, the fleet-footed creature having no trouble negotiating its way through the wilderness. Henry was over in the Roaring Lion and Annie was by herself at Asbestos Cottage when the cataclysmic 7.8-magnitude Murchison earthquake hit at 10.17AM on 17 June 1929. Annie watched in horror as the hills all about seemed to tumble, the valleys roared and the ground heaved in solid waves. Trees thrashed around in a violent state of agony, their branches crashing to the ground. In the hut, many of Annie's precious preserves and jams were smashed.

Henry's powers of observation were astounding. Many people who met him have testified to his intuitive approach to prospecting, saying it was like he could almost see what lay beneath the earth. But it was his musings on nature in the late 1930s and into the 1940s that earned him the byline 'The Hermit of Mt Arthur' in his regular contributions to 'Nature Notes', a syndicated column that ran in several weekend newspapers throughout the country. As part of another series of articles called 'Jagged Peaks – Exhilarating and Beautiful Sights', a piece headed 'The Windless Valley of the Roaring Lion' was published in the *Star-Times* on 28 July 1938. In it, Chaffey introduces the extensive valley as one that has never been fully explored, 'in fact, it has not been seen by many persons'.

Chaffey goes on to outline how he first began cutting his trail through to the Roaring Lion in 1923, starting up Chaffey Stream, a branch of the Cobb River, and crossing over 'Anderson Pass' at 1,400 metres, after which the descent to the river took him around three hours. He alludes to a considerable amount of prospecting over an area of 75–100 square kilometres, where he identified several gold-bearing reefs as well as outcrops of other minerals, including 'molybdenite, wolfram [sic] and tatanium [sic] in an albite feldspar formation'. But it was the gold that was his primary focus, because only that would give him a fairly immediate return: 'Some of the 60 to 80 feet terraces of debris carry alluvial gold, perhaps in sufficient quantity for large scale operations.'

Postulating about the economic advantage of gold mining in the area, Chaffey poured forth about how rapidly the national wealth could be advanced, including a saving of taxation from other directions. He cited how money continued to pour into Australia, chiefly from England and America, to help with the development of 'new propositions', and how all that would serve to transform our trans-Tasman neighbour into a far richer country than us. However you think about it, Chaffey was a visionary here, for Australia's early investment in extracting minerals did just that.

Although Chaffey advocated that the Roaring Lion's mineral wealth was of great consequence, a prelude to permanent production there and in the surrounding mountains, he does go on to describe the alluring valley as it was when he visited. And this description still fits today:

> *The floor of the valley at the lower end would be about 800 feet above sea level, and rises only in gentle slope to the head of the main stream. Many large fertile flats and terraces are in evidence, especially for the first 7 or 8 miles from the mouth, and the ground is covered with large ferns of many varieties. The forest is composed of rimu, matai, hinau and the various species of beech; the soil is rich in potash mica.*

Chaffey's natural inquisitiveness comes out in his writing, and he talks about how there were many exhilarating and beautiful sights to enjoy en route from the Cobb Valley, notably an ascent of Mt Ranolf on the right side of Anderson Pass, which can be completed in around an hour: 'As this mountain stands out by itself and clear of any adjacent mountains, the finest panoramic view, north, south, east and west, can be obtained.'

Dave Heraud shows off items from Chaffey's camp, including his camp oven and prospecting pick, enamel bowls and basins, a coil of wire rope, and a section of drainpipe (lower right) with glass at one end that Chaffey used to spot gold in the deeper pools. Photo: Dave Heraud

He refers to the jagged peaks of the Dragons Teeth, to the north, as the 'Super-Remarkables'. They are indeed a sight worth seeing, especially when the sun is setting behind them: 'A splendid view can be obtained from my old camp on the edge of the bush below Mt Ranolf.' More often than not, this camp was Chaffey's pitching spot on the two-day haul to and from Asbestos Cottage.

Right up until the 1980s, there was an identifiable beech tree at the edge of the bushline on the Cobb side below Anderson Pass, directly above Chaffey Stream. It was identifiable because it featured a rudimentary map carved by Chaffey with his knife, showing his route over and down into the Roaring Lion. The tree is still there, but the map is no longer obvious, the bark no doubt having grown over it with time.

Trampers still take a similar route today to get into the Roaring Lion from the Cobb Valley, bush-bashing up Chaffey Stream, sidling around Mt Ranolf and then heading down the obvious Kimbell Spur to end up in the Roaring Lion. The elevation at the start, where Chaffey Stream flows into the Cobb River, is around 900 metres, whereas the exit point on the Roaring Lion River is only at 400 metres, so the return involves a strenuous eight-hour climb back over.

In his 'Jagged Peaks' article, Chaffey says that two huts had been built up the Roaring Lion, one by him and another by some friends of his. That other hut and its position have long been forgotten. From his camp, Chaffey cut a trail up to the tops on the western side of the river, from where it was possible to look over to the Ugly River catchment and across the many granite peaks surrounding it – 'all unexplored country'.

Sitting on his own by the campfire up the Roaring Lion gave Henry much cause for reflection:

> *In this wonderful region where, far from the insane desire and race for wealth, 'meditation may think the hours down to moments, and the heart may give a useful lesson to the head', as Cowper says any intelligent individual with equanimity divest himself of vanity – by gaining understanding, and it would be unnecessary 'to ask for saintly souls to guide him on his way, or male and female devilkins to lead his steps astray', as Rudyard Kipling puts it.*
>
> *Well, well! Perhaps some day in the not too distant future some enterprising people may seek to open up this region. Or perhaps, some Government may become curious to its possibilities.*

In September 1942, Chaffey made a point of adding an 'Addendum' comment to his 'Jagged Peaks' series, inspired by the changing circumstances brought about by the war:

> *Transport by plane will be simple and cheap after the war – our airmen will not be absorbed into other industries. The mountains and valleys of New Zealand, which are one sixth of the area, are due for exploitation. Tracks should be made and not roads; landing-grounds established, development and production with transport by air will follow. It will be a wise policy to give our returning men the chance to follow their own inclinations.*

Those inclinations would not so much be taken up by returned servicemen as by foreign mining companies, which came to northwest Nelson to carry out 'systematic reconnaissance exploration', mainly for base minerals, in the late 1960s and early 1970s. Using the latest geotechnical methods, around 20 overseas companies were active in the area around this time, including Sarco, Amoco, Anglo American, British Petroleum, BHP and Kennecott. The rising price of gold in the late 1970s and early 1980s changed the focus towards exploration for the precious metal, bringing in CRA Exploration, which made prospecting forays into the Roaring Lion. But it would be the gold deposits discovered at Sams Creek off the upper Takaka Valley that was their eventual area of focus.

Many of the gold companies scaled down their operations in the early 1980s, leaving remote valleys like the Roaring Lion open once again to hopeful amateurs like Dave Heraud and Michael Clark. Those two never came out rich, of course, but they did have a great time trying, and were particularly pleased to find Chaffey's camp. At the end of their trip, the two men stashed all their gear in a hollow tree, including Chaffey's cast-iron camp oven, and so needed only one helicopter trip for the journey back out. Heraud would go back another three times in all, but he made the mistake after the first trip of telling some hunting mates where the gear was stashed. 'That was a mistake because that was the end of it, Henry's camp oven as well. All gone.'

Today, the sprawling Roaring Lion catchment makes up around a tenth of the Tasman Wilderness Area, which was gazetted in 1988. This whole area – 87,000 hectares of it, and originally advocated by the Maruia Society – was chosen because it had largely escaped the ravages of civilisation, being just too isolated for all but the most rugged of individuals. You still won't find any tracks or routes marked on maps of the area – bar one, the old McNabb Track, which leads up Bellbird Ridge from Heaphy Hut to the Gunner Downs, and permitted only because it existed well before the wilderness designation.

Landing helicopters was also banned as part of the wilderness area designation, leaving the Roaring Lion the preserve of hardy trampers and anglers. The river is well known for its numerous trout, mostly within the 1.5–2.5-kilogram range, although a few trophy-sized giants do exist in the long, powerful glides, rapids and deep pools. Wet flies are particularly effective here, especially when fishing the evening rise. Some anglers go to huge lengths to get to the Roaring Lion in order to experience its uniquely remote challenges.

Around a dozen international mining companies became active prospectors in the North-West Nelson Forest Park in the late 1960s and 1970s. CRA Exploration prospected the vast Roaring Lion catchment for gold, but finally settled on Sams Creek, where they set up this drill rig.
Photo: Graham Drummond

Well-known local trout fishing guide Tony Entwhistle once took a Japanese client in by helicopter as far as the top of Kakapo Spur – as close as they could get to the wilderness area – then they bush-bashed their way down to the Roaring Lion, coming out at Cub Stream after a 1½-day struggle. As he recalls, 'It was one of the hardest trips I ever took.'

Carl Walrond worked for Fish & Game in the early 1990s, when one of his jobs was to survey the trout population up the Roaring Lion. One year, a beech mast had led to the forest being overrun with mice, and he witnessed the unusual sight of trout patrolling the river to snatch any young mice that fell off the overhanging tree branches. One trout he cut open had two dozen young mice in its belly. Another interesting observation Walrond made was that there were lots of weka in the Roaring Lion, but it wasn't until he crossed over into the catchment of the Ugly River that he saw kiwi.

Anyone who makes it into the remarkable and remote Roaring Lion catchment can claim to have had an adventure indeed – a true wilderness experience.

CHAPTER 15

MODERN CONTROVERSY

THE LAND MAY BE ANCIENT, but Kahurangi National Park is essentially a modern concept. The boundaries of New Zealand's 14th national park and our second largest (after Fiordland) were drawn up in 1994 after 14 months of often testy consultations. Objections to 'locking up' the land came from both individuals and wider business interests. In the end, some 60 separate blocks of land, totalling 20,000 hectares and not including the Buller Coalfield, had to be excluded to allow for existing uses around the edge of the park. In dribs and drabs, these historical titles – which were put into the limbo of conservation land status – are slowly being cleared up and added to the park. Past Conservation Ministers have all taken credit when these additions periodically occur, but each has been a long time in the process.

Existing uses included grazing leases, the ElectroCorp (now Trustpower) hydroelectricity operation up the Cobb, *Sphagnum*-moss-gathering operations and small mining claims. Farewell Spit was excluded because it was already well protected and contiguous with the rest of the park.

Despite the well-publicised opposition to the gazetting of Kahurangi National Park, support was overwhelming, with 80 per cent of submissions in favour. The fact that most supporters came from the top half of the North Island irked many West Coasters, who thought their submissions should count for more than those of people who lived far away and wouldn't be so affected by the changes. In the end, nationwide democracy won, and the North-West Nelson Forest Park was no more.

The dissatisfaction around the process with which Kahurangi was created ended up being documented in several reports and theses. Canterbury University Master's student Simon Prowie was the first, in 1997, to investigate the environmental politics involved in the set-up that led to the creation of the national park. This included claims that some stakeholder groups had manipulated the consultation process by organising bulk submission forms. Prowie's study was followed in 1999 by that of Nicholas Taylor, Janet Gough, Julie Warren and Wayne McClintock, who conducted a socioeconomic assessment of the park three years after it was gazetted. Issues identified included the dissatisfaction of locals over the upkeep of tracks and huts, and concerns about the future viability of extractive industries that utilise natural resources. Other issues involved concessions, roads, helicopter access, hunting, mountain bikes, pests and weeds, poison drops, mining, forestry, water resources, eeling and gathering *Sphagnum* moss. It's a fact of life in our modern, overcrowded world that the stakeholders in our public lands are many and often in conflict.

Another report, by J. Buchler in 2000, analysed the results of a quantitative survey of Karamea residents on their perceptions of the impact of Kahurangi on their lives. Interestingly, it turned out that many of those who took part felt they hadn't been greatly affected by the establishment of the park, although many still harboured concerns about how the consultative process had been carried out. Locals perceived that visitor numbers were rising, but to them the benefit was not especially attributable to the park because, apart from the Heaphy Track, it lacked star attractions, needed to develop a national or international reputation.

All these reports were incorporated into one encompassing look at the subject put out by Lincoln University in 2004, titled 'Love They Neighbour? The Relationship Between Kahurangi National Park and the Border Communities of Karamea and Golden Bay, New Zealand' and written by Julia McCleave, Kay Booth and Stephen Espiner. Together, the studies pinpoint the issues and pitfalls associated with the creation of Kahurangi National Park, allowing more equitable consultation processes to be carried out in similar cases in

The Old Ghost Road (OGR) is New Zealand's only officially recognised cycle track that traverses subalpine terrain. Some conservationists took exception to the scarring caused by cutting the high-level route around the previously virgin Lyell Range, but ironically that route was chosen after Forest & Bird objected to the original plans to track the OGR through the Mokihinui Forks Ecological Area. Photo: Gerard Hindmarsh

the future, especially when dealing with the 'locking up' of public lands. The subject is complex and not within the scope of a book like this, but one thing is certain: controversy will continue no matter what.

One recent controversy on conservation land adjoining Kahurangi National Park involved the creation of the longest track through a protected area in this country for decades. This was the 80-kilometre-long Old Ghost Road (**OGR**), a mountainbike and tramping track connecting the Lyell historic area, on the Buller River, with Seddonville, in the lower reaches of the Mokihinui River north of Westport. When I first visited in March 2013, it had taken advance work crews three weather-thwarted attempts to finalise the 'marked route' through the last and most difficult 21-kilometre-long middle section between 'Ghost Lake' and Goat Creek, joining the two already completed sections of the track, totalling 59 kilometres, that had already been put in

A mountainbiker's dream – the OGR loses 800 metres in altitude as it heads down from the Lyell Range towards the Mokihinui River. Photo: Gerard Hindmarsh

from both ends. These were not hand-cut paths created with a slasher and shovel – although plenty of arm-wielding grunt was involved – but a modernly executed road-building project, the width of the road being that of a narrow-tracked digger aided by plenty of explosives and shovel work.

There were final delays, including clearing up significant rockfall hazards alongside the Mokihinui River, but finally it all came together. The track was upgraded to intermediate mountainbiker standard (grade 4), with the middle, mostly forested, section being suited to more advanced riders only. A mountainbike track it may be, but a doddle it surely isn't. Officially opened for business on 15 December 2015, the OGR has attracted many rave reviews from users ever since.

Without a doubt, New Zealand's latest and longest single multi-use track was a truly massive project, and is a credit to those who undertook such a venture in wet, dripping and often exposed wilderness conditions. Roughly equivalent in length to the Heaphy Track, it was four years in the making. The massive volunteer contribution alone has been quantified succinctly as

415 locals giving 28,000 hours of time. The final cost came in at $5.9 million, although that doesn't take into account the ongoing expense of maintaining the track in such a high-rainfall environment. To make a whole trail like this in one go is unique in New Zealand. Admittedly, around half of its length is an upgrade, but tracks invariably come about in a more organic fashion, as extensions and improvements of existing historical thoroughfares.

Starting at the Lyell historic area campground, the benched, beech-lined first section follows 17 kilometres of the Old Dray Road to Lyell Saddle Hut (11 bunks, altitude 885 metres), the first of four new huts built along the route. All the materials for these shelters came from Solid Energy (before its great demise), at a cost of around $347,000. Cycle Trail funding is for track formation only, not huts, so additional sponsors were needed for these amenities.

You don't need to imagine the past up here, as the trail is a veritable outdoor mining museum. Historical artefacts litter the side of the track – a two-man crosscut saw, an iron kettle and even an old anvil can still be spied. It took me a few seconds to figure out that the mousetraps screwed vertically to the end of every bunk in Lyell Saddle Hut were there not to catch climbing rodents, but to conveniently display your hut ticket.

From Lyell Saddle, the track climbs gently through another 6 kilometres of mountain beech and neinei (*Dracopyllum* spp.) forest, before breaking out onto the splendid tussock slopes of the Lyell Range. While both ends of the OGR have made use of old dray roads and bridges (indeed, four mining settlements once existed along these routes), the middle section was carved through untouched wilderness. It's not the first time it's been eyed up though: an 1870s map reveals a reconnaissance survey for a Lyell–Mokihinui road to connect the two promising goldfields.

To be fair, the Old Ghost Road name is a modern marketing invention, fancifully referring to the ghosts of miners past, which this pathway supposedly evokes. As opponents to the track have pointed out though, the mining settlements and tent camps were only situated at either end. The new Ghost Lake Hut sits atop a crag overlooking an idyllic and previously unnamed mountain tarn, now dubbed Ghost Lake. The name also evokes another Ghost Lake, the much larger one that was to be made by the creation of the Mokihinui hydro dam, proposed by Meridian Energy but canned in 2012.

This 85-metre-high dam and external-link generating plant, estimated to cost $250 million, would have drowned 330 hectares of forest, river terraces and the river gorge itself, creating a 14-kilometre-long finger lake back up the valley. Opposition from conservation groups was immediate, and even the normally conservative Buller District Council ended up objecting to the proposal, saying that the size of the dam did not even comply with its district plan. They went on to point out that the dam would destroy forest and vegetation, alter a special landscape, and could increase coastline and riverbank erosion downstream. Some species, including blue duck, might not survive the loss of their habitat, and changes to river flow would almost certainly disrupt whitebait catches downstream. The development would also damage the proposed site's historic values, and affect long-standing recreational activities. In addition, the council said Meridian had not proposed enough mitigation, focusing mainly on the short-term impact of construction and not enough on the radical long-term changes to the Mokihinui area. The West Coast Regional Council backed up their Buller colleagues, saying the dam and its associated infrastructure were entirely inappropriate for the area. The plan was nothing short of madness – Mokihinui madness.

From the new Ghost Lake, unspoilt views stretch around in all directions from the OGR, New Zealand's only subalpine mountainbike track. Rocky Tor (1,456 metres) now has a metre-wide track gouged around its imposing summit, thanks to small but liberally applied doses of gelignite, or 'rock solvent' as the track-making crews I came across affectionately called it. But the unspoilt views are only one way, detractors say. Up on the Thousand Acres Plateau, the wilderness panoramas are no more – the gougings along the Lyell Range are highly noticeable from here and will be for years to come. Ironically, it was Forest & Bird objections to the low-level route that forced the track-builders to change their plans and reroute around the tops.

From Ghost Lake Hut, the new track loses more than 800 metres of altitude in the next 9 kilometres to reach the north branch of Stern Creek. Two lots of rock protection have already been deposited in front of the new hut here to stop floods eroding any more of the bank. It may be nearly 90 years since the big Murchison shake devastated this wilderness, but the earthquake country hereabouts is still spooky to traverse and the damage wrought by nature puts into perspective the piddling effects of man. The open meadows are still littered with debris and jagged house-sized rocks tossed down from the surrounding mountaintops. It is both humbling and a relief to be past the worst of it.

At some unnamed twin lakes, the newly marked track switches back into climb mode to reach the saddle that leads over to Goat Creek. DOC's four-bunk Goat Creek Hut was the first ever in New Zealand to have its materials bundled up and air-dropped by a fixed-wing plane. Many of the bundles broke on impact, and the hut today still reflects how the original builders were forced to cobble together the damaged timbers as best they could. An upgrade to original Forest Service specifications is eventually planned, and the shelter will stay in DOC ownership and remain free to the public as a backcountry hut.

The massive podocarp forest of mataī, rimu and kahikatea in the ecological area along the south branch of the Mokihinui River makes for enchanted walking. Many of the trees have trunk diameters greater than a metre, with more than a few exceeding 1.5 metres. At one point the track weaves around the 'Resurgence', a sizeable opalescent spring just off the river. Eventually, the valley widens into the massive open area around Mokihinui Forks, where the north and south branches converge into one mighty grade 4 raftable river. When I passed through here last, there had been a late-summer population explosion of native bumblebees, which were seemingly as numerous as the sandflies!

This majestically expansive forks area was once grazed, hence all the blackberry, gorse and thistle that took off here. More recently, the tail of a Cessna 185 plane used to protrude occasionally like an aluminium tombstone from the gravel flats here. The plane, loaded with eels, crash-landed after being struck by a downdraft on take-off. As it was being dug out, heavy rain started to fall and the aircraft ended up covered in gravel. A long succession of venison hunters, possumers and eelers long used this stretch of pebbly riverbank as an airstrip. One possumer up here told me that years ago he'd bagged an astounding 25,000 pelts from the surrounding backcountry and flown them all out.

Sitting on an elevated toe of land overlooking these expansive gravel flats is Mokihinui Forks Hut, enlarged from six to ten bunks by the OGR team. Once a public hut, it is now part of the OGR network under a management

Citing safety concerns, DOC authorised the OGR track crew working at Mokihinui Forks in mid-2012 to cut down the 60-metre-high kahikatea growing behind the recently enlarged hut there. The forest giant had towered over the surrounding forest and was a marker for passing travellers. More than 20 people attended the tree's 'tangi', held around its sawn-off stump over the weekend of 6–7 April 2013. Photo: Gerard Hindmarsh

agreement with DOC. This arrangement – part of the department's 'Developing new partnerships' strategy – allows DOC backcountry hut passes to be used at the hut as it has fewer amenities, notably no gas burners for cooking.

In mid-2012, DOC authorised the OGR work gang based at Mokihinui Forks to cut down a towering 60-metre-tall kahikatea that stood triumphantly beside the hut, citing safety concerns over the tree's proximity to the small rebuild extension and potential wind-throw from boughs overhanging it. It was a massive tree, dominating the forest for acres around, a natural marker to the hut and providing protection from bad weather. When I heard about the plan, I couldn't help but think of Max Polglaze dealing to that big red beech towering over Crow Hut (see Chapter 9), but those were very different days and public perceptions have changed.

The felling of the kahikatea by Mokihinui Forks Hut, smack bang in the middle of the ecological area, proved a lightning rod, attracting the ire of conservationists, local iwi, veteran trampers and even an old venison hunter who had spent years in the area. It culminated in a symbolic tangi (funeral) for the tree over the weekend of 6–7 April 2013, attended by 20 people. DOC did later issue a statement saying that they had invested some $75,000 in transforming the 1960s forestry hut, and that moving it would have been 'phenomenally expensive' in such a constrained site. For them, removing a tree that posed a risk to the public was standard operating procedure.

The Mokihinui is the West Coast's third-largest river. At the forks it gathers all its water to begin a determined charge down the gorge, pausing in huge elongated, opalescent pools along the way. The three 'Suicide Slips' along here, brought down during and since the 1929 earthquake, once made this section especially hard to traverse. Indeed, two crosses at the start of the track at the Seddonville end remember 23-year-old James Russell and his brother David (12th Reinforcements Canterbury Infantry), who were crushed here along with their packhorses by the earthquake. Now those slips are traversed with impressive suspension bridges, which were flown in and then assembled and bolted to the bedrock. A boulder-strewn side creek further down the gorge has also been bridged.

I felt relieved to get beyond the slips and make the new Specimen Point Hut, but found it locked. I heard later that the OGR work crew stored their explosives inside. I carried on, weary now. Slowly, the hills become lower and open sky appeared ahead, and I knew I was nearly out at last.

Ever since the disastrous 1929 Murchison earthquake, access up the Mokihinui River has been restricted by the 'Suicide Slips'. As part of the OGR project, steel bridges bolted to bedrock now allow trampers and cyclists an easy passage. Photo: Gerard Hindmarsh

The process of how the OGR came to be is interesting, and was a new one for backcountry New Zealand. The entire route beyond the Mokihinui Forks, which crosses a large swathe of previously pristine wilderness forming part of the Mokihinui Forks Ecological Area, was originally included as part of the New Zealand Cycleway (later Cycle Trail) project, a 2009 joint National/Greens initiative pushed by Prime Minister and Tourism Minister John Key. Initially intended as a continuous concrete strip running the full length of the country, the thoroughly impractical idea of a single cycleway was soon modified in favour of developing 'promising individual links through scenic areas'. Key dubbed these 'Great Rides', alluding to New Zealand's Great Walks system of tramping and hiking tracks.

The eight-person Mokihinui–Lyell Backcountry Trust (MLBT) was the charitable community trust formed to take responsibility for the OGR under an agreement with DOC. It was an ambitious project for its members, who are mostly local businesspeople based at either end of the track. Their efforts go back to around 2006, when their initial search phase was funded by Meridian Energy, who supported the investigation of recreation opportunities in the area as part of their mitigation process for the proposed Mokihinui Dam. Encouraged by the prospect of development and seed money, the MLBT presented their ideas to the public at the Westport Motor Hotel in July 2008, later applying to the Ministry of Economic Development (MED) for approval and funding under the Cycleway project. They were granted $2.15 million under the scheme, and received another $750,000 from Development West Coast, $250,000 from Buller District Council, $43,000 from the Gough Group and $41,500 from Walking Access Aotearoa.

Without a doubt, the project solicited huge local support, as evidenced by all the volunteer labour and the significant regional funding. But late in 2014, as the work was progressing, some conservationists started crying foul, calling the project 'The Ghastly' and complaining of excessive tree felling and slope debris, along with degraded mountain landscapes. They questioned the trust's arrangement with the MED, which they claimed had overridden DOC's conservation management strategy (CMS) for the area. This concern was originally aired by the West Coast Tai Poutini Conservation Board chairperson in 2011 in comments that were later notably rescinded from the record. The OGR became a touchy subject on the upper West Coast for sure.

DOC's West Coast managers stayed staunch supporters of the OGR, saying that the track was all contained within the Kawatiri Place conservation block. This 68,000-hectare chunk was originally left out of Kahurangi National Park pending assessment of its hydro potential, a plan first initiated by the Ministry of Works back in the 1970s and later reactivated by Meridian Energy. Said DOC's Westport area manager Bob Dickson, 'Our priorities now are not only to encourage people into the backcountry but to generate income for remote communities.' Once again, DOC's position was in line with its new 'Conservation for prosperity' slogan.

'Control where the water goes' was the advice of early track-builders. That meant laying down a corduroy of cut vegetation, covering it with water-table diggings and rounding it off with gravel. Inclines were kept at 4 degrees or less, so people and horses could maintain a steady pace. Today, methods have changed somewhat. Three blasts on an air horn warned me of another imminent blast as I made my way down the Mokihinui. I took cover behind

Two lone crosses at Welcome Creek at the start of the track leading up the Mokihinui River remembers father and son team, David and James Russell, who were up in the backcountry here when the 7.8-magnitude Murchison earthquake struck at 10.17AM on 17 June 1929. No sign of them, their gear or their packhorses was ever found, likely buried under one of the massive landslides that crashed down from the mountains that day. Photo: Gerard Hindmarsh

a huge rock bluff and waited. Boom! The valley rattled and shook, then returned to a numb sort of silence. I met a track gang and we stopped and chatted. They were proud of their work, without a doubt.

The last person I met in this wilderness was Bill Milligan of Westport, in a hard hat and carrying a big jerry tin of petrol. He was foreman of the crew who were putting the last touches to the revamped track down the true left bank of the Mokihinui. At age 65 and just about due to retire from a lifetime of such work, this was Milligan's last big job and definitely his most satisfying: 'Biggest sandpit I've ever worked in, this has been really something to go out on. Whether they come on foot or cycle, New Zealanders will love this bit of backcountry.'

No doubt they will, but similar future ventures that pass through conservation land may well be subject to more monitoring as a result of the OGR project.

A Federated Mountain Clubs of New Zealand (FMC) 'position paper' on the OGR, written by Patrick Holland in July 2013, acknowledges that the new track 'does make more accessible some beautiful and historic backcountry', but adds that the role of CMSs in the brave new world of 'Conservation for prosperity' will need a bit more clarification.

Expansive wild places always inspire. The Masai word Serengeti means 'the place where the land runs on forever'. Exactly when New Zealanders' own concept of preserving wilderness originally came about can only be speculated. It has been postulated that our national appreciation of backcountry areas stems in earliest part from the influence of the English romantic poets like William Wordsworth and Samuel Coleridge Taylor, who in the early nineteenth century raved about returning to pristine environments as an antidote to the sprawling environmental depravity of the Industrial Revolution. A succession of New World poets, explorers, writers and philosophers subsequently popularised the word 'wilderness', evoking the idea of a land untouched by man.

The United States created the first national parks. These sprawling, wondrous wildernesses formally became the nation's common ground, set aside for all its citizenry and even visitors from overseas to appreciate freely. For many, best of all was that the old notions of gentry and class didn't apply in national parks – they were places where everyone was equal. The US certainly touted its 'natural' cathedrals up against the medieval cathedrals and monuments of old Europe.

Some say that the US concept of wilderness was exported to New Zealand. In the 1930s, the American environmentalist Aldo Leopold brought a bunch of like-minded wilderness aficionados to check out our mountain scenery, and their persuasive arguments won over influential politicians here along the way.

As in the US, our national park focus has changed from preserving epic scenery to the higher purpose of preserving nature's diversity – defined as the whole mix of native flora and fauna, ecological processes, pristine free-flowing rivers and even geology, all brazen and raw. Blatantly, national parks should not represent economic opportunities, because that's not what they are all about. Ownership brings with it responsibilities, and New Zealand's citizens as owners of its conservation estate may find that they have to rise to the high ideal of further defining the preservation they want in the future.

Kahurangi is a kind of pathway along which we wander, glimpsing back at an ancient past as well as forward into the future, inspiring, invoking curiosity and reminding us how it all was before cars and roads and buildings ruined the natural landscape. More than anything, we need to keep vast and relatively untouched places like Kahurangi as examples of the Earth's interactive complexity, balanced and in harmony.

BIBLIOGRAPHY

CHAPTER I ANAWEKA WAKA

Beaglehole, J.C., *The Journals of Captain James Cook on His Voyages of Discovery. Vol. 3: The Voyage of the Resolution and Discovery*, Cambridge University Press for the Hakluyt Society, Cambridge, 1967.

Best, E., 'Some Place Names of Islands of the Society Group. Supplied by Natives of Those Isles at Wellington, in 1916', *Journal of the Polynesian Society* 26(3): 111–115, 1917.

Department of Conservation, 'Summary of Events, Taitapu', Department of Conservation Takaka Office historical file notes, n.d.

Heaphy, C., 'Notes of an Expedition to Kawatiri and Araura, on the Western Coast of the Middle Island', *in*: Taylor, N. (*ed.*), *Early Travellers in New Zealand*, Clarendon Press, Oxford, 1956.

Johns, D., 'Cultural Conservation of Ancient Waka Heralds a New Chapter in Understanding Maori Maritime Technology', *in*: *University of Auckland* [website], https://www.auckland.ac.nz/en/about/news-events-and-notices/news/news-2014/10/cultural-conservation-of-ancient-waka-heralds-a-new-chapter-in-u.html, 6 October 2014.

Johns, D.A., Irwin, G.J. and Sung, Y.K., 'An Early Sophisticated East Polynesian Voyaging Canoe Discovered on New Zealand's Coast', *Proceedings of the National Academy of Sciences of the United States of America* 111(41): 14728–14733, 2014.

Kane, H.K., *Voyagers*, WhaleSong, Inc., Washington, 1991.

Kane, H.K., 'In Search of the Ancient Polynesian Voyaging Canoe', *in*: *Hawaiian Voyaging Traditions* [website], archive.hokulea.com/ike/kalai_waa/kane_search_voyaging_canoe.html, 1998.

Kay, R.F., *Tahiti and French Polynesia*, Lonely Planet, Melbourne, 1992.

Manguel, A., 'South Pacific Paradises – Bora and Huahine', *Islands* (supplement), 1995.

'Mau Piailug', *in*: *Wikipedia* [website], https://en.wikipedia.org/wiki/Mau_Piailug, 2017.

Pope, D. and Pope, J., *Mobil New Zealand Travel Guide: South Island, Stewart Island and the Chatham Islands*, 5th edition, Heinemann Reed, Auckland, 1990.

Porter, D.D., *Memoir of Commodore David Porter of the United States Navy*, J. Munsell, Albany, 1875.

BIBLIOGRAPHY

Priestley, R., 'Homing in on Hawaiki', *New Zealand Listener*, 17 November 2012.

Rose, P., 'Conservator Gives First Aid to Waka', *Motueka-Golden Bay News*, 26 January 2012.

Rose, P., 'Picnickers Dig Up Remains of Ancient Waka', *Nelson Mail*, 27 January 2012.

Smith, S.P., *Hawaiki: the Original Home of the Maori, with a Sketch of Polynesian History*, Whitcombe & Tombs, Christchurch, 1904.

Walls, J., 'A Maori History of Golden Bay', unpublished paper, 2012.

Withers, T., 'Les Oiseaux Marins/The Seabirds', *Air Tahiti Magazine* 93, January–March 2017.

CHAPTER 2 HOPELESSLY LOST

Arnold, N., 'Without a Trace', *New Zealand Geographic*, August 2016.

Hill, K., 'Tramper Fit After Grim Bush Ordeal', *Nelson Evening Mail*, 19 February 1980.

Hill, K., 'Joyful Reunion at Bedside', *Nelson Evening Mail*, 20 February 1980.

'Silent Plea by Missing Tramper', *Nelson Evening Mail*, 13 February 1980.

Simpson, B., 'Ferns, Worms, Raw Fish Kept Him Alive', *The Press*, 19 February 1980.

Spink, E., 'Tramper Winched from Kahurangi Park', *Nelson Mail*, 29 February 2016.

'Tramper Lifted Out After Month's Ordeal', *Nelson Evening Mail*, 18 February 1980.

Vincent, R., 'Tramper's Mother Tells of Long Vigil', *Sunday Times*, 24 February 1980.

Walrond, C., *Survive! Remarkable Tales from the New Zealand Outdoors*, David Bateman, Auckland, 2008.

Walrond, C., 'Peter Le Fleming', *Tales of the Lost*, RadioLIVE, 2 November 2014.

Young, D., 'Peter Le Fleming: Back from Beyond', *New Zealand Listener*, 24 May 1980.

CHAPTER 3 TAPLIN'S HUT

Atkins, R.J., 'Memories of the Past. Vol. 2', unpublished family memoirs, *c.* 2005.

Shaw, D., *North West Nelson Tramping Guide*, Nikau Press, Nelson, 1991.

CHAPTER 4 LITTLE BIDDY'S STORY

'Alpine Company, Lyell', *Westport Times*, 24 June 1879.

Department of Conservation, 'Rogues and Ruffians', interpretation panel at Lyell Campground, n.d.

Hindmarsh, W., *Tales of the Golden West*, Whitcombe & Tombs, Christchurch, 1906.

New Zealand Walkway Commission, *Lyell Walk*, brochure, New Zealand Walkway Commission, Wellington, 1984.

Rob (RKC), 'Gold Nuggets of New Zealand', *in*: *Gold Dredging Forum* [online forum], http://golddredgingforum.proboards.com/thread/72, 2008.

CHAPTER 5 THE STOREKEEPER'S LAMENT
Barne, J.H., *History of Taitapu Estate*, New Zealand Forest Service, Wellington, 1986.
Moffatt, H.L., *Adventures by Sea and Land*, Nelson Historical Society, Nelson, 1966.

CHAPTER 6 THE FLYING CRAY FISHERS
'Flotsam Washed Up on West Coast, Combined Fishing Flying Abilities, Nelson Police Take Over', *Nelson Evening Mail*, 19 October 1972.
'Hope for Missing Men Recedes', *Nelson Evening Mail*, 20 October 1972.
'May Continue Search Next Weekend', *Nelson Evening Mail*, 25 October 1972.
Ministry for Primary Industries, 'History of Fishing in New Zealand', *in*: MPI Fisheries Infosite [website], http://fs.fish.govt.nz/Page.aspx?pk=51&tk=166, 2009.
'Part of Bow Recovered', *Nelson Evening Mail*, 19 October 1972.
'Search Area Extended', *Nelson Evening Mail*, 21 October 1972.
'Taylorcraft Auster', *in*: *Wikipedia* [website], https://en.wikipedia.org/wiki/Taylorcraft_Auster, 2017.

CHAPTER 7 RIVER PORTS
Chalmers, B., 'Karamea's Forgotten Footprints', unpublished manuscript, 2004.
Chalmers, B., 'The Heaphy and its People', unpublished manuscript, 2004.
Cowan, J., 'Famous New Zealanders. No. 6: Three West Coast Explorers: Thomas Brunner, Charles Heaphy, James Mackay', *New Zealand Railways Magazine* 8(5): 25–28, 1 September 1933.
'Ghost Ships Only Callers', *The News*, 18 July 1991.
Jenkin, R., *New Zealand Mysteries*, A.H & A.W. Reed, Wellington, 1970.
'Karamea Welcomed Admiral with Dining and Dancing, Recollections of Mr George Johnson of Karamea, as Told to a Staff Reporter', *Westport Times*, n.d.
Leahy, P.J., McDougall, R.J., Matravers, W.G. and McClean, G.J., 'For the Record/ Karamea Shipping Company', records compiled for the New Zealand Ship and Marine Society, Wellington, *c.* 1980.

CHAPTER 8 MINING MAGNESITE
'Cobb Valley Soapstone – Lives and Gives Forever', *Guardian (Motueka)*, 12 September 2012.
'Concern Over Potential Steatite Mining Application in the Cobb Valley', *Guardian (Motueka)*, 5 September 2012.
Dodson, A.D., 'On the Traces of Ancient Glaciers in Nelson Province', *Nelson Examiner and New Zealand Chronicle* 30(4), 13 May 1871.
'Golden Bay Soapstone Scheme Gets Government Support', *Guardian (Motueka)*, 29 December 2008.
Henderson, J., *The Exiles of Asbestos Cottage*, Hodder & Stoughton, Auckland, 1981.

McDowell, R., 'Steatite Mining Proposal Raises Conservationists' Fears', *Golden Bay Weekly*, 14 September 2012.
'Park Has $50b in Minerals', *Nelson Mail*, 5 October 2009.
Petyt, C., 'Cobb Magnesite Mine', unpublished notes, 2016.
'Quarry Application', *Motueka-Golden Bay News*, 29 March 2012.
Rattenbury, M.S., Cooper, R.A. and Johnston, M.R., *Geology of the Nelson Area*, Institute of Geological and Nuclear Sciences Ltd, Lower Hutt, 1998.
Roland S., 'Mr Teale – Quarryman, *School Journal* 1(2), 1976.
Van den Burgh, R., 'Myers Praises Mineral "Stocktake"', *Business Day*, 9 January 2010.

CHAPTER 9 RANGER'S DIARY
Polglaze, M., 'Karamea Work Diary', unpublished report for the New Zealand Forest Service, 1981.

CHAPTER 10 HERITAGE HUTS
Ashley, A., 'John Gordon Rees ("Jack") McBurney 1919–1978', *New Zealand Entomologist* 7(1): 111–112, 1979.
Henderson, J., *The Exiles of Asbestos Cottage*, Hodder & Stoughton, Auckland, 1981.
McBurney, J., 'Cobb Valley Diary, June 1952–June 1956', unpublished reports for the New Zealand Forest Service, 1952–56.
McBurney, J.G.R., 'Notes on the Life History and Distribution of *Anagotus helmsi* (Coleoptera: Curculionidae)', *New Zealand Entomologist* 6(2): 177–181, 1976.
Squire, C., 'NZ's Only Tent Camp Restored', *Nelson Mail*, 5 November 2014.
Taylor, J., 'Cobb Valley Tent Camp Restoration', *in: Conservation Blog – A Behind-the-scenes Look at DOC's Conservation Work* [online blog], https://blog.doc.govt.nz/2015/01/13/cobb-valley-tent-camp-restoration, 13 January 2015.

CHAPTER 11 TRACTS OF IRON
Bell, J.M., Webb, E.J.H. and Clarke, E. de C., *The Geology of the Parapara Subdivision, Karamea Nelson*, Government Printer, Wellington, 1907.
'Collingwood's Golden Days', 'Colonial Album' series, *Nelson Evening Mail*, 20 August 1988.
Jenkin, R., 'Under the Korowai', unpublished notes/draft material, 2016.
McGowen, H., 'Gold Found in Massacre Bay River: The Rest is History', *Golden Bay Weekly*, 14 March 2008.
Newport, J.N.W, 'Some Industries of Golden Bay', *Nelson Historical Society Journal* 3(5): 5–23, October 1979.
St Just, F.J., 'The Future of Onekaka', *Better Business*, May 1947.
Washbourn, E., *Courage and Camp Ovens: Five Generations at Golden Bay*, A.H. & A.W. Reed, Wellington, 1970.

Washbourn, H.P., *Reminiscences of Early Days*, R. Lucas & Sons, Nelson, 1933.
Washbourn, H.P., *Further Reminiscences of Early Days*, R. Lucas & Sons, 1934.

CHAPTER 12 CARBON FOOTPRINTS

Browne, G.H., 'First New Zealand Record of Probable Dinosaur Footprints from the Late Cretaceous North Cape Formation, Northwest Nelson', *New Zealand Journal of Geology and Geophysics* 52(4): 367–377, 2009.

'Coal Mines in the Nelson Province', *New Zealand Coal* 15(2), October 1970.

Department of Conservation, *Westhaven Inlet Marine Reserve*, information brochure, Department of Conservation, Nelson, 1994.

Dyer, P., *Coal Mines of Puponga*, River Press, Picton, 2003.

Park, G., *Ngā Uruora – The Groves of Life: Ecology and History in a New Zealand Landscape*, Victoria University Press, Wellington, 1995.

Roberts, H., 'Devanny, Jean', in: *Te Ara – Encyclopedia of New Zealand* [website], http://www.teara.govt.nz/en/biographies/4d13/devanny-jean, 1998.

Roberts, W.H.S, *Southland in 1856–57, with a Journey from Nelson to Southland in 1856*, Southland Times Co., Invercargill, 1895.

Roberts, W.H.S, *Nomenclature of Nelson and the West Coast*, Otago Daily Times, Dunedin, 1912.

Smith, S.P., 'Captain Dumont D'Urville's Exploration of Tasman Bay in 1827', *Transactions and Proceedings of the New Zealand Institute* 40(22): 416–447, 1907.

CHAPTER 13 CHASING THE KĀKAHI

James, M.R., 'Ecology of the Freshwater Mussel *Hyridella menziesi* (Gray) in a Small Oligotrophic Lake', *Archives für Hydrobiologie* 108(3): 337–348, 1987.

Ogilvie, S.C. and Mitchell, S.F., 'A Model of Mussel Filtration in a Shallow New Zealand Lake, with Reference to Eutrophication Control', *Archives für Hydrobiologie* 133(4): 471–482, 1995.

Phillips, N., *Review of the Potential for Biomanipulation of Phytoplankton Abundance by Freshwater Mussels (Kakahi) in the Te Arawa Lakes*, NIWA Client Report HAM2006-125, prepared for Environment Bay of Plenty, National Institute of Water and Atmospheric Research, Hamilton, 2007.

CHAPTER 14 ROARING LION GOLD

Chaffey, H., 'The Windless Valley of the Roaring Lion', 'Jagged Peaks – Exhilarating and Beautiful Sights' series, *Star-Times*, 28 July 1938.

CHAPTER 15 MODERN CONTROVERSY

Abbott, M. and Reeves, R. (eds), *Wild at Heart: The Possibility of Wilderness in Aotearoa New Zealand*, Otago University Press, Dunedin, 2011.

BIBLIOGRAPHY

Aulakh, B., 'Gorge No Longer So Suicidal', *Westport News*, 18 December 2012.

Buchler, J., 'Community Perspectives About Karamea and Kahurangi National Park', Bachelor of Science with Honours thesis, Victoria University of Wellington, Wellington, 2000.

Fulton, K., 'Track Will Put Westport on the Map', *Westport News*, 5 February 2013.

Henzell, J., 'Dismay on Mokihinui Over Dam', *The Press*, 7 April 2007.

Holland, P., *The Old Ghost Road Cycleway Project*, FMC Position Paper, Federated Mountain Clubs of New Zealand, Wellington, 28 July 2013.

Inta, F., 'Nga Haeranga: Destructive or Constructive?', *Te Awa/The River* 37, February 2013.

'Large Exclusion from Park Investigation', *Bush Telegraph* 43, September 1991.

Lusk, P., 'Ghost Road Frightener', *Wilderness*, March 2013.

McCleave, J., Booth, K. and Espiner, S., 'Love Thy Neighbour? The Relationship Between Kahurangi National Park and the Border Communities of Karamea and Golden Bay, New Zealand', *Annals of Leisure Research* 7(3–4): 202–221, 2004.

Mills, L., 'DOC Drops 500-year-old Tree', *Greymouth Star*, 22 February 2013.

Powrie, S., 'The Environmental Politics of the Creation of Kahurangi National Park', Master of Arts thesis, University of Canterbury, Christchurch, 1997.

Quammen, D., 'This Land is Your Land', *National Geographic*, January 2016.

Scanlon, L., 'Tree Felling Upsets Conservationist', *Westport News*, 31 January 2013.

Scanlon, L., 'Conservationist Says Hut Privatised', *Westport News*, 15 February 2013.

Scanlon, L., 'DOC Hut Handover Criticised', *Westport News*, 16 February 2013.

Scanlon, L., 'Lusk Wrong, Says DOC Manager', *Westport Times*, 21 February 2013.

Taylor, C.N., Gough, J., Warren, J. and McClintock, W., 'Social and Economic Impacts of Kahurangi National Park', *Science for Conservation* 119, Department of Conservation, Wellington, 1999.